PHOTOGRAPH OF WITTER BYNNER

BY CARL VAN VECHTEN, 1933

PROSE PIECES

THE WORKS OF
WITTER BYNNER

GENERAL EDITOR, JAMES KRAFT

PROSE
PIECES

·  ·

EDITED, AND WITH

AN INTRODUCTION, BY

James Kraft

FARRAR · STRAUS · GIROUX / NEW YORK

Library of Congress Cataloging in Publication Data
Bynner, Witter, 1881–1968. / Prose pieces.
(The Works of Witter Bynner)
Includes bibliographical references.
I. Kraft, James. / II. Title. / III. Series:
Bynner, Witter, 1881–1968. Works.
PS3503.Y45A16 1978 / 814'.5'2 / 78–11441

This book is published with the aid of a grant from
The Witter Bynner Foundation for Poetry, Inc.

Contents

· ❧❦❧❦❧ ·

Poets and Scholars

The Mirrored Self

REVIEWS

ESSAYS AND

OCCASIONAL PIECES

The Spectra Hoax

Pueblo

At War

Some Roots

On Writing

Introduction

· ❧❧❧❧❧❧ ·

"THE POETRY OF REALITY":
WITTER BYNNER'S
PROSE PIECES
BY JAMES KRAFT

Written mostly for his own pleasure, in an easy, conversational tone and style, and largely without any particular attention to what was current or fashionable, Witter Bynner's prose pieces are an unusually direct expression of his distinctive character. One finds throughout these essays Bynner's special interests: his pleasure in the expression of human character, especially when it shows the minority viewpoint; his commitment to democracy and humor—concepts he considered related; and his affinity for Mexico and China as societies that offered important alternative ways of looking at the world.

The first essay in this volume, "A Word or Two with Henry James," is the report of a series of conversations that took place late in 1904 and early in 1905. As one of Witter Bynner's first prose publications, it illustrates an element that is found in most of these selections of his prose writing over a period of sixty years. So often his own work reflects the qualities that exist in fine conversation: the individual character alive with witty, intuitive insights; a lightness and ease of style, almost a casualness; and the absence of overly serious academic analysis. Through conversation one encounters the human voice, which remained for Bynner the great indicator of character and quality in the human being.

Clearly Henry James delighted in the twenty-two-year-old American: tall, handsome, extremely witty and urbane, from a good if unconventional New England family, with an uncle who had been a successful historical novelist. Bynner admired the senior man of letters and found charming his grand manner and convoluted style. Though they shared a commitment to conversation as an art to be ardently pursued, James and Bynner could not have represented two more divergent characters. James was so much what he was—the European artist, thoroughly engrossed in his career, so serious and intense he seemed never to relax; Bynner was easier in manner, so confidently American in his style that he often appeared casual. This difference suggests why the direction James took—toward the older, more intellectual Europe—never occurred to Bynner as a pattern for his own life, any more than the Jamesian mode of thought or style seemed to Bynner anything less than brilliant, although needlessly complicated and verbose.

This and another essay on James written in 1943 directly illustrate Bynner's interest in the human voice as the essence of character. Throughout his career, Bynner sought to express in his prose pieces the voice of the writer, but he was equally concerned to convey his own distinctive voice and character. This collection reveals the warmth, humor, and tolerance in Bynner himself, but behind the apparent ease of his conversational style are certain strong and very personal critical convictions.

·

Bynner began his professional career as an assistant to the editor of *McClure's* magazine, as a reader of manuscripts, and as the magazine's poetry editor. Usually he wrote his own prose pieces for other magazines (they are listed with each essay), and he was generally able to write whatever he wished because payment for his work was not essential. Most critics are associated with special interests and approaches—Bynner later became a China expert—but it is part of his fascination that Bynner could choose subjects as diverse as meetings with Henry James and D. H. Lawrence; Arthur Waley's version of *The Tale of Genji*; his own translation of Euripides, which he did for Isadora Duncan; John Dewey and Bertrand Russell in Peking; Pueblo children's paintings, Indian dances and jewelry; Edgar Lee Masters, Ezra Pound, Willa Cather, Robinson Jeffers, Edna St. Vincent Millay; the effects of Prohibition; bullfighting; and Chinese culture. One encounters here topics as various as Bynner's eulogy for a minor Swiss painter, Paul Thévenaz, and his report of a youthful visit to the major English writer George Meredith. As different as all the essays are in period, style, intent, and effect, each illustrates Bynner's personal interest and reveals, through the voice of the subject, the unique human. qualities of that individual.

The case of Thévenaz is interesting. His name is now generally unknown, yet he once worked in Paris with Cocteau and Stravinsky, painting portraits of them, of the Countess de Noailles, and of others; he also designed interiors of several New York houses, and had exhibitions at Knoedler's in 1917 and the Chicago Arts Club in 1921, just before his death at thirty-one. He is a figure in several of Florine Stettheimer's multi-character portraits of creative life in New York City, which suggest, as Paul Rosenfeld said, "slyly humorous autobiographical canvasses narrative in the naïve manner of the medieval draftsman; presenting separate events or successions of them simultaneously within the limits of single designs." Here, with Thévenaz, are Marcel Duchamp, Carl Van Vechten and his wife Fania Marinoff, the photographer Arnold Genthe, and the sculptor Elie Nadelman.

Bynner's eulogy of Thévenaz, in prose and poetry, was published in *The New York Times* just after Thévenaz's death in July 1921. From this man, Bynner—the puritan New Englander—learned to accept openly his emotional nature and to enjoy life with ease and lightness. (In his long, self-searching, autobiographical poem, *Eden Tree* (1931), Bynner recorded his nature as bisexual.) Thévenaz was no more "serious" than Florine Stettheimer and her art were, but each suggests something about the time and the period and about an approach to life and art that is, indeed, quite important. Their art touches upon an aspect of our existence that is childish and delightful but still powerful in its youthful, romantic abandon to fun, friendship, and a form of spontaneous creativity. Such art is naïve and "light," but if we ignore it, we will miss a significantly human and creative expression. Thévenaz said: "If one has personality, it will come through, no matter what one does"; the expression of personality was as important to him as to Bynner. One of Bynner's poems to Thévenaz, published in *Caravan* (1925), contains lines that suggest the painter's unusual qualities:

Tradition he would set at naught,
And never shed a tear:
No scripture we were ever taught
Accords with his career.

Persons who conserve the race
With families and fatigue
He would encounter face to face
And never care a fig.

He would snap his fingers at the young
And thumb his nose at the old,
Believing in some of the things that are sung
But in none of the things that are told. . . .

The essay "A Young Visit with George Meredith" is a very different piece. Bynner begins by naming his three literary heroes:

As a freshman, in 1898, I had read *Diana of the Crossways* and had at once fallen under the Meredithian spell with much the same excitement as that which came to me two years later from Walt Whitman and three years after that from A. E. Housman, an odd but complementary trio: the patrician self, the democratic self, the ascetic self, similar to one another only in sheer individualism and resultant creative artistry. For my young taste and response there had been since Shakespeare no writer until Meredith whose English could make characters come so alive and large in an atmosphere of acute and steadfast thought.

While at Harvard Bynner had started a club which read Meredith's novels aloud, and in his senior year he wrote a prize essay on Meredith's style. Bynner had gone to England in 1902 specifically to visit Meredith, and he recorded the day in a notebook: "Echoes of Meredith's voice made for me a recording in that book, as actual voices were later to do on discs." The events remained very much alive in Bynner's mind, and finally, in 1956, he published his recollection of the visit in *The Virginia Quarterly Review.*

This essay is a delightful evocation of a young man's admiration of an established artist and portrays Meredith vividly, but it is especially his interest in a writer out of vogue that reveals Bynner as a critic. Bynner often seems out of step in his critical interests: a bit behind, or ahead, but never much concerned with current taste. The list of examples is long: he arranged for Pound's first United States publications in 1910 (and then tired of him as a poet, but not as a man); he first introduced A. E. Housman to American readers and continued to regard him as one of the great poets; early on, he praised and supported Edna St. Vincent Millay and Vachel Lindsay; he began to discover the quality of Chinese verse as early as 1917 and became a fine interpreter of China to the United States. Also, he began to support women's suffrage in 1898; he worked actively for black equality and Indian rights in the 1920's and stated in the early twenties that the United States must be able to defeat Communism by democratic and not by totalitarian methods or there was no justification for democracy. Another of his discoveries was the nineteenth-century poet Frederick Goddard Tuckerman, whom he considered to be one of America's finest poets. Bynner left the literary establishment of the East and went west to California, made two trips to China, and finally in 1922 moved to Santa Fe, where he lived until his death in 1968. While Pound and Eliot found European culture a necessity, Bynner found no significant reason for an American to aspire to its attitudes or standards and never went to Europe from 1902 to 1950. He was a pacifist in World War I and hoped that America's entrance into World War II would end white racial imperialism throughout the world.

Bynner had written in his 1902 prize essay at Harvard that Meredith's novels contained "the poetry of reality." The phrase was used to describe Meredith's complex sensibility and style, and it was Bynner's interpretation of this writer's important grasp of reality: not only what was, but human existence allowed to grow and become all it could be. Perhaps nothing so fully conditioned Bynner's thinking as this one commitment. He had faith in the quality of human potential if it was released through the democratic experience. Then the poetry in life existed; one was able to be oneself, to be a "character." As incidental an essay as that on Santa Fe, "A City of Change," shows how he believed in democracy and in its power to transform the simplest event into a matter of human significance. He saw humor as the great democratic leveler and equalizer—the single most commonly shared and unifying human experience. This delight in humor runs throughout his prose as the central means for creating the climate of democracy and his poetry of reality.

·

Beginning in 1923 and continuing until the late 1960's, Bynner went regularly to Chapala, a small town just south of Guadalajara, on Mexico's largest lake. He spent close to ten full years of his life in Mexico, including a year between 1923 and 1925 and two and a half years during World War II. Mexico had a great influence on him. He first went there with D. H. and Frieda Lawrence, and this visit resulted in a personal encounter with

D.H., a lifetime of friendship with Frieda, and a book, *Journey with Genius*, describing the trip and these relationships. Some of Bynner's best poems were written about Mexico; he thought of it as the source of human qualities in which he took great pleasure: "the courtesy, the innate intelligence, the quiet force, the ease, the quickness, the sensitiveness, the endurance, the smile of these people." To this must be added: "Be it said at once that I am for the most part puzzled by Mexican aristocracy and officialdom and by the bourgeoisie. These classes seem in many ways unworthy of their supposed inferiors. With notable exceptions, they turn to Europe or to the United States for inspiration or example, when, obviously, they need to trust and cultivate the basic qualities of their own race."

Like other observers, including Mexico's Octavio Paz, Bynner saw that the nation had "a subtle touch of cruelty." Bynner's essay "Bull-Rings"* depicts the actual and symbolic aspects of this dark side of the Mexican (and the human) character. Observing the fervor of the period of social revolution in the early years of this century, Bynner overestimated what Mexico could (or would) do for its ordinary citizens, but he saw in Mexico, closer at hand than Europe and more truly revealed in its Indians, an alternative culture with values which could counter certain material and mechanical efficiencies of his own civilization. He believed there was a great deal there to be learned. He never gave up this idea—that Mexico is an important antidote to our particular kind of societal arrogance.

·

Bynner was in China less than two years, but it was one of the major influences on his life. China became the measure for what he did: he had formed a concept of poetry before he went there in 1917, and again in 1920–21, but from the Chinese, and espe-

---

* "Bull-Rings" (1924) has the added interest of being Bynner's account of a bullfight he, D. H. and Frieda Lawrence, and Willard "Spud" Johnson saw on Easter Sunday, 1923. Lawrence used this event to begin *The Plumed Serpent* (1926), in which Bynner is a minor character, Owen Rhys.

cially from the T'ang poets, he took as his model the short precise lyric, easily accessible to the reader. He called it "a record of human feeling and thought so simply and rightly expressed as almost to conceal its artistry . . . no ponderous or intricate symbolism, no foppish babble, but the grace of an art in which a man's mind never grows childish and a child's heart never dies. . . . Whether or not Po Chü-yi, as is said, tested his poems by reading them to his cook, they are as human and simple as if he had done so. . . ."* Bynner's most well-known books are his translations from the Chinese, *The Jade Mountain* (1929) and *The Way of Life According to Laotzu* (1944), and his best critical work is on China, the Orient, and the nature of translation.

His enthusiasm and knowledge are evident throughout his many articles relating to China. One feels the sharp pleasure of his experiences, and his descriptions convey a strong feeling for the people and the country. He never knew the Chinese language, but he often traveled with Chinese friends (for example, with Kiang Kang-hu, who was his co-translator for eleven years on *The Jade Mountain*). He was able to place himself outside the usual tourist experiences: he often stayed at hotels designated for Chinese rather than for Westerners, and he enjoyed eating the local Chinese food whenever possible. He was also able to travel quite extensively through a large country; he made a point of finding out how the common people lived; and he studied and collected the art of China. He did all this at a time when the "Yellow Peril" was a prevalent prejudice. By today's scholarly standards, Bynner was not an expert on China. By other standards—experience, intuition, concern, and care—his knowledge and appreciation were immeasurable. An understanding of the background against which his knowledge was to grow is found in this opening paragraph of his essay "Do We Know the Chinese?" (1949):

---

* Witter Bynner, "Remembering a Gentle Scholar," *The Occident* (Winter 1953), reprinted in *The Works of Witter Bynner: The Chinese Translations.*

As a boy, I knew nothing about the Chinese other than that they were "Chinks," a more menial race than even Micks or Dagoes, that they were mostly laundrymen who wore pigtails, pushed wooden balls across framed wires, and gave out red tickets with black marks on them, were gibbering heathen (even worse than Catholics; I was bred near Boston), who spat on clothes to wet them for ironing, and who ate rats. Once I joined a juvenile gang which threw stones at laundry windows and then fled the monsters in holy terror. College likewise taught me nothing of the Orient, though there was Lafcadio Hearn, and there was *Madam Butterfly*; but gradually through the next fifteen years I came to know, or to think that I knew, a little about Japan, not only because they had long been experts at woodblock printing but because they were beginning to be experts at propaganda. It was not until 1917 that I had my initial glimpse of the two countries.

He felt that the United States had little in common with the Japanese character and much with the Chinese. Living in a vast, sprawling country, the Chinese were easier, warmer, more humorous, and more tolerant than the Japanese; more like Americans, he believed. Of the Chinese and the American he said in 1949: "Names, phrases, labels are of little significance . . . as compared with the spirit of a people which, through any form of government, is what actually and finally governs." He quoted his own translation of Laotzu as expressing the individualism he so admired in the Chinese.

Rid of formalized wisdom and learning
People would be a hundredfold happier,
Rid of conventionalized duty and honor
People would find their families dear,
Rid of legalized profiteering
People would have no thieves to fear.
These methods of life have failed, all three,

Here is the way, it seems to me:
Set people free,
As deep in their hearts they would like to be,
From private greeds
And wanton needs.

Bynner's individual quality as an amateur sinologist and an unconventional viewer of his world is evident in "The Chinese Brush," which appeared in *The Atlantic Monthly* in 1949. This essay expresses an appreciation of Chinese calligraphy in its own right, as an art equal to that of painting. There was little about calligraphy for Bynner to have read, and it is not likely that he could have known from his limited Chinese studies that "calligraphy establishes the criteria for the judgment of Chinese painting, which came to be appreciated because of its affiliation with and dependence upon the brush strokes of calligraphy."* The first exhibition in this country solely devoted to calligraphy took place in 1971, three years after Bynner's death, but he was able to write with real appreciation of the art of calligraphy in China many years before that. He spoke of a scroll he had obtained, called "Two Fishermen," as having been painted in a "minimum of broad, bold strokes" and showing that the artist had "affixed his brush name . . . in strokes so similarly broad and bold that they less resemble writing than they do his wen and the gourd he always carried in his sash." He described a piece of great calligraphy he saw in China as taking away his breath. Calligraphy was the voice of the artist speaking. Bynner had seen Charles Freer's collection before it went to Washington, had lived in China, had collected his own scrolls, and had talked to scholars. The fine eye of the intelligent amateur, with its appreciation of the unusual, had done extraordinarily well for the poet-critic.

·

* Shen C. Y. Fu, *Traces of the Brush: Studies in Chinese Calligraphy* (New Haven: Yale University Art Gallery, 1977), p. ix.

The qualities most evident in Bynner's essays, in his sketches of writers, especially of poets, and in his book reviews, are the same as those in his more personal pieces: ease of phrasing and lightness of tone, intimate relationship with his subject, unconventional stance, liking for what isn't always acceptable, insistence on the human qualities in the subject and disappointment at the absence of such qualities. His insights are not those of the scholar, or of the literary critic in the usual conception of his role. (He seriously condemned two biographies of Willa Cather as written for "libraries rather than for persons, for studious reference rather than for quickening warmth.") He was an educated and unconventional Easterner who moved West, who wrote classical lyric verse in an age of extreme poetic experimentation, who himself lived an independent existence and advocated total equality for women and for blacks, who never failed in his confidence in the American character or in his belief in man's ability to create a decent world in which to live. For Bynner the human spirit was fulfilled and sustained by humor and by the democratic commonality of human experience (if not of politics), and through the belief that man by the essential goodness of his nature always would transcend any particular venality. In this largely non-judgmental sense of human potential, he saw an opportunity for a free expression of all people. His relationship to the nineteenth-century New England tradition of individualism and democratic self-determination is evident. People endured in spite of what was done to them, and the spirit of their endurance showed their oppressors the dignity of the human being. Bynner believed that it was in the viewpoint of a small, elite group that the imperial prejudice rested and that it was through the figure of the individual that most people could discover the image of true human quality and the means to human self-fulfillment. Bynner delighted in the eccentric, even in those truly mad: he felt that they were entertaining—that they enlarged the area of the possible and made our own "madness" and sense of guilt for our inadequacy less disturbing. They—the mad, the eccentric, the individual—are what improve and sanctify the race; they humanize it and, in the long course of our history, sustain and increase the democratic potential of life.

Mention should be made of Witter Bynner's apologia for his life's work, an essay called "The Persistence of Poetry"; and comment should also be made on his most famous prose work, *Journey with Genius*, not included here.

"The Persistence of Poetry" was published in 1929 by the Book Club of California in an edition of 325 copies, and the latter part of the essay was used as an introduction to *The Jade Mountain*, published the same year. Bynner begins by speaking of the impossibility of defining poetry and then suggests as a definition the phrase "passionate patience"; passionate because, like music, poetry lies closest to the heart and "No one would question passion as the prime element in live things"; patience because that is what man must have to meet the great "cosmic silence" he faces. Poetry creates this passionate patience: "it is the rhythm by which men feel their own impulses, their own emotions, their own thoughts." Bynner calls A. E. Housman and Edna Millay the two great lyric poets of his time, and designates Amy Lowell as an example of what appeals immediately but does not sustain; he calls her one of the "haberdashers for contemporary culture." He acknowledges the Greek and Hebrew philosophers and poets as the sources of Western poetic tradition, but urges serious consideration of the values in the Chinese poetic tradition, in which folk art and cultural expression are naturally combined and poetry becomes a part of life: it is the "element common to us all."

> Through the Asian centuries, everyone has written verse. In fact, from early imperial days down to these even worse disordered days of the republic, the sense of poetry as a natural and solacing part of life has lasted among the Chinese people. . . .

It has been an age-old custom in China that poets, even the best of them, have devoted their earlier years to some form of public service. Century after century, Chinese poems reflect this deep devotion of their authors to the good of the state,—their unwavering allegiance to righteousness. . . .

These various remarks bind together, I think. I have been trying to focus my thoughts on the place of the poet and poetry, in a time of cumulated and over-materialistic culture. I have remarked that the art of a poet is by no means only craft, but inheres in his life; that there is a special gift by which a particular poet now and then expresses the poetic impulse in the hearts of other men; but that the element is common to us all, and is an element inextricably mingled with the element of life itself.

He goes on to make a most eloquent defense of the T'ang style of poetry: "The Chinese poet seldom lets any portion of what he is saying unbalance the entirety. . . . Chinese poetry rarely trespasses beyond the bounds of actuality. . . . The great Chinese poets accept the world exactly as they find it in all its terms, and with profound simplicity find therein sufficient solace. Even in phraseology they seldom talk about one thing in terms of another. . . ." And then, in speaking of the Chinese, he defines his own poetry: "They perform the miracle of identifying the wonder of beauty with common sense. Rather, they prove that the simplest common sense, the most salutary, and the most nearly universal, is the sense of the beauty of nature, quickened and yet sobered by the wistful warmth of human friendship." It is his self-defense, made with grace and ease, as he says, with "that passionate patience which is the core of life."

Journey with Genius, which first appeared in 1951, was reprinted by Octagon Books in 1974. It is a long prose work, imperfect yet always stimulating. For one reader this biographical-critical study of D. H. Lawrence is brilliant, if limited; for another, malicious, and not without justice. Bynner admires

Lawrence's style but not his character, and presents him as a brutal, erratic, difficult genius, capable of human kindness when not debilitated by physical illness. Frieda Lawrence is the "hero." The interesting point is that Bynner and Lawrence saw one another during a period of less than six months, although they were in almost daily contact for most of that time. Bynner described the encounter as an unbearable battle. Yet they later corresponded, and Lawrence's letters to Bynner—few of Bynner's to Lawrence have survived—are full of warmth and pleasure. Bynner's poetic portraits of Lawrence are severe, but Lawrence appreciated them. Bynner said of Lawrence and himself that they were like the light and the dark, but it may be closer to the truth to say that Bynner hid his own darkness and Lawrence could not enjoy his own lightness. The book is highly personal in its perceptions, full of warmth, alive—and, in this case, filled with a sharp envy stirred by the presence of the penetrating intellect of Lawrence. Bynner saw much that others ignored, and the poetry of his way of looking at the world always made the reality beautiful to him, just as Lawrence's vision seemed to darken life for him. Bynner's sense of reality is one to be savored for its lightness, a lightness that is tinged with sadness. (Speaking of the Chinese, in an essay included in this book, he said, "Facing and acknowledging the irony of life, they accept what it offers of good as outweighing what it imposes of ill.") Perhaps a poem of his, typical in subject matter, language, length, and tone, best suggests the special voice and insight that characterized his writing.

At the Last

There is no denying
That it matters little,
When through a narrow door
We enter a room together,
Which goes after, which before.

Perhaps you are not dying:
Perhaps—there is no knowing—
I shall slip by and turn and laugh with you
Because it mattered so little,
The order of our going.

INTERVIEWS, PORTRAITS, AND REMINISCENCES

New York and London

· ✹✹✹ ·

A Word or Two with

Henry James

· ❧❂❧ ·

Mr. James was in New York for practically the first time in almost twenty years. As we walked he told me of his first flying visit a month or two ago, and thence the talk led to various topics:

"My renewal of acquaintance with New York was not to begin with altogether happy. This second visit is more satisfactory than that first pause of a day or two. I arrived in the sultry last part of August and was absolutely overwhelmed with the heat of the city and its other terrors. It was not at all the place I had known as a boy.

"My friends elected luckily to bring me straightway to the Players Club, which I then thought and think still an oasis of quietness and atmosphere. It suggested to me, as I looked about, the Garrick Club in London and its fine collection of paintings. Amid the abundance of portraits and photographs in the Players, I came upon a case of daguerreotypes full of faces so many of which were familiar to me, that I realized I must have been fortunate enough as a boy to be in the hands of parents who were fond of the theater. They must have taken my brother and me to the playhouse rather prematurely, I judge, else I should not have known all those faces and recovered so many half-lost sensations. Leaning stiffly on pillars, for instance, there were two girls with long hair, the Bateman sisters, whom I used to see on the stage. I remembered them, of course, the better, in having known them, since those times, as two very charming women in England. But there were others, such as the Florences, who once impressed me with their singing; Maggie Mitchell, over whom I went fantastically mad, though she was undoubtedly a barbarian and would nowadays be taken for such; and there was one woman with the face and curls of a schoolmistress, draped in some ghastly pseudo-classic hangings short at her shapeless knees, whom I indubitably once took with admiring seriousness. Those were emphatic events in my boyhood, those visits to the theater. I remember wondering how I could possibly live the time through from a Tuesday to a Friday, and then, when once I was seated in the theater with my eyes on the old green curtain, feeling quite convinced that in the few minutes before that curtain should rise, I was doomed to be removed by accident or death or some unforeseen punishment. Those were palpitations that are immemorable; I seem hardly to have been done with them yesterday.

"Equally as recent seem the old sensations produced on me by my previous life in New York. Gramercy Park and such other places as I found unchanged stand about me this time and give me the same sense of existence as though it were last week instead of twenty years ago that I was calling on a relative or on the way to my own home. I was born in Washington Place and lived afterwards in Fourteenth Street near Sixth Avenue. Those parts of the town are, of course, all gone,—that is, as I knew them. I cannot give you an inkling of what a queer, ghostly, melancholy experience it is to go about a town and find here and there a piece of it, a fragment of it, so to speak, with great stretches between, where it has crumbled away and been replaced by size and strangeness. Suddenly while walking along, as we are walking now, I will come upon a house, or a block of houses or even a section, unchanged, and will discover and snugly recognize, be aware of the old town again, only to lose it all the next minute and to seem almost not on *terra firma*.

"Naturally I cannot know in a day what there is to be known about New York; even to know again what I used to know about it would take many days. Although I have an exemplary memory for rubbish, more important facts do not seem to stay by me. Not that I must complain of my memory; I suppose it has served me well, accurately, ardently for the writing of picturesque trash. During that day or two in New York before I left for Boston, I had, for instance, in the Players I believe, a dish that I have not tasted in over sixteen years and remember, not only as an American food but, if I mistake not, as an idiosyncrasy of New York—brandied peaches!

"In the Players Club, as in other New York clubs (and there are so many!) I was impressed with the sociability of club life here in America. The clubs in London, as I at least have observed them, serve purposes rather of utility and political coagulation than of consociation. Men take meals at their clubs in London, it strikes me, much as they would eat at a small and absolutely nice hotel, whereas here I notice that you eat in groups and have altogether amiable, chatty times together. That's the point,—you are more gregarious, more sociable at your clubs, more *en famille.*

"After the shock of New York in those one or two hot days, I was glad to be back again in Boston, the city with the charm exclusively its own. Its distinction is, of course, its oneness, its completeness, its homogeneity, qualities it has retained almost precisely as it had them when I was a boy, and it was a rural, or rather a rustic city, the conservative, collective and representative capital of New England. One feels, to be sure, the disadvantages of such advantage. Boston's standard of comparison is bounded entirely by its own precincts. It is given to bidding you to swan and setting you goose. But this very stiffness, stuffiness, this very inaccessibility to a breath of outer air, produces, in however close an atmosphere, a demeanor of self-respect and of patrician dignity.

"How many men, by the bye, New England contributes to New York, and how few New York to New England! It would seem to me that, when I was a boy, not so many would leave us for New York. I remember feeling the proximity in Boston of its imposing figures, with most if not all of whom I came, through my father, in some touch, except, I believe, with poor Hawthorne. My father used to take me now and again to luncheons of the Saturday Club, active, at that time, with its gifted founders.

"Writing seems nowadays so different a matter from what

it then was. I judge it may have come to much the same pass with you in America as with us in England, where training in journalism and, before that, training in public schools, has given, to a multitude, a sort of pseudo-form, a largeness, looseness, and elasticity of talk which has flooded the country with an enormous sea of chatter. As soon as any man has anything at all to say to anybody, it is puffed about the country in distended and distorted shape. To blame for this, of course, there is the accessibility of print on the one hand, and the dissemination of it on the other. All this chatter must have its uses. There must be a public for it. Indeed I have a reason or two to believe there persists a public for it.

"But I must make no statements! Sometimes I think I shall never speak again; particularly, that is, when some remark or other which I have made in all obviousness, is fostered, to my detriment, annoyance, and ill-temper by persons who have mistakenly interpreted it as a clever saying. I had that trial, for instance, with a chance and simple remark about my friend, Henry Harland. I make mention of it since the ghost of its murdered sense has pursued me even to America. With somebody of presumable intelligence, I was speaking of Harland's last three books and, in common with all the world, was admiring his ability to make one situation serve him thrice. I stated the mere fact that in his first book a nobly-descended young Englishman hires a castle of an Italian or Austrian princess and that the two fall in love, that in his second book, the princess hires the house of the nobly-descended young Englishman and that the two fall in love, and that in the third book, the princess and the nobly-descended young Englishman are together hiring the same house and that the two fall in love. It is as though there were a red glass, a blue glass, and a green glass, rearranged in various order. And to the artist who can rearrange the combination with, each of three times, an equally charming effect, there is deference. Nothing in what I said is to be translated beyond appreciation of Harland's handling of his material, which, after all, is the material he knows and loves and can write best about. One may anything in the nature of an interview, report, reverberation, that is, to adopting, endorsing, or in any other wise taking to myself anything that anyone may have presumed to contrive to gouge, as it were, out of me? It has, for me, nothing to do with *me—my* me, at all; but only with the other person's equivalent for that mystery, whatever it may be. Thereby if you find anything to say about our apparently blameless time together,—it is your little affair exclusively."

—*The Critic*, February 1905

be entertained with his skill of trickery, but the man who laughs aloud at my little word of observation is a silly donkey.

"There is something wonderfully engaging in Harland's fresh boyishness. Never so young as with pen in hand, he is, after all, the eternal boy! It is a disappointment to me that now when I have come to America he has returned again to England. He desired me to visit him in his beloved Norwich and I should so much have liked to see him there. Probably no one ever bore towards Norwich so strong an affection as Harland's for the town. Probably Norwich feels that in his love for her there is untoward excess—something not wholly proper, not wholly licit.

"The poor man has not of late been well. It was suggested to me that he should seclude himself for a period in one or another of the dry Western States, but it is altogether likely that the mental emigration, segregation, deprivation therein would be too much; he could not be without his grand duchesses and his princesses and his nobly-descended young men.

"Partly it's a great compliment to his books that I remember them so clearly; for, on the whole, I seldom can recollect as stories even the books that I most enjoy. On the other hand, for my comfort on this score, I am convinced that many of the best effects derived from reading or, it may be, from experience, come to us by a process quite distinct from that of remembrance. Germs of evil influence we remember all too clearly, but salutary effects softly enter into us without our realizing just how or when. One does not much remember the plot of a book by Meredith, for instance, but looks back on it, finds retrospect, retains vision, in something deeper than memory.

"I believe this is the afternoon when I am to be taken to hear *Parsifal*, to which I have agreed to go on the condition that I be not expected to return for the second installment."

He relieved me with the dexterity of a pickpocket, while we shook hands, of my scruples as a highwayman:

"May I add, since you spoke of having been asked to write something about me, that I have a constituted and systematic indisposition to having anything to do myself personally with

On Henry James's Centennial

· ❧✖❧ ·

I first met Henry James in New York in the summer of 1904. He was a thick-set, slow-moving presence of sixty, with a nervously benevolent face and the hesitantly considered, clausified speech which I might have expected from acquaintance with the literary style of his later days, save that most authors do not speak as they write. He did.

At the risk of seeming to exaggerate, let me, from notes made after we parted, record the first paragraph of length which I heard from his lips, a troubled paragraph about a cold he had contracted between the train from Boston and the New York house where he was visiting. I make no attempt to reproduce with punctuation or syllables of pause his vocal gropings and painstaking allotment of words to their places.

I had brought availably with me [he said] two overcoats, one somewhat heavier and one somewhat lighter, and in Boston I had worn with comfort the somewhat lighter over-coat and was carrying, for possible immediate need in New York, the slightly warmer overcoat on my arm. All had gone well, until I found myself here, seated in a cab beside my friend, David Munroe, known to you doubtless as a fellow-editor, albeit much older, editing, yes, *The North American Review*, and so faithfully replete with welcome and so instantly exacting of responses that I was only vaguely, though venially, aware of my impulse and need to doff the somewhat lighter overcoat and to don the slightly heavier overcoat, which I by all means should have done, to be sure, on account of a rapid change in temperature, or else a difference in temperatures at the place where my journey began and the place where it ended, or perhaps merely a change in hour, but a change all in all,—and, as I have noted, my good friend, David, so engrossed me in greetings and reminiscences and interrogations that I continued, despite a disquieting chill in my marrow, to wear the somewhat lighter overcoat, protecting only one arm with the slightly thicker overcoat, which I should assuredly have been wearing in order to avoid this probably thus avoidable touch of influenza with which I must begin my—under otherwise auspicious aspects—visit to New York, and all, let me charge, on account of your beastly, and by me long foresworn, climate.

Anyone doubting my approximate veracity in this attempt to reproduce the involved plaint made to me many years ago might consult Edith Wharton's account, in *A Backward Glance*, of Henry James inquiring directions on a motor-drive in England. Mrs. Wharton and the Appleton-Century Company have kindly permitted me to quote from her.

My good man (James would like to inquire of an aged countryman) if you will be good enough to come here, please; a little nearer—so. My friend, to put it to you in two words, this lady and I have just arrived here from Slough; that is to say, to be more strictly accurate, we have recently passed through Slough on our way here, having actually motored to Windsor from Rye, which was our point of departure; and the darkness having overtaken us, we should be much obliged if you would tell us where we are now—

and still other winding approaches to his final question, the whereabouts of the King's Road, a question answered by the countryman, "Ye're in it."

To my friend, Henry Harland, was due in large measure

Henry James's cordial attitude toward me both before and after our meeting. Harland had warned me that I might find James fidgety and at first difficult. Even after a seasoned liking between the two novelists in England, the Harlands had told me of the older man calling on them in a cottage there and, saying always that he could stay but for a moment, remaining for an hour perched uneasily on the edge of a piano stool, overcoat still buttoned and hat in hand. I could not but remember this unhygienic procedure of his in England when I heard later about his overcoats in New York. Yes, James had odd mannerisms; but from the first to the last of my exchanges with him in person or in letter, I was never sensible of constraint either on his part or mine. Once I hopefully sent him my first book, *An Ode to Harvard*. Here are some excerpts from his response:

What an inhuman brute you must long have thought me! I have been, have had to be, deadly silent all round for the last couple of years—for I have been immersed in a job of which the sustained rigor, admitting of no compromise and no break, has dishumanized or dissevered me (from the life about) in a monstrous or remorseless fashion. I undertook some time since a collection (or *selection*) of a revised edition of my productions, with long prefaces, to the extent of 23 thick volumes, & the pressure of this (my minuteness of revision proving a colossal task, as I think it is in fact an absolutely unique achievement—which ought to incur some critical attention worthy of the name—) drove correspondence & contacts & social joy—all other employments of the pen, at any rate, in particular, completely to the wall—so that I had simply to stop my ears & blind my eyes; groaning at the odious appearance I presented, but nevertheless holding my course. My letters are all unwritten & my friends mostly alienated & vindictive; but the particular job I recklessly (as regards labors involved) proposed to myself is performed (all will very presently have been) to the last shade of a shade.

After our first luncheon at The Players, I secured James a card to the club, and several times he arranged our late lunching there, "giving me very mercifully till *two* o'clock," he would write, "and then we can make out a genial hour together." Nearly two years later, October 27, 1905, he sent me this word from the Reform Club in London. "I have lost no echo of that kindly buzz of The Players, no moment of my immersion in which failed to fall on my ears like genial music." At one of these luncheons he had remarked.

> You are insolently young, but I approve of you. You do not treat me as I was recently treated in Boston by some vague and amiable young men, who grow always more vague and more amiable, I imagine, toward eleven o'clock in the evening. Bidden to set a night for dining with two or three of them, what was my stupefaction when I found myself confronted by a huge banquet, with peaches on the table, and a toastmaster, and that sort of thing—extravagant magnification.
>
> 'Twas my most troublous experience since being lured into a reception somewhere for one of your considered poets. I had pictured a handshake and two or three minutes involved, for I had elsewhere to go; but there was a very long wait irresistibly enforced on us until arrangements had been concluded for him to commence droning a poem, something about the wind it was, and there for a full quarter of an hour, while we were obliged ruefully to contemplate our broken engagements, he continued droning, slower and slower, on only three notes.

When James said something I wished to remember, I would later jot down not only its substance but, as nearly as I could, its rhythm. I was constantly fascinated by his precise manner in speaking. He selected words as a cat does morsels of food from a plate, occasionally shaking one of them away with delicate distaste. He would even flush over a slip into the wrong word and would flutter and hem and haw till he had righted himself. I wish I could remember some of those instances of oral editing; but I was so impressed each time by his discomfiture, his mortification that I would forget the occasioning word. This matters less than if he had regarded me as a receptacle for momentous utterances.

On old envelopes and slips of paper, yellowed with these thirty years, I have recently come across a few scribbled words against which I had set the initials "H. J." There was a phrase about H. G. Wells,—"immensely ingenious," and a description of a well-known American as "a virtuous little citizen afflicted with clubs for working people, with numerous and unsightly children and with rabid declarations." He complained at the world's being full of "lady-novelists who victimize the supine public" and on another occasion he branded the public as "a great unthinking beast." He enjoyed The Players as "a corner of calm" and musingly murmured, over the photographs which lined its halls, "relics of mummers!" Once, after returning from the Middle West, he gave me the comment, "Chicago is full of the world;—the farther they go from it, the more they appropriate it." May it have been that Chicagoans in the epoch tried to harbor more of "over-ripe" Europe than New Yorkers did? And always I remembered, when he would send me reports from this or that section of America, his having written me from England before the visit, "All I can say at present is that I *desire* to vibrate as intensely, as frequently and as responsively as possible—and all in the interest of vivid literature." Most vivid to me of his sayings in New York, though I left it out of the apocryphal interview I subsequently published and had almost left it out here, was this: "Women are cats, and men are women."

When Miss Jeannette Gilder, editor of *The Critic*, suggested that I contribute an interview with James, I told him of my having from time to time recorded what he said and asked him if I might try to compile from my notes a few pages in the form of more or less connected monologue. He acceded,—writing

(December 24, 1904), "I find it in me to melt and relent toward you—so put me to what further ordeal (of sending on proof and suchlike) you absolutely must." Later he wrote (January 5, 1905), "*Don't* submit it to me—I shouldn't know how to participate little *enough*, and I had much rather participate, frankly and freely, in you as yourself than in you—as not yourself!" Before long "A Word or Two with Henry James" had appeared in *The Critic*, and he wrote me about it from the South.

> Forgive me this horrible public paper, the sign of my demoralized & travel-stained state. I am leaving this place in an hour or two & can't again unpack anything properer.
>
> I have your note telling me that the thing is out at large & am moved while thanking you for the information, to reply that if you can stand it—this more or less indecent exposure—I will try to. Don't please, however, ask me to read it—even to "see" it: I gather in fact that you have that superiority. There are things I won't see.—Success in life today, I think is measured by the degree of one's cultivation of the art (an exquisite one) of not seeing. All except here, for instance, where there is real balm for the rightly averted & the rightly directed eye. . . . I could even now wish you the blessing of a taste of this Florida pleasantry of air & sea & of all nature. Still, your youth doesn't require the fontaine de jouvance in the degree of the battered age of
>
> > Yours ever,
> >
> > Henry James

And here, reprinted from *The Critic* for February, 1905, is an "interview" with Henry James which he forgave, but, as far as I know, never read. He had come back to his native land after an absence of nearly twenty years. . . .

—*The Saturday Review of Literature*, May 22, 1943

Bertha Kalich,
the Yiddish Actress

· ❧❦❧ ·

"If Gentiles cared to come to the East Side and hear me act in Yiddish, I was glad to have them come. But I would not carry Yiddish uptown where it does not belong, and expect them to listen." That is why Mme. Kalich, though she has been playing in New York for nearly ten years, has not before this given us, in the vicinity of Broadway, a complement in some woman's role to Jacob Adler's masterly Shylock.

Reports of a great actress at the Thalia Theater, radiating from the light of Jewish conviction, have, for some time, been reflected and intensified by the enthusiasm of such Americans as would leave the beaten path and dare the unfamiliar speech. Exhorted two years ago to act in English, Mme. Kalich protested, over a glass of Russian tea: "It is the desire of my heart to succeed upon the American stage! I wonder, would they laugh at my English? Would they understand our way of acting? And our idea that to be an artist is to be *real*?"

"Lemberg, where I was born," she said more recently, "was the birthplace of Modjeska and of Sembrich, and I hope that for me too that will be a good sign. When I was about twelve years old, a rich woman there sent me to learn singing. At about sixteen, I got a place in the front of a chorus. Later, when the prima donna grew sick, I played Carmen, and made at once a success. Queen Carmen Sylva was kind to me. Then I came here, and first I sang in operas; then I took to plays, and began to be urged, by Gentiles who saw me, to come on the English stage. But I would not come and speak Yiddish, so till now I have waited."

In the Jewish theaters, Thursdays to Sundays inclusive make up the week of performances. Mme. Kalich has in this way had an opportunity to see acting on our stage. Some prejudiced view that we demand in our actresses an extravagance of emotion and an artificial constancy of movement may have been at the root of her apprehension, two years ago, of not being elaborate enough for us, and may on May 22d have been the cause of a surprise for some of her Gentile admirers who, in her accomplishment, had found likeness to the simplicity and easy sureness of Duse. At her entrance on the night of her debut, a startling spontaneity and solidity of applause leaped to her from the house. It was tribute sufficient to thrill the nerves and impel the tempo of any actress. Mme. Kalich struck at once an emotional pitch that left her no margin. But her audiences gave lively response to her high-strung representation of Fedora, and may have stiffened her prejudice as to what is dear to the Gentile.

"I shall like better when I play some humble character as in Mr. Gordin's or Mr. Libin's plays, or like Magda, who came from a poor family. I cannot be sure when I stop to think about Fedora, especially when the Gentiles are critically watching me; for she was a princess."

As far, though, as can be judged, Fedora has brought Mme. Kalich striking success. The public endorsed the divining instinct of her manager, Mr. Fawcett, who had never seen her act. Her engagement was extended. The critics bowed her a welcome with branches of noble adjectives.

Mme. Kalich is at the vibrant time between youth and maturity. She is sincere. She is ambitious. She has mental energy. She has temperamental grace. With a securer sense of English,—her first use of it was but slightly foreign,—and with a chance for naturalistic rather than hectic acting, she is bound to give English-speaking theatergoers a worthier brief than *Fedora* could be for her reputation as an actress of superior singularity.

—*The Critic*, July 1905

A Poet's Tribute
to a Painter

· ❧❦❧ ·

He danced through life, lighter than any dancer—
Until you spoke his name, that broken word
For which I asked again, although I heard
And did not dare to hear nor you to answer.
Is this a dart from some dark hand in hell,
Or is Heaven's archer so averse to joy
That he spares no music in a laughing boy,
But leaves him silent and invisible?
Perhaps from Heaven—perhaps, himself, he knew . . .
Because he was a playboy and a molder
Of many images in morning dew
To enchant such youth as his from being older.
I noticed yesterday, and so did you,
The winds of Spring forever at his shoulder.

On an old tomb in Arabia is graven the grim inscription:
"This indignity has my father visited upon me, I upon none."
Those who know the young Swiss painter, Paul Thévenaz,
vibrant with life, strong of heart and limb, creator of beauty and
its shadows, are haunted now by his bright image challenging
this final shadow but compelled by the same indignity against
which years ago was uttered the Arabian protest. He died at the
Greenwich Hospital July 6, bringing to a sudden end, at the age
of 31, a career already brilliant. Hardly since the death of Rupert
Brooke has so sunlit a youth been eclipsed among artists.

Five years ago Thévenaz had come to America. He had
rapidly made friends here and won for his art a wide circle of

admirers. He was unmarried, and since the recent death of his parents he had transferred his life and interests to America. Though a French-speaking Swiss, he had volunteered not in the French but in the American Army and was proud of the association.

Of Italian descent, Thévenaz was born at Geneva, Switzerland, on Feb. 22, 1891. He developed in boyhood talents of a painter; and, soon proceeded to Paris to study and earn a living. He was self-taught, except for two years at the Beaux Arts School of Geneva and except as he had learned secrets of color and motion and vigor from Alpine heights and valleys. Only ten days after his death, he was to have sailed for Europe with American friends, mostly for the sake of a walking trip among his native mountains. And how he could walk! I remember, on an all day's jaunt one snowy Winter day along the Palisades, how he skimmed across the drifts as though on snowshoes, while I plodded and stumbled after him. And he would face the coldest weather in glowing exhilaration, with no overcoat, no waistcoat, only a single layer of silk between his chest and the elements he loved. But before his days of silk, those first months, those first years, in Paris, had meant many hardships. Progress was slow. Like other young painters there, Thévenaz led a hand-to-mouth existence, often wondering what lay ahead of him, not what life, for he knew that, but what livelihood. Yet afterward, laconic and with a slight smile, he said of that precarious time: "It did me good."

During his six years in Paris and an incidental journey to Russia, the pre-war Cubistic movement was strong enough to claim him, according to his recent statement through Elizabeth Crump Enders, "so that he became known as a Crystalist, Prismatist, and so on. He met Igor Stravinsky and Jean Cocteau, and both exercised a strong influence in his artistic development. His long talks with the former convinced him of the necessity for a knowledge of geometry, mathematics and the absolute mastery of technique; and a thorough grounding by Eurythmics at the Dalcroze School of Music in Switzerland had laid the foundation of a clear musico-rhythmical knowledge, which he carried through all his work." For a while, until the war interfered, Thévenaz was devoting his energies to the production of ballet, in collaboration with Stravinsky and Cocteau.

Meantime he had gained recognition in France as a portrait painter, among his successes being portraits of Stravinsky, Pierre de Lanux, Cocteau, Countess de Noailles and Comte Etienne de Beaumont. In spite of his modern geometric technique, he had an uncanny aptitude for creating vivid likenesses, behind which, instead of background—with which he mostly dispensed—there gleamed, like a spark in the eye, the salient quality of his sitter. I might have ventured a guess that this faculty was not in spite of his sharp, precise technique, but owing to it, if I had not seen at his studio last year a portrait he had done of himself in the traditional manner, with solid depths of realistic color and warm, rich modeling, against a carefully painted Florida landscape background. Thévenaz was his own severest critic; and, though his self-portrait was to my eye a masterly image of him and sadly to be missed now, yet it went the way of two portraits he had made for me and of many other canvases—he slashed it out of existence.

He may have been in too exacting a mood when he destroyed, or it may have been the result of slow judgment. I never heard him repent. Once gone, the rejected painting seemed forgotten, and toward the task of recreating it he evinced no dismay. Graceful and gay as most of his work was, and even at times flippant, yet in his art he was Spartan, with a conscientious courage akin to that of Saint-Gaudens, who, after three years' work on the model of his Sherman statue, came to look at it one morning and, to the consternation of his assistants, hammered it into fragments. A number of the Thévenaz portraits were shown at his New York exhibition at Knoedler's in 1917 and at the Chicago Arts Club in May of this year. Among the best of the many painted or drawn in America are portraits of Miss Elsie de Wolfe, Mrs. Simeon Ford, Miss Lauren Ford, Mrs. Ruby Rose Goodnow, Mrs. Gardner Hale and Miss Fania Marinoff (Mrs.

Carl Van Vechten) of New York, Miss Mary Brown Warburton of Philadelphia, Mrs. John Alden Carpenter of Chicago and Mrs. Abraham Stern of San Francisco.

Memorable among his works, and different from most of them, are two paintings, made in 1920, of Christ-themes. One is a portrayal of the boy Christ in the Temple. Over his head in a shaft of light a cherub is holding a crown of thorns; His mother, proud at His elbow, is yet anxious and touched with presentiment; and in the young face is a pure and surprised serenity as He holds His own against the legalities of a pompous, bewigged Judge on one side of Him, the sophistries and pedantries of two skull-headed scholars on the other and the orthodoxy of an angry old Pharisee confronting Him. The bony fingers of six hands are already reaching for Him like talons and the Judge is permitting the law to have its way.

One day Thévenaz handed me a photograph of the other of these two paintings and then turned to a page in *The Beloved Stranger* and indicated this two-line poem:

Peace

When I am crucified upon his brow,
Will the strange god be at peace?

An emaciated, drooping Christ hangs from the brow of a great long-eared face which broods and smiles and is the entire background of the picture. The sensual and the spiritual are blent in the eternal mystery of pain and peace.

But, in spite of such accomplishments, the artist had long felt, as he phrased it himself, "that decoration is the most abstract form of art, the most musical, the most creative, and that it requires more intelligence, more tact, more knowledge than any specialization in a portrait-form of landscape or of still-life or of portrait." He "realized," writes Mrs. Enders, "that he was not painting a canvas to be hung first in one room, then in another, but with the architect was making the wall a veritable part of the house itself, no monotony, no false note of color, no undue proportions, but all in harmony." And, as joy of life was vibrant in his physique and character, so was the intense joy of the artist vibrant in the bright, pure tones and daring, vivid arrangements of his mural decorations.

"No matter what the subject is," said Thévenaz, "decoration is related to music and the higher mathematics." And, as he turned to his mural undertakings in this country, he explained further that "the educated artist of today knows too much in too subjective a way, limiting himself often to one form of expression and doing the same thing over and over all his life. So-called 'personality,'" he continued, "is too frequently a question of strokes, tricks, more or less self-conscious, for most modern artists. If one has personality, it will come through, no matter what one does. In doing decorative work the artist is given limitations by his customer's tastes or wishes, he has to fit his personality into the new shape every time, thus enlarging his field of expression and discovering that variety is not the enemy of style but, quite the contrary, its friend."

In accepting commissions Thévenaz set himself unusual and difficult tasks. "It was like ice skating with red hot skates," said he, when he painted recently for a dining room in the house of Mrs. Frederick Havemeyer a nineteen-foot frieze on white oil cloth; and it was characteristic of him to choose for his subject the skyscraping City of New York as seen from the East River, for he was a keen disciple of the beauties of Manhattan. Totally different was his treatment of the swimming pool in George Blumenthal's New York home. With magical design of water and of all its curious contents, mermaids, deep sea fish, tall iridescent flowers, jeweled shell and sunken ship, he created of the pool an undersea garden in gorgeous poetic motion. For a moving-picture hall in Miss Alice De Lamar's home on Long Island he alternated with comic rhythm charcoal and colored panels. On the former appear Charlie Chaplin, Theda Bara, Mary Pickford, Douglas Fairbanks and others; and on the latter appear such subjects as Punch and Judy and a Tyrolean fantasy called *The Final Kiss*.

To quote Mrs. Enders once more, "he was not afraid of anachronisms. By employing any experience of the past, of the foreign, of life or of nature anywhere, he could infuse into one painting all that the varied musical instruments may bring into a symphony." Among those who own mural decorations by Thévenaz are Mrs. George Vanderbilt, Mrs. Sidney Fish, Mrs. Richard Hudnut, Robert Handley and Rodman Wanamaker, while there are two specimens of his work on the walls at John Wanamaker's. There will be a memorial exhibition of his work next season, held by the Junior Art Patrons of America, founded by Mrs. Albert Sterner.

By quotations from Thévenaz as to his art tenets, I have given evidence of his prompt use of English to express the sensitive notions of his mind. Letters of his which I have seen on varied topics might well be collected into a distinguished volume of swift observations and gay wisdom. When he made a trip to the Pacific Coast, he wrote briefly of the Grand Canyon the nearest description I have ever seen of it. I liked it so well that I asked him to give me the phrase. I cannot remember his exact wording, which this time was in French, but these were his images: "It is the dead sex of the earth, in which at noon the sun still revels. It is the sarcophagus of mountains, into which peers the moon."

Even during his first year here he knew how to make English words and American words shine and move, as in a description he wrote me of a performance at the Hippodrome: "Maelstrom of joy—forty Arabian boys red and gold—sparkling like as many suns—jump and whirl in a rush. And from the sky dive girls—slender black arrows—in a 'spectral' extravagance of colors and water and noise and rays and clowns. Gee! I had a good time at the Hippodrome." On the same page he said of a poem I had shown him: "It makes me think. And I do not like to think. Laughing is better. And you will laugh in reading this letter that I wrote in English, with the very sweat of my brow as ink." Though later he became more willing to "think," he seemed a little sad about it. And of his death, of this he doubtless would have said to us: "It makes you think. And I do not want you to think. Laughing is better."

—*The New York Times Book Review and Magazine,* July 24, 1921

A Young Visit with George Meredith

· ❧❀❧ ·

Looking through family papers, I found a post card I had written my mother from London shortly after my twenty-first birthday, in 1902: "England is pretty big in spite of its size. But the biggest town in it is Box Hill, Surrey. Two hours, tea and cigarettes with him! He's deaf, so I sat and listened. His face is beautiful, and what he says and desires is sadly vigorous in so old a man, with no more use in his legs."

As a freshman, in 1898, I had read *Diana of the Crossways* and had at once fallen under the Meredithian spell with much the same excitement as that which came to me two years later from Walt Whitman and three years after that from A. E. Housman, an odd but complementary trio: the patrician self, the democratic self, the ascetic self, similar to one another only in sheer individualism and resultant creative artistry. For my young taste and response there had been since Shakespeare no writer until Meredith whose English could make characters come so alive and large in an atmosphere of acute and steadfast thought.

The proctor at Stoughton Hall, where I lived through my college-time, was Charles Townsend Copeland, an impressive wag, a genius at reading aloud, an instructor in English, liked by students but accepted by some of the more academic professors with a tolerance only half-amused. I remember the curl of his moustache when I pitted the importance of George Meredith against that of Thomas Hardy. I took his attitude as a sort of challenge: and it was not long before a freshman on the ground floor of Stoughton was reading Meredith to a few of his classmates, while in the room above, to crowded groups of older students, the proctor continued reading Hardy.

Out of this impudent emulation grew "The Meredith Club": twelve or fourteen of us organized for readings aloud from the genius who was to us what Proust and Joyce and Eliot have been to youths born later. At Boston in 1900 Meredith, like Brahms, was said to be occult; but neither of them was occult to us. And how could they have seemed occult to a boy named Lyman Beecher Stowe, to George Clair St. John, future head of The Choate School at Wallingford, to Barry Faulkner, future muralist, to Karl Young, future scholar at Wisconsin and Yale, to Arthur Davison Ficke, future poet, or to me? I wonder how many of us who are still living take *The Spirit of Comedy* as seriously as we did then?

We met one evening a week for our readings, with beer and pretzels, in this or that room hung solid with framed photographs of paintings, sculpture, architecture, or classic ruins, and on the mantels family photographs. Our grates held glowing coal fires, chairs were comfortable then (usually there was a Morris chair for the reader close to his student lamp), and during our four-year existence, especially during the earlier half of it, we covered much Meredithian ground. I recall that later, when freshman and sophomore seriousness was waning, the accent of the evenings shifted somewhat from our seer to our beer. Meantime, through a system of dues and fines, we made more or less available to members a growing stock of the green Scribner volumes, each with a golden tree of life on its cover. The system was simple. Whenever a member was absent from a meeting, he paid the treasury a dollar, which would be added to his monthly dues until enough had accumulated to buy him a volume. Of course a flaw in the system was the fact that the two or three of us who cared least for Meredith were soonest possessed of his books.

The hail and farewell of The Meredith Club was set for an occasion when I, its president in my senior year, was to read to a public audience in Massachusetts Hall my Bowdoin essay, a performance exacted by the terms of the award. It was a laborious essay on "The Style of George Meredith." The occasion was officially advertised, Mr. Copeland was especially invited, the club was proud. And then when the hour struck, I strode upon the platform, with my heart sinking into the spacious emptiness of the room. There was no escape. Bitterly, doggedly, I read my paper to eleven embarrassed faces. Four faithful members of the club were sitting in a tiny cluster. In another cluster were my mother; an uncle whom the rest of the relatives had bullied from his office; two stiff-set aunts; a sullen, athletic brother from Yale; a meek girl cousin; and also a girl from Brookline, not quite at ease with my family. The club members had already heard my essay more than once and assured me later that they still admired it; but four of the relatives, vindictively disappointed by the vacuum and profoundly uninterested in Meredith, were done with their duty. To this day I remember that while my voice echoed in the empty room, my thanks were going up to God that Charles Townsend Copeland was not present.

This debacle, however, only stiffened a youth's faith in his idol; and my main purpose, on a trip abroad that summer, was a pilgrimage to Meredith, with a letter from a mutual friend of the novelist's daughter as my open sesame. In London I received word of an appointment and a marked timetable.

The day came.

On leaving the train at Box Hill, I felt my heart fiddling and thumping. Could a man just of age experience in the 1950's any such tremors, on any such pilgrimage, as those that stirred me on mine at the turn of the century? Are young men today, about to meet Picasso, Malraux, or Stravinsky, as shaken by such excitement? The younger generation seems cool today. Perhaps younger generations always seem cool. Several times along the walk from the station I stopped to make sure that the person moving was I. My heart was not only in my throat but in my ears, half-deafening me as I approached the presence of one who, to his disciple, was a supreme being in the heaven of letters. The sensation returned and then slowly subsided on my train trip back to London, during which a still hypnotized hand managed to draw from my brief case a black-and-white checkered notebook with a Spencerian label, *Compositions*, and joggle into it paragraphs remembered from the afternoon. Echoes of Meredith's voice made for me a recording in that book, as actual voices were later to do on discs.

Through fifty years I never recopied the jottings. Meredith had been caustic concerning an American woman's "interview" with him. But now, reading the notes again, I find, spoken to me: "If you should care to quote me . . . wait till I am dead," and my conscience is cleared by his permit from the grave in which he will soon have lain for half a century.

Twenty-five miles out of London, in a Surrey countryside looking like southern New Hampshire but cosier and neater, the walk from the railroad station to Flint Cottage was by a sylvan roll over dwarf hills. I passed an inn where Keats was said to have begun "Endymion." And then, before long, I came to a lane branching with a private air as into some large estate. A hearty passerby told me that Mr. Meredith lived but a step or two down it. There may have been other buildings on it. I see only two: Flint Cottage, square and small, with a simple front of ivy-covered block stone; and still smaller, above it to the right, the miniature chalet, like a Swiss dollhouse, where Meredith had long done his writing.

From the lane, three tall parallel green hedges made a triple crescent, enclosing two paths. The one I followed led me to the kitchen. A maid, who was in the yard tilting a copper pan against a post, set me right as to the way I should have taken and, passing through the house while I went round, had the front door open to me before I reached it.

I stepped into a low, easy-feeling room, where I thought to gather my wits, and stood face to face with Meredith. I had known but forgotten that he was partially paralyzed, so that he could not stand. Leaning forward as though the upper half of his body rose and indicating with a quick gesture a chair across from his, "Be seated," he said, "pray be seated."

The voice, though large and commanding like that of an

old-time Shakespearean actor, was warm. The face was reassuring, the expression, the eyes. There was none of the remoteness of age or importance but a clear close look of welcome, or human parity. A small dog—a dachshund, I think—was dancing round me with barks. Just as I began to realize the barks and wonder how long they would last, a half-indignant, half-indulgent "Go to!" cut them short. Tender and repentant, the little animal went to, choosing a place close to its master's chair where it became an appreciative, though only slightly animate, footstool.

With slippered, slack-stockinged feet propped on the dog, Mr. Meredith asked in a companionable way questions I could readily answer through the daze that was still on me: where I had been, what I had seen, what I was planning in England and "Have you other engagements for the afternoon? . . . Then will you wait for a train which, giving us a pleasant interval, yet reaches London in good time for dinner?" While I was still nodding, he rang for the maid, the same one. "We shall have tea, Frances, at four." And mentioning the hour of the train's leaving, "You will take care," he told her, "of tea and of the clock." Seeming to feel relief at having fixed the schedule for the afternoon, and perhaps at having made me sure that I might stay two hours but not for dinner, he settled back in his chair, with his head turned slightly in my direction.

I had already heard of the sculptural beauty of his bearded head. I heard later that the Meynells had set at the end of their swimming pool a stone Spanish Christ of the seventeenth century with head and face remarkably like the young Meredith's, and that Rossetti, in his painting, "Mary Magdalene in the House of Simon the Pharisee," had modeled the Christ after Meredith. But it was not as a Christ that I saw him, not as the son of either carpenter or tailor. It was as a blend of Hebrew prophet and Greek youth, Moses and Alcibiades. His brow at seventy-four had a scholarly cast but none of the contracted importance of an academician's. I was not aware of wrinkles. And, within the white halo of hair and beard, the newness of a child's face came through his chiseled, classic features. It was as though a purity of white marble had flushed alive.

He spoke awhile of his daughter's American friends; and his speech, to my surprise, was very slow. From a man with mind so swallow-swift I had expected darting, intricate speech. On the contrary, his phrases were measured, were almost drawled, the syllables not blurred but lengthened; and his voice was certain and firm, easy, deliberate,—not loud, but a slow and powerful pomp of sound, musical, melancholy, deep, like a contented funeral march.

Knowing of his deafness, I was not surprised to notice, standing vertically by him on the table, above volumes of Aristophanes and Racine and a copy of *Hamlet*, a curious hearing aid which looked like a cymbal of yellow metal with, for some reason, a diminutive lace handkerchief hung over its top. And I noticed that he wore a rough suit of light gray, with a red tie.

He scarcely a moment sat still, constantly shifting his hands, his head or, with more effort, his legs, which fell most of the time into a diagonal position from one side or the other of his chair.

In answer to my eagerly articulated account of our Meredith Club at Harvard, he said: "I always welcome an American. Yes, such audience as I have had in England I owe to you Americans. Long before my countrymen would hear of me, certain good Bostonians received my writings with a friendly ardor. And the English have followed but slowly. Perhaps because of this, I am not in general over-fond of my countrymen. I sometimes have to resist a feeling that I cannot bear these English and must keep away from them."

"Because they haven't liked your work?" I ventured, not quite pleased that my hero should be so human.

"No, no," he mused. "I'll tell you. I'll try to illustrate. Their disagreeable narrowness. Their insularity. I remember in my young manhood, when I was studying in Germany, a marked instance. I was on a walking trip alone and had climbed the steps that led to a high terrace by one of the castles on the Rhine. I found sitting there a family of Germans," which he so pronounced that I at first thought he said Drummonds. "After a moment they spoke to me in fluent English; and we were still amiably conversing when a great red-cheeked English girl came bouncing up over the edge of the parapet. She stopped short, stared at us and, being in advance of her family, called loudly down to them: 'Oh, father! Some of those beastly Germans are here! What are we to do?' The answer came distinct: 'I suppose we must go down again.' And down they went. An extreme instance this may have been and it happened many years ago; but there is still too much, ah, far too much of that spirit in many an Englishman. The English never know when they are beaten. They come back from a trouncing. That I am proud to say of them. It is a good quality, but it is not all, it is not all. I am afraid these English are not—not open to ideas." (Five years later, in a letter to *The* (London) *Times* concerning the violent tactics of the suffragettes, Meredith referred to John Bull as "a still unburied old gentleman, though not much alive," who would "not move sensibly for a solitary kick" but only for a "repetition of that manner of enlivening him." And two years after that, in 1909, a few months before his death, he told an interviewer: "I am by temperament an optimist. I believe in the future of the race, in the progress of mankind and in the inviolability of the soul. But I am a pessimist in one direction, because I see looming in the distance, not the very far distance, a great tragedy, the Armageddon of Europe. . . . We in Britain need a great stirring up, a great crisis, to rehabilitate the qualities of our race." On the other hand, he predicted that militarism in Germany would "produce a sort of barbaric courage, dead to all the higher instincts of man.")

While he was still shaking his head over "these English," I mentioned his severity toward them in his novel, *One of Our Conquerors.*

"Yes," said he, "in the opening of that book I gave them, perhaps, too much of a drubbing. I no longer care whether or not they like my drubbing or me or my work. But I can still be irritated by them. Even amongst the Englishmen who choose to admire my books there is an attitude, a custom I dislike. Do you know that even men of letters will write me asking that I send here or there photographs with my name on them? That I will not do. If they wish my books, let that be. But my life, let that be too."

He spoke of a "brilliant young critic"—Richard LeGallienne —who had come to call on him and, upon being offered a manuscript poem, had said that he would rather have a page of one of the novels. Meredith confided with a pleased chuckle: "He was given nothing."

The maid brought him four or five letters. "May I open them?" he asked. And then he glanced up from one of them a little wearily. "Even Maeterlinck asks for a photograph. But they should leave my life alone. I should not be troubled by it now. It is in my books."

Another of the letters, he said, was from "a kind person, an American woman. She too wishes a photograph! While she was here, in Box Hill," he continued, laying down her letter, "I was not well. She was at the Inn and sent me bouquets, for which I had no use. But she was a kind person. I think she shall have a photograph. You see, I like Americans. Will you write your name large on this card? And will you lay it on the edge of the chimneypiece—there where you see several papers—thank you, —papers and notes that are of importance to me. Are you of Celtic descent? Yes? I thought so."

I had myself been on the edge of asking for a photograph with his signature; but since I was not particularly "kind" and neither a woman nor Maeterlinck, I decided against it. Afterwards, in America, I received the sensitive Hollyer photograph, unsigned. It was not, however, because he had read my thoughts and responded to them; it was because I had written his daughter of my hope that he might have read them when he asked for my Celtic name on his chimneypiece.

He questioned me again about my travels. I told him that in

shop windows, not only of cities and university towns but of villages the country over, I had seen sets of the new pocket edition of his works, placed alongside sets of Scott, Fielding, Thackeray, and George Eliot. I did not realize at the time that Meredith's first book, *The Shaving of Shagpat*, had been published in 1855, before any of George Eliot's. The quick gleam which came to his eye contradicted, it seemed to me, his remark that he was indifferent to English dislike of his work. "I am glad," he said quietly, "of any reason for my writings to be reprinted."

He implied the unlikelihood of another novel from him: "I can no longer use my hand. I tried dictating only once and gave it up. I have to write directly from myself to paper, with no intervention." Later, understanding that his never-finished *Celt and Saxon* was written after that, I wondered by what means.

By now I was brave enough to bring back the name of LeGallienne and to praise his book, *George Meredith, Some Characteristics*, which had appeared a decade before. "I liked it," said Meredith, "I told you that I thought him a brilliant young critic. An American critic," he went on, "has bound an essay concerning me in a volume with essays concerning Carlyle, Thackeray, Ruskin, and the others. He named it *Victorian Prose Masters*. I am sure that is good of him. But I believe he calls me perverse," (pronounced *par-varse*) "and I believe therefore, he will not *see* what I mean, prefers *not* to see." I was disturbed by this, since I had met the critic, Mr. W. L. Brownell, a potent figure at Scribner's, and been impressed by his great and proper reverence for Meredith, whose major quality he had described in the book as a "celestial sunlight of the mind." If my host had not been deaf, he would have heard Mr. Brownell defended, but the back and forth of it would have been too difficult; I had done enough, advocating LeGallienne. So I substituted a question which sounded to me and, I feared, to him, like words from the most mechanical of reporters. I tried to hold them back, but out they came: "What criticism has pleased you most of all you have ever received?"

The little dog might have yawned while his master paused

and then at quick random, I think, picked this: "An eminent Australian surgeon wrote me that there was no medical treatise in existence containing a truer exposition of a certain kind of mental disease than my account of Victor Radnor's case in *One of Our Conquerors*. It pleased me particularly, since I knew nothing whatever about that kind of disease."

He gave patient answer to the query often made in those days as to why, in *Diana of the Crossways*, his heroine should have sold for money the confidence of the man she loved. I spoke of a woman's telling me that "Diana would no more have done it than she would have eaten with her knife." Meredith smiled. "The Celtic mind," he explained, "in man or woman, is peculiarly constituted. After a nervous cataclysm, a bolt such as had shocked and rent Diana to the depths, the Celtic temperament goes blind, the Celtic mind drops into a swoon from which it wakens slowly and dully. Then from the deathly impress of darkness it flees in panic towards light, towards the first light that appears. And this is what happened with Diana."

I feared that I was tiring him, but how could I leave before train-time and how the devil could I make myself interesting? On I went as if a machine possessed me: "I have often heard you criticized, Mr. Meredith, for treating only of the upper social class."

"Ah, yes," he smiled. "Why will I write only about educated persons? I am accused of being supercilious and narrow-minded or interested only in the one class. It is not that. It is merely that I believe ideas to be more truly the man than are his arms and legs. With the lower classes one must treat mainly of primitive passions. Once I did it, but not with enjoyment or success." This reference, I think, was to his Hardyesque novel, *Rhoda Fleming*, which Robert Louis Stevenson had called the best drama since Shakespeare.

I regained my ease by interrupting as little as possible. Meredith appeared to enjoy talking and I knew now that his difficulty in understanding annoyed him. I did venture, though, to mention my having won a prize at college for an essay on his style and concluded with the practical point which even he might expect of an American: "So you see, Mr. Meredith, you have been worth forty pounds to me."

"Indeed?" he answered, glancing around genially. "There on the table is a photograph of one worth sixty pounds." I looked toward the table in bewilderment. He was apparently indicating a framed portrait of what seemed some fancy breed of dog! Perhaps my eye, as I spoke, had rested on the dog at his feet and he, not hearing my prelude, had thought I referred to the value of some pet of my own. Or was it amused and gentle discipline?

Having said earlier that he liked a cigar I had brought from America, he now pushed a box toward me, remarking: "Will you pardon me for offering you one of mine? It is a Swiss product of a kind that was given me once in Venice, where I could not bear the native cigars. I smoke them now not so much because I like them as for association."

To my comment that there was little mention of tobacco in his books, as contrasted with the memorable passages on wines and ales and beer, he nodded and said: "Yes, I discovered, reading over *The Egoist* lately, that I made Dr. Middleton zealously fond of port. Do you know? I cannot bear port!"

"What *is* your favorite wine, Mr. Meredith?" I asked, for his sake more than mine.

"If I but think of burgundy," he answered, "I care for nothing else."

"Sparkling burgundy?" I asked in eager innocence.

"Ah, no, no! Would you intrude upon the peace of Bacchus a bouncing trull! Renounce degraded burgundy! Sparkle is better in Moselle, and best in champagne. But they serve champagne too cold. No ice should touch it. Use the pump on it fifty times, or wrap it in a thoroughly wet towel and place it in a draft. Perhaps with Hamburg champagne ice is an improvement. Ice may help it into you; getting it out is another matter. But as I say, I like nothing else if I but think of burgundy. Yes; there is one case downstairs. I am not sure what is left in it. It has been there for years, heaped with dust. It is something rare and will just about last me. The way to have a good wine is to buy the vineyard." His smile wandered to an unspoken reminiscence.

He came back, smiling still. "Do you know that liking good women is consistent, though it may not seem so, with liking good wines? A little more sense of humor among women and a little less tendency among men to dissemble and exaggerate would make evident the justice of my conviction." To this day I am not quite certain what he meant by this; but it is what he said.

While the maid at four o'clock served tea, Meredith, tapping a magazine on the table, declared: "Your *Nation* used to be the best-written journal I knew. But now that it has lost Godkin, I find nothing so good as *Le Débat*. And, besides, of all modern languages, I judge none so fit a medium of expression as French prose, in which the stress is not arbitrary but compliant to the sense."

He then pointed out a coffee cup which the maid had brought half full of lemon juice: "I wonder if you have ever seen lemon juice used in tea? It is a custom introduced to me but lately." Seeming surprised that Americans shared with him this peculiarity of taste—though I did not mention our use of slices, for the taste of the rind—he asked for more juice, and into his own tea he poured both lemon and milk! Over his mixture, which I politely matched, and our thin-cut slices of buttered bread, he spoke suddenly, with no apparent connection:

"An Italian woman said to me once that she would rather marry a monkey than an Italian. But an Italian countess whom I knew fell in love with an English debauchee, a divorced rake, fell sick and pined for him. Every string was pulled for the Pope's sanction. They eloped without it. After regaining her family's good will, she finally secured a Papal dispensation. All this she did for a man who was worthless. Later, at Florence, I myself saw the Englishman helpless and pushed about in a wheelchair, hopelessly an idiot. He had been misusing women for years. Women are given men as an everlasting test and, where men are not monkeys, as an everlasting blessing. An honor to the race are the children of a race which honors women. I believe that the nation which first permits its women to be independent enough to choose their mates or to live alone in comfort and security will stand at the world's helm. The fact that your race leads today at the forefront of civilization is due to your magnificent women, sound in body and mind."

He spoke warmly of Gertrude Atherton, I cannot recall whether in literary or personal approval. "And do you know Emilie Grigsby?" he asked. "You do not? Then you shall have a letter to her. I call her my auburn dove!"

"American women are not all so wonderful," I said. I have forgotten whom I was remembering. It was not the girl in Massachusetts Hall.

"No, not all," he granted. "Your S. S. McClure—fine fellow, though too busy—served me unkindly once. He sent a woman to me, a fair woman. She came in July, dressed in furs, and posed by my fireplace and stuck out her foot. She told me she was engaged to be married to one possessed of all that delights the female heart, a journalist, she said. And she said that she too was a journalist. 'You are not having an interview with me?' I pleaded. 'Oh, but I am,' she laughed. 'Oh, but you are not,' I decreed. And I said not another syllable until she pledged that she would keep our afternoon private. In less than a year she had the brave assurance to send me an entire printed page of more or less possible remarks, purporting to be mine." It was then, with a twinkle, that he added: "If you should care to quote anything that I have been saying or not saying, wait till I am dead. I shall be then quite willing."

There was a sound at the door. He half rose, with an effort, to greet two visitors, a young woman and a man, and named us to one another. "We cannot even sit," she said. "We have a long walk ahead but have dropped in for a moment, because I wish to thank you for your introduction to the Egyptian letters."

"I have contributed," explained Meredith, "a feeble expression of my knowledge of her great-aunt, Lady Duff Gordon, whom I loved and reverenced,—a silvery dominant woman."

They did sit a while and invited him for a yachting cruise on the Mediterranean. He accepted, stipulating that he be allowed to sleep most of the time, perhaps all of it, on deck. I asked if that were a measure against seasickness, and he answered with a slight grimace, "I sometimes bend the knee when Neptune nods." (I wish I might have told Meredith then about a note I was to receive in 1903 from Lady Duff Gordon's daughter, Mrs. Janet Ross. It was after I had joined McClure, Phillips and Company, publishers of Lady Duff Gordon's *Letters from Egypt*, and had sent Mrs. Ross Mark Twain's enthusiastic comment in which he called them "a literature in themselves." I was answered from Firenze: "I am obliged for yr. quotation of Mr. Clemens letter but am at a loss to understand yr. fancying you brought out the book, as it was published by Brimley Johnson in London, & noticed with the highest praise in nearly every newspaper in England. I am expecting Mr. Clemens here next month." Mrs. Ross must have thought American publishers nonexistent or only branches from Britain; but in this instance I believe Meredith would have been amused by the indignant English "insularity.")

After Miss Duff Gordon and her companion had left Flint Cottage, he spoke of their long walk—of long walks he had himself taken and of others he would like to take. "I am told that your Hudson is even more beautiful than the Rhine, and I have always said that someday I should walk along the Hudson and see for myself." And then he looked down at his legs.

I suggested motorcars.

"Bicycles! Motorcars!" he exclaimed. "Yes, yes, but all the world will return to walking. I shall not be here. But that will hardly matter. All the world will return to walking. Meantime for me a donkey cart."

"Do you live alone in Box Hill?" I inquired.

"I do. And I am accustomed, after all, to my own society. Through many years I have learned that the levels of constant social intercourse usual in ordinary life are not beneficial to a writer, certainly not to one," he smiled, "who seeks to soar. Here I have my gardener to talk with. And my girl, my daughter, is only two miles away at Leatherhead. My gardener has been with me four and twenty years. We discuss politics."

As the time for my going drew near, I asked him about a story I had heard of his sharing, with the Rossettis, with William Morris and with Swinburne, quarters on Cheyne Walk in Chelsea. Visiting Carlyle's house a few days before, I had stepped around the corner for a look at the Rossetti house, not a comely memorial like Carlyle's but an ill-featured dwelling.

He sat back, gave a deep gentle laugh and then with a note of indulgence exclaimed, "Gabriel!" He paused, as if to collect details, and then proceeded. "This is the story. Gabriel had written that he and his brother were taking a house in Chelsea, that Swinburne and some of the others might join them, and had suggested that I too should have rooms there, where I might find congenial company when I should be in London. I think that I vaguely assented and told him I would soon wander out and discuss it with him further. I started early one morning and walked to London and beyond to Chelsea. There I found Gabriel in the dining room, but hardly out of bed, and before him on the table a large slab of ham that had hung at the butcher's too long, been kissed too warmly by the all-kissing sun, and over the ham bled five great eggs. I sat down, looking at him in astonishment. 'Gabriel,' I asked, 'You will eat that?' He said he would. 'Gabriel,' I asked, 'You have exercised?' He said he had not. Wherewith he fell to and in a trice had consumed it all. That, I found, was much the way he lived: after the meal an excess of work till six o'clock when he would eat an excessive dinner; and then he would walk to London to one of those cellars where they sang madrigals and glees and loutish ballads. Thackeray put an end to the worst type of their songs by having Colonel Newcome rise up and walk out. I cannot bear the cellars. But some men can. Thackeray could. Gabriel could." Whether Morris could or Swinburne and Watts-Dunton could he did not tell but continued: "Gabriel would come back, fall into a stupor of sleep, waken to fall upon another such breakfast and then fall into a stupor of work. I think I did engage my rooms for the quarter, though I had little use of them."

The Southwest

A City of Change

· 〰️〰️〰️ ·

Now and then, since a decade ago, travelers who had been taking a little extra trouble had been telling me of their reward. They said that Santa Fe, lying eighteen miles off the main line, had held its own against man and his mechanisms, had remained a city different from the rest, had escaped the American cookie-cutter which turns out cities one after another in approximately the same pattern. I was conscious of the sad fact that New Orleans, San Antonio, San Francisco and even Charleston had been changing, had been taking on, more and more, the one likeness. And when, three years ago, I came to the little ancient Capital, I came in time.

To be sure, the great oblong Plaza reaching the Cathedral had long since been cut in twain: half of it, the Cathedral end, solidified now into a Grecian bank, a Middle West department store and a New Mexican post office. On three sides of the surviving plaza were the usual haphazard and hideous fronts of an American business street, but on the fourth side the old Governors' Palace, massive adobes, seasoned pillars and *vigas* still held its ground; its *portales*, like a public cloister, still shaded one sidewalk, as they had formerly and properly shaded all four; and its *patio* was still a garden-spot with trees. On Sunday evenings when the band played, youths would stream in one direction round the Plaza and in the opposite direction maidens, just as apart from one another and just as aware of one another as I have seen them in Mexican cities. Older women moved nun-like, on Sundays or weekdays, with soft black shawls over their heads, the fringe hanging down their dresses. Burros came daily in droves with round burdens of firewood, or with riders from the country whose heels bumped lazily from a jiggling trot. Though there was no longer an open market in the Plaza, there was one street left where wagons, from ranches or from Indian villages, held corn, tomatoes, apples, melons and other fresh produce to be bought directly from the dark-eyed drivers. On the roads radiating from town were many views and few signboards. In doorways, on street corners, were many groups speaking Spanish and few speaking English. In the Legislature were interpreters nimbly moving from one member to another and nimbly rephrasing remarks into English or Spanish. On the outlying hills were venturous artists in sombreros, corduroys and bright neckerchiefs. When Holy Days came, there were bonfires and the Virgin or St. Francis was carried through the streets by walking worshipers. And round about the landscape, in their snug, earthen pueblos, were Indians, guarding the dignity of their race and instinctively living the beauty of their religion and their art, as they had been doing for hundreds of years.

I had come in time.

Soon I had found my own adobe, one of the oldest, with a broad-beamed roof to shed homely dirt on me in windy weather and primitive rain in wet. I was above the troubled world. I was washed clean of the war, I was given communion each night when sunset would elevate the host on the Sangre de Cristo mountains. I was writing to friends who lived on another planet. I had found something not to be found elsewhere in These States, a town too much itself to be feverishly imitating its neighbors. Nothing strained, nothing silly, just an honest-to-God town, seasoned and simple, easily breathing its high air.

And now what?

We Americans from the outside have quickly made of Santa Fe the city of our discontent. It must be boosted, paved, enlarged, it must be Americanized. The streets which were rough and made us go slowly are smooth now and make us go fast. The native earth which used to touch our feet on the edge of the Plaza is being sealed out of sight, out of touch. These pavements may grow machines now, but not persons. The little adobe houses near the Plaza have cast down their grassy crowns before a bulk of garages, garages in the Santa Fe style, yes, but inviting blatant vehicles which hurry people's errands and harden their faces. Even the Virgin this year, because it rained, took her annual outing in a limousine. There is a red airplane in town. Will she come to that, if it rains next year? The Ascension of the Virgin! A faint ambition to restore the *portales* encounters practical objection from the shopkeepers; but it may in the end be realized, not because *portales* lend beauty but because they attract tourists. Someone built a movie house in the style of a Pueblo Mission; someone else hired it and closed it to prevent competition with a movie house built like an oven. The band still plays on Sunday evenings, but the boys and girls walk now as they like. There are fewer and fewer black shawls, fewer and fewer burro riders. The free market place opposite Burro Alley is a thing gone and forgotten; it was unfair to the grocers. There are no more Indian pots to be seen and advantageously bought in the patio of the New Museum; it was unfair to the curio-dealers. The outlying views are flecked and flanged now with billboards. There are campgrounds for the tourists and the con-tourists. Spanish gives way to English on the streets and soon in the Legislature. Eagle-eyed artists have motors and gather visitors into exhibition-parlors. Even those who persist with the som-brero and the flying scarf serve, it seems, a commercial end. "At first," said an old resident, "we respectable people used to resent the freakish, free-and-easy clothes you artists wear about town; but we have found that it attracts and amuses the tourists; and if you can stand it, we can."

We are all doing it. We cannot help ourselves. We are attracting people here. We are advertising. We are boosting. We cannot care enough that, by professionalizing the apparent dif-ference of Santa Fe, we are killing the real difference. We are crowding out the natives, to make room for improved houses with artificial warpings. We are changing our town from the city different to the city indifferent. Even the Indians are feeling us, are yielding to us. Being Americans, we have to manage our neighbors. And it is always for their good. A few years ago, the Pueblos conducted their own deliberations and maintained their own character. Because of their simplicity, they were threatened with unjust loss of their lands. Not only Santa Fe but the country at large came to their rescue, spurring Congress to pass at last needful legislation. As to their lands, the Pueblos are much better off than they were a few years ago; but almost any month now, a non-Indian with a childlike face and a flowing tie may be found steamrolling an Inter-Pueblo Council according to his whim and writing letters for them in imitation Indian. Other outsiders, to serve other ends, are following his example. And what shall it profit the Pueblos to win their land if they lose their way? We in Santa Fe, for the sake of their health and their lives, are persuading some of them, in spite of their medicine-men, to benefit by the services of a visiting nurse. And while we thus discourage a therapeutic element of their religion, the Protestant missionary, less tolerant than his Catholic brother, is urging the Indian bureau to discourage an aesthetic element. While our own white medicine-men are saying to the Navajo, "Come away from the former things, you cannot be a guest at the heathen sings and be a member of Christ's church in good standing," our archaeologists, artists and merchants are busily summoning Indians to Santa Fe and to Gallup for a theatrical presentation of the dances and ceremonies which have hitherto been a communal and at their best a spiritual exercise. Last year, for this friendly exploitation, we cut down trees in the patio of the Governors' Palace and made it bleak with bleachers.

To "attract and amuse the tourists," to make a show of our town, are we cutting down and withering its beauty? Are we killing and embalming the best qualities of Santa Fe, in order that a long line may come and look?

Enough of pessimism.

Not long ago, at a meeting in Santa Fe, when a project was broached that some of the ablest Indian painters be sent as art teachers to the pueblos, a zealous collector of old pottery objected on the ground that such teachers might spread among the villages designs which belonged from antiquity in one or another particular region and which should therefore be sequestered at the source. As though the source were not Montezuma or Kubla Khan or the sun itself!

And so it is with Santa Fe. I have been talking like a collector of old pottery, of old shards. I have been talking as our friend did at the meeting, when he concluded, "It is unfortunate but true that art grows."

Cities grow, for the worse and for the better. A motorcar will some day be as quaint a sight as the old wagon over Candelario's. And he who rode in that old wagon was doubtless a shrewd trader; he may have told Indians about the Gospel and corrupted their art with beads. The wagon in its time took man away from the touch of the earth, so that he transferred healthful exercise from his own legs to those of a horse. No wonder the skull of the horse is still laughing, alongside the motor-road.

Lovers and old women and artists and Indians! Why should youth forever follow an ancient and unnatural custom? Why should the boys and the girls pass on opposite ways of the street? Why should old women be draped funereal before the *velorio*? Why should artists, or merchants either, be grudged their livelihood? Why should Indians give their corn or their cattle for a song that fails to cure? Why should those dance faith who had rather dance jazz? Are unbelievers more dignified in a dance than they are in a pew—or are believers less dignified in Santo Domingo than they are in Washington? The Pueblos have long danced their dances before Catholic altars and added an older beauty to the beauty of the saints. Will it hurt them to bring some of that beauty into an American town, just as the Acoma Mission has come beautifully to town in the shape of the New Museum? Or will it hurt the town to take what it likes from the Indian, from the Spaniard, from the Greek, from the Mexican, from the Middle West? There are more kinds of vitality here after all than are dreamt of in a sentimental philosophy. It is an abode not only for a collector of pots but for a collector of life. And as Heraclitus noted long ago, and a collector of pots long after him, life changes.

—*Laughing Horse*, September 1924

Mexico

· ❧❧❧❦ ·

Bull-Rings

· 〜✕〜✕〜 ·

I

All through the week we had been setting foot into churches.
Mexico City in its business section had reminded me of the Bund
in Shanghai, of Berlin in its public buildings, of Los Angeles in
its residences, of Brooklyn in its parks; but in its churches—
perhaps because I have never been to Spain—it was Mexico City.
In the massive Cathedral, in the Sagraria, with its great trickles of
carven stone, in every church on every street, there had
been thousands of kneeling figures: women with black shawls
over their heads, not quite hiding their wistfully wrinkled faces;
an occasional fashionable widow; men of the world in North
American dress; ragged peons and their wives in bare feet or
heavy sandals. On Good Friday it had been a long, thick ooze of
people, in at one door and out at another. And inside, always,
that sound as from somewhere else, that murmur of praying
voices with a faint dominant treble, like doves at evening or like
the one breath blent from many bells on a pagoda. At the cinema
we had seen The Passion of Christ: we had seen the figure of
Jesus come forward with a lamb on his shoulders, forward into
the very hearts of the audience, while the orchestra played, on a
marimba, a gaily swinging tune to welcome him. The fact that
even during the Crucifixion the tune happened to be "Three
O'clock in the Morning" seemed in no way to lessen the emotional reverence of the Mexicans.

And so, on Easter Sunday morning, having been to churches
all the week and to a sacred movie, we arose with the bells of
resurrection and went to a bullfight.

There were five of us: from Poland an experimental psychologist; from England a novelist, from Germany his wife; and

from the United States an editor and a poet; the psychologist continually sympathizing with Soviet Russia, the novelist continually sympathizing with himself, the wife and the two Americans sympathizing variously.

At the entrance of the arena, we had all, but the wife and the poet, been searched for firearms. It had been announced that President Obregon would preside at the spectacle, much as President Coolidge might preside at a ball game. But there was neither firearms nor, eventually, their possible target. President Obregon was too busy explaining to a province of the Kingdom of Oil some of the developing doctrines of democracy.

Since places cost half as much in the sun as in the shade, we were sitting in the sun; except that this day there was no sun. Below us, surrounding the great empty ring, was an inner rim, a circular five-foot fence with here and there a gap two or three feet wide, and in front of the gap, on the same level, a slightly wider six-foot fence, making in each case a safety-box for hard-pressed toreadors. We sat within five rows of the ring—sufficiently elevated for security of limb, but sufficiently depressed, even at the outset, for insecurity of nerves. The crowd about the ring, seeming less an assembly than a monster, was already, with its murmurs, growls and occasional yells, twisting our nerves a little; and we noted on face after face of the Mexicans, however prepossessing and amiable at first glance, a subtle touch of cruelty. Never a hard eye. Seldom a hard mouth. But, almost always, that tiny telltale dent above the nostril.

There came, opposite us, an abrupt crash of many voices. Somebody's hat had been seized and was tossed among scrambling groups. Other hats. Even a shoe. And orange skins were aimed from behind at tempting heads.

Three bands appeared, one at a time, each band in its own smart uniform, and were promptly barked at for "musica." When at last a Spanish melody came swooping down from one of them, the vocal din was only thickened, accelerated. They had wanted, not music, but a sharper and heavier tempo of excitement.

What looked like a folded coat was thrown into the ring. It

seemed a signal. Instantly the mass of men in unreserved seats swelled over the reserved section like black water from a broken dam. Most of the seatholders who came later were vain claimants.

On the very moment advertised, a square procession entered from the gate and marched trimly toward the Presidential box: two wide rows of toreadors with cloaks of yellow, magenta, blue or green, above their salmon-colored stockings; then mounted picadors; then banderilleros, their short jackets and caps embroidered in silver; then matadors, embroidered in gold and with red cloaks; and then, finally, in red harness, two teams of three mules each, a comical, grim promise of the dragging of bloody carcasses.

Heroes received plaudits, the procession dispersed. And, with no warning, no noise, a great white bull had swum into the ring and stood a moment apprehending his enemies. They were there, the first of them: two stationary horsemen. When he lowered his head and made clumsily for a horse, the rider warded him off with a goading lance. The second rider did likewise. And then into the ring came the toreadors, to allure him, to nag him, with their bright mantles. He saw them one at a time. He snorted. He charged a cloak. It was whisked over his head. He curved quickly and charged again, spearing the air under a swing of color. To and fro about the ring it continued. Now and then he would corner a toreador, who would either dodge into one of the safety-boxes or lithely vault the arena fence. All of a sudden the bull, too, had struggled into the circling alley. Followed a scurrying of attendants, a closing of gateways to cut off a section of the alley, then a subsiding of excitement. A cloak teased him out again into the ring: he stood still, waving his tail. His belly lifting, lowering with tired breath, he looked slowly around; then again he leapt the fence, this time breaking it. Once more the closed exit, once more the flashing taunts, the trim weavings and wavings of five toreadors; once more his return to the ring, his half-seeing eye, his vain charges, his wasted wrath.

But now a change, now a chance! A horseman comes toward him. A picador with armor under his trousers urges a decrepit mount to expose his poor old belly. The crowd is hushed, expectant, on the edge of the seats. This encounter is not at the center of the ring, but close to the fence, with no room for the horse to escape; and though the picador is supposed with his blunt lance to ward the bull off, the crowd knows better. The baited bull paws up the earth, slowly bends his head, expects results, and gets them. The lance is futile. The horse rears and flounders. In and up goes the horn. And, while the picador tumbles against the fence and sheepishly finds his feet, the bull shoves and gores and rips. The crowd heaves a sigh of relief; and by the time the toreadors have again drawn their stupid prey toward the cloaks and the picador has remounted and forced his dazed animal into motion toward the exit, the horse's bowels are bulging, almost to the ground, great, hideous, pale gourds and vines of pain. And see! Somehow the bull is not where he should be. Just before the picador reaches the gate, there is another snorting plunge and this time the entire covering of the horse's belly is ripped off. The sacrifice is down and dead; and his contents are out on the ground stinking. Earth is thrown over them. The whole proud front of the bull—head, neck, chest, leg, hoof— shines crimson in a moment of sun. How throaty the crowd is, how satisfied! There has been something phallic in this fierce penetration, this rape of entrails, this bloody glut of passion.

Warnings had not prepared us. Dark with anger and shame, the novelist and his wife are on their feet and gone. And at the same moment there are large drops of rain. Then a shower. Then a downpour. Many of the onlookers scatter for cover. Others, including our own remnant, remain, huddling from the wet. And, in spite of rain and mud, the show continues.

A banderillero advances, with no protective cloak, but holding up in each hand a pink-stemmed barb. He yelps at the brute, hops in the air with feet clicking together below and barbs clicking together above. Now on this side, now on that, he waits and watches till the bull gathers its heavy wits again and charges. In a flash the man has leaped aside, and in the same flash has planted two barbs at a neat upright angle just between the shoulders. He does it again with green banderillas, shorter ones: an alert and precarious performance. We may have applauded with the crowd. I am not sure.

For a moment the animal shakes his shoulders and bellows a little: hurt, angry, baffled. And then comes the matador, his scarlet cloak hung athwart a long sword. His taunting and cheating of the bull by dexterous lifts and twists of the red cloak is a gayer, nimbler feat than that of any toreador. Again and again he cheats the tired brute; till, finally, choosing a moment when the horns come toward him at precisely the proper slant for an opening, he plunges the sword half to its hilt, between exposed shoulder blades. There, with the banderillas, it joins a deadly nimbus of steel: ironically like a section of the nimbus surrounding Our Lady of Guadalupe, the patron saint of Mexico.

How can these pains have reached him, these mortal thrusts? He pauses; he wonders. For a last moment or two, before the end, he follows his bright enemies, but with weaker and weaker lunges. His knees crumble. He sinks. He is up again, but only for a second. He is a ghastly image of a bull at rest in a meadow. His eyes see nothing and everything. He knows that he is dying. He accepts. Thereupon, with one swift jab, the obscurest of the butchers dispatches him. In come the mules. Proud and stalwart until now, now limp and ignominious, the bull's body is dragged out at one gate, and out at another are dragged the horse's body and entrails. And the rain-drenched crowd is ready for scene two at the popular slaughterhouse.

With the rain over, people are gay again. The poet's bald head becomes a target for wet wads of newspaper. He takes it in a daze, feeling rather the banderillas and the sword; but when he puts his hat on again, the crowd is appeased and spares him. He thinks he is smoking.

Another bull, another of the six—a small black one. Another spectacle of brilliant brutalities; a dull, dark weight of brutality against a keen, bright ease of brutality.

In the second round, the creature seems more sagacious. He continually backs away from his persecutors, sees through their game and despises it; but to no avail. He is helpless against their intentions and against the blood-lust of the onlookers. Reluctant, if-you-make-me-I-will, he finally charges first one horse that is edged toward him by his picador, and presently a second. In each case and several times, the horse, given a chance not so much by the rider as by the bull, uses his hind legs to good effect, fights free and stalks off with an air of doddering valor, all the more pathetic in the fact that he has postponed his disembowelment until the next holiday.

Only the first bull was white. The third, like the second, was black, and three others that followed were black, too, or partly black. This one, weighing a ton and a half, promptly killed a horse; and then, before long he himself was killed by a matador who, in the very act of executing the master-stroke, a deep thrust of the sword into the vital spot, slipped and fell and might have been injured but that his huge victim at once drooped and stood quiet, stricken from within by a mortal vent of crimson, triply spilling with his breath from his throat and nostrils. In a few moments he was humbled and dead by the one stroke, and the matador was gracefully acknowledging applause from section after section of the amphitheater.

In the fourth round, one of the horses, receiving a horn in the chest, managed to walk all the way out with a steady spurt of blood from above his forelegs, like a jet from a fountain wall. In the fifth round, the favorite matador, Juan Silveti, yielded to one of his fellows a bull not fierce enough, not foolish enough, for heroes.

Then, in the sixth round, the banderilleros inserted their gay barbs as neatly as ladies adjusting long hairpins. And the matador waited on his knees for the clumsy beast to attack, as ever, the cloak of the man instead of the man himself; by a clever twirl, the master attracted two charges in the time of one; he walked nonchalantly away, dragging his mantle at his heels, with his back to the bull; he placed on the ground a handkerchief and succeeded in so manipulating the victim's attack that the perfect sword-thrust was given with the matador not stirred from his white foothold. Surely, by this time, the game needed these graces, these variations—since there was no mastodon at hand to spill the bull's entrails or his own.

The editor stayed stoutly to the end with the psychologist. They even paid homage later at the home of the toreador. The poet did not see the last dead carcasses hauled away by the mules. But, outside the Toreo, he saw the live carcasses being hauled away in automobiles, the dapper teasers and murderers, through a crowd of adoring faces and voices, not to their butcher shops, but to their beds and their liquor and their tobacco.

II

Later that evening, the novelist remarked to his wife that we had seen "the grandeur that was Spain soiling its breeches." Still later, the experimental psychologist brought a Mexican friend to join the original group.

"It was my sixth bullfight," gloated the Pole. "You become used to it. Did you see how happy the bulls were, shoving it into the horses! I'd like to have you meet my . . ."

"No," said the novelist, firmly. "I do not wish to meet your friend, nor anyone else in this loathsome country. And I have seen, as well, all that I wish to see of you."

A pause. A separation. The Mexican remarked quietly, "Because he has judged all Mexico by one bullfight, must I judge all England by one Englishman?"

No. Rather by the one bullfight let us judge the one Englishman and his like. A believer in Empire, in master and slave, in the subjection of India; but a pitier of horses and bulls. Or let us, by one bullfight, judge the President of the United States supporting a navy that tortures Haitians to make a national business-day. Or let us judge almost any American tolerating a Congress that delivers over thinkers to be held in prison pens, or Negroes to be burned alive by mobs—the national sport of America. Or Americans tolerating the president of a great university who expels a boy for refusing to stick a bayonet into a dummy's entrails, for refusing to accept instruction in Anglo-Saxon manhood.

Bull-rings, bull-rings! India, Egypt, Belgium, the Ruhr,

Haiti, California, Mississippi. And with men for victims. At least the bulls of Mexico are openly intended for market and are given a chance, if they care for it, somewhat as soldiers are, for "one crowded hour of glorious life" before the sacrifice. But the horses were given no chance, nor the Hindus, nor the Egyptians, nor the Haitians—with their picadors astride them. Bull-rings, bull-rings, true to form.

The poet dreamt, that night, of Christ with a lamb in his arms; and the lamb changed into a bull; and the bull changed into a Hindu; and the Hindu changed into the burnt remnant of a Negro. After all, the Mexicans, with as much joy as they liked, might have killed all the black bulls, if only they had shown a sense of the fitness of things, spared the white bull and hung it with roses dipped in the blood of black calves. But, no. The dream concluded with one more tragic change. The burnt remnant of a Negro became the dead body of a white soldier.

A night or two later Rodolpho Gaona, the most popular matador in the Republic, left Mexico City on his way to Madrid. The station was thick with his admirers. There was a military band. It played the gracious melody, "La Golondrina." Thousands of hats waved farewell to the great torero on the Pullman platform. "Viva Gaona! Feliz viaje! Regresa pronto!"

Matador means murderer.

From Mexico to Spain, the triumphal tour of Señor Gaona, the matador; from France to America the triumphal tour of General Foch, the matador; from Britain to America the triumphal tour of Lord Balfour, the matador; from America to Europe the triumphal tour of General Pershing, the matador.

Bull-rings: the spectacular slaying of stupid, helpless animals or of stupid, helpless men who have been teased to their death with bits of bright cloth.

Can our gods be as false as we have made them, in our chapels by the bull-rings?

"Yours is a morbid religion," said a Chinese scholar once, when the poet had questioned him as to Christ. "Why are they so glad that Christ has risen?" he went on. "Because they are ready again, as always, for the crucifixion." A morbid religion, a bloody religion: this blood-lust of Europe and America, this religion of the blood of the lamb.

—*Pearson's*, June 1924

While the Train Pauses
at Torreón

· ❧✦❧ ·

Federico Gamboa, when a member of Huerta's cabinet, worsted Wilson's Secretary of State, Bryan, in an exchange of notes; but, better than that, he is a Mexican author.

I happen to be on the same train with him when he arrives at Torreón in the State of Chihuahua. At the station, an expert band is playing him welcome; and between banners which hail him as "la gloria de las letras Mexicanas," he is being led by officials, on a national holiday, into this town of cotton, flour and iron mills.

What such flowering of the spirit has my own country to offer amidst all the massive mechanics of its civilization?

When we Americans come to Mexico humbly, when we forget to criticize the railroads, the hotels, the clothes, the mechanical status of the country, when we open our hearts and minds to the conscious earth that resists vulgarities, to the courtesy, the innate intelligence, the quiet force, the ease, the quickness, the sensitiveness, the endurance, the smile of these people, we shall begin to appreciate the nearness to our borders of a natural university for our youth. Unfortunately, the nearer Mexicans come to the aforesaid borders, the more rapidly they learn the gist of what we to the north of them know and the more deplorably they forfeit both outer and inner grace.

All this is being jotted down while the train still pauses at Torreón, while Gamboa's gesture of appreciation is still in the air; but the record is no momentary impulse, it is the result of a year of months spent in Mexico during 1923 and 1925.

Be it said at once that I am for the most part puzzled by

Mexican aristocracy and officialdom and by the bourgeoisie. These classes seem in many ways unworthy of their supposed inferiors. With notable exceptions, they turn to Europe or to the United States for inspiration or example, when, obviously, they need to trust and cultivate the basic qualities of their own race. It is the Mexican Indians who challenge and deserve homage: human beings as graceful and rewarding as corn, as self-sustaining and self-defending as cactus, as violent and quick to change as Mexican sky, as firm and slow to change as Mexican mountains. From them, be it hoped, comes future Mexico. From them comes a spirit of civilization strange to motorists. From them come wisdom and laughter, a proportioned sense of the values of life, a power to work when work is necessary, a power to endure when endurance is necessary, a power to oppose when opposition is necessary, to smile and live and fight at happy intervals and to loaf magnificently when the earth commands.

Yes, these are qualities under the sun and moon. But under government, under the economic harness in which the world is driven, how are they then, these Mexicans? How are these estimable Indians as officials, as governmental instruments? They are like the Chinese. They are often enough honest grafters. They speak hypocrisies on occasion, but they also take occasion to wink. They fill the heart, the stomach and the pocket as conveniently as they can, but almost always they exercise therewith the morality of humor. They are not like Anglo-Saxons, "weaned on pickles," grimly swallowing scruples and using a Christian cookbook to explain unholy diet. Our American humor is too frequently a humor of fear lest the other fellow laugh first, a defensive humor lest we be thought slow or stupid or sensitive or tender or decent or just. Mexican humor, humor among the Mexican Indians is more natural, more vital, more imaginative. The Mexican Indian is often obscene, but with the earth's obscenity, often cruel, but with the earth's cruelty; lest he might succeed in becoming pompous or pretentious or greedy, in ways false to his bit of substance with the earth.

Besides his sense of humor, he has an awareness that, in

the long run and in the large sense, justice is inevitable. Revolutions may have helped in the lesson. He may close one eye, but he seldom closes both eyes.

It has been said of Señor Calles, President of the Republic, that he manipulates the national law to indulge his own career and pocket and of Señor Zuno, recently Governor of Jalisco, that he put the Guadalajara streetcars out of business because he controlled the supply of buses; just as it has been said of Mr. Coolidge, President of the United States, that he would have preferred to retain rascals in his cabinet and of Mr. Mellon, Secretary of our Treasury, that because he and his family are major beneficiaries of the aluminum trust, he grossly favors it.

Let us assume, for purposes of comparison, that these charges are true, both in Mexico and in the United States. In Mexico there is an important offset. The public, the consumer, may in both countries be robbed with the left hand. Obregon and Fall may both own ranches which they never earned by service to the state. Yet in America, the aggrandizement at the moment is all one way. President Coolidge removes from this and that public commission members who might act as watchdogs for public interest against private interest. He has given, otherwise, ample evidence of believing that there is no public interest of the many, except through the preferred private interest of the few. His disregard of the ordinary citizen's welfare is implacable, whole-souled and complete. In Mexico a few important pockets may be neatly and unduly lined, but on the whole the ordinary citizen looms higher and higher as a conscious and considerable decider of Mexican destiny. The Mexican laborer is being handed the beginnings of a real education, not merely pious bunk but the facts of economics and the satisfactions of art; land has been given him, and now he is to receive the water and the tools to make it yield; the professional military college is to be closed or curtailed and the workers of the country are to be depended upon for an army. In a word, the Mexican people, against temporary obstacles and confusion and outside interference, are more and more becoming the state. North of them, the state is more and more being substituted for the people. There may be more melancholy on the Mexican Main Street than on ours; there is also more happiness, more awareness of lasting values in other things than oil. And though America may officially protest to Mexico that its appropriation of moneys for educational purposes is excessive, Mexico insists upon teaching its own people in its own way.

It is conceivable that Gamboa was being welcomed to Torreón as a politician; but it is not inconceivable that the banners meant what they said, that he was being welcomed as a man of letters. It is conceivable that ex-Governor Zuno of Jalisco may not have been averse to his own welfare; it is incontestable that, besides easing and bettering the life of Jalisco laborers, he has reopened the University of Guadalajara after its long desuetude and has even offered a free Mexican trip to the winner of an American poetry contest. American Governors please notice.

There are bandits in the United States as well as in Mexico. There is oil in Mexico as well as in the United States. There is civilization in both countries, each after its kind and each complementary, though not always complimentary, to the other.

—*Laughing Horse*, Autumn 1927

China

Translating
Chinese Poetry

· ❧❧❧ ·

Blithely, three years ago, I undertook with the eminent scholar, poet and publicist, Dr. Kiang Kang-hu, a translation of three hundred poems from the Chinese, thinking that twelve months would see my labors ended. Through twelve of the thirty-six months I have worked from eight to ten hours a day on nothing but these poems and through the other twenty-four have been continually devoted to them, even accompanying Dr. Kiang to China for a year of closer cooperation. And they are still unfinished. I might have read a lesson from the history of as short a piece of translation as Fitzgerald's *Omar Khayyam*; but I was rash and, better than that, fascinated. Prior to the present undertaking, I had translated with the help of a Chinese student a few poems from the Confucian *Book of Poetry*. Those few had been enough to stir my wonder at the quiet beauty and deep simplicity that are as much qualities of Chinese poetry as they are of Chinese painting.

Stephen W. Bushell, in his book on *Chinese Art*, speaks of some early painter as typifying the aim of painting with the phrase, "to note the flight of the wild swan." It "shows already," says Bushell, "the preoccupation of Chinese art with the motion and breathing life of animals and plants, which has given their painters so signal a superiority over Europeans in such subjects." When one remembers that in China the wild swan was traditionally the messenger of the heart, the phrase might be used also to typify Chinese poetry: "the motion and breathing life" of a world in which man is the animal and nature the plant. But the wild swan was not merely a messenger between young and passionate hearts. Chinese poetry begins, in a way, where ours ends. When I felt a certain monotony of subject matter in a section of the volume I was translating, the parting and separation of friends and the solace of the everlasting hills, I turned to the *Oxford Book of English Verse* and found there an equal if not greater monotony in the succession of poems dealing with the extravagant passions of youth. Wordsworth, in his lyrics, is the most nearly Chinese of our poets. The poetry of the Chinese is, like his, the poetry of the mature, or, better, of grown children. It sings not the rebelliousness of youth, but the wisdom of age; not the excitement of artificial life, except for the elevation brought by wine, but the quiet of nature; not the unsteady joys of passion, but the steadfast joy of friendship. It is attached to actual daily life and not reserved as an ethereal pastime. A Chinese poem sounds often like the heart of a letter—and so it was: a condensed and thoughtful message.

Tu Fu of the T'ang Dynasty is generally accounted by the Chinese as the greatest of their lyric poets, though it was said of him and Li Po, "How shall we tell, when two eagles have flown beyond sight, which one has come nearer the sun?" From Tu Fu's grandfather, Tu Shên-yen, the editors of the anthology I am translating selected a single poem, in which his quiet voice echoes all the way from the sixth century to undo a persistent delusion, prevalent among certain poets of the Western moment, that beauty is to be found only in the unfamiliar. Incidentally, the poem illustrates the difficult game of "harmonizing a poem," which poets sometimes played with their verse: one poet would respond to a poem from another by adopting the other's rhyme-words in the same or altered arrangement. Tu Shên-yen's poem is called

> *On a Walk in the Early Spring*
> (*Harmonizing a Poem by My Friend Lu Stationed at Ch'ang-chou*)

> Only to wanderers can come
> Ever new the shock of beauty,

Of white cloud and red cloud dawning from the sea,
Of spring in the wild-plum and river-willow. . . .
I watch a yellow oriole dart in the warm air,
And a green water-plant reflected by the sun.
Suddenly an old song fills
My heart with home, my eyes with tears.

"To understand the circumstances of mortality," says a writer in *The Nation*, "to know what such a being as man can expect, and then to contemplate such knowledge—that is as near as art can get to any steadiness of joy." And that is where T'ang poetry had arrived a thousand years ago. The T'ang poets do not fool themselves with illusion but, seeing things as they are, find beauty in them—and thereby bring the high, the deep, the everlasting, into simple, easy touch with the immediate. They are masters of momentous minutiae, the small things that make the big. They know and record the immense patience of beauty. There is sadness in that patience, but it is an honest, a hearty, an even relishable sadness. One feels that they had sent their souls out through all the intricacies that are now confusing this Western generation, through all the ways of experience and imagination, and had then recalled them to the pure elemental truths, had received them again, peacefully cleansed of illusion and restlessness, and content in the final simple beauty of their own dooryards. To be sure, they knew where to place their dooryards. But so might we all, if we would.

I was fortunate enough to spend three months on a Chinese mountaintop, with a poet and his family, in the kind of retirement the old fellows loved and wrote about, overlooking a landscape the like of which I had never seen from any dwelling on earth. There were Sung mountain paintings glimmering from our peak all the way to the Himalayas; there were tremendous rainbows, sometimes leaving a bright section in the heart of a towering white cloud after the rest of the bow had faded; there were countless bamboos glistening after brief showers; there were the cicadas, ten thousand Chinese actors on one note at top pitch; there were the waterfalls along our paths; there were slow changes of incredible mist, spellbinding the dawns and the twilights; there was always, below us, the vast plain—rippled with hills, varied with purple shadows of cloud, veined with jade-green rice fields; and there were remote silver gleams of river and lake and even of sea—the whole level eastward horizon seeming often the actual ocean and our mountain the brow of the earth. It is no wonder that I became imbued with the spirit of the poets who had lived in just such places—with the "huge and thoughtful" patience of China: the kind of patience that is wisdom; the kind of wisdom that is submersion of one's self and its little ways in the large and peaceful distances of nature. And just as that landscape moved and breathed, so do the Chinese poems from line to line. And just as man becomes natural and simple in a presence like that, so did the Chinese poets. And in all the chaos of contemporary China that spirit is alive. In Peking last winter, fine old Admiral Tsai Ting-kan said to a friend of mine, "The older I grow, the more contempt I have for the processes of human reason and the more respect for the processes of the human heart."

Dr. Kiang has said much the same thing to me. And against various odds, he has practised what he preaches. Appalled at times by the stupendous task confronting those who would ameliorate conditions in China, he has begun, as the sincere and simple altruist always begins, with his own conduct and his own circumstances. Some years ago he founded a girls' school and gave his own dwelling in Peking to house it: the first girls' school in the country founded by a Chinese. He inherited a fine library and a distinguished collection of paintings. Some of the latter are in museums in Japan, the Nipponese having been the most intelligent of all the looters after the Boxer uprising. What was left of the library he has given to the University of California. His share of other property inherited from his father he has renounced in favor of his brothers. When Yüan Shih-k'ai usurped the throne, Kiang risked his life by challenging the act and finally fled to America. Now that he can be of service again in China, he has relinquished academic opportunities in the New World, to return to his own people. In other words, he is a man of the same nature as the noblest of the T'ang poets and, as such, better fitted to interpret them than if his only qualification were the title he won under the Empire, when literary knowledge and even poetic ability were requisite for passing the old Government Examinations.

When Dr. Kiang and I were colleagues on the faculty of the University of California, he led me to an anthology, compiled several hundred years ago, of poems written during China's golden age of poetry, between A.D. 600 and 900: *Three Hundred Pearls of the T'ang Dynasty*, an anthology better known among Chinese than *The Golden Treasury*, or any other collection of English poetry, is known among us. It is in the hands and heart of every Celestial schoolboy. One afternoon in Peking, I was to address a large audience and read some of my translations at the Higher Normal School, a Chinese institution for the training of teachers. Dr. Kiang was my interpreter for those of the students not proficient in English; and he was to read the originals of the poems. At the last moment we found we had not brought the Chinese book; and it had to be hastily bought at a shop close by. Laughing at my surprise that so important a volume was not in the school library, President T. Y. Teng explained, "We do not need it there: everyone has it."

The Chinese call this poetry, written thirteen hundred years ago, "modern poetry." In this "modern poetry," in spite of the constraint of rules and regulations unparalleled in the prosody of the West, I found the same human pith, the same living simplicity and directness, the same fundamental beauty, as in the ancient "unregulated" verse of the Confucian *Book*, and the added power of an austere and consummate art.

T'ang poetry, like all Chinese poetry—even of the contemporary poetic rebels, who correspond in spirit to our writers of free verse—used rhyme, or what we should call assonance. Rhyme in itself, however, is not enough. There are "drum tales," containing thousands of lines all on a single rhyme, which calls each time for an accompanying drumbeat; and these achievements are not considered poetry. Besides rhyme, there are rules of tone and balance which I have space here only to intimate. A

Chinese character may be inflected, in the dialect preferred by *literati*, according to five tones—one level, two rising, one sinking and one arrested. The first three are called "even tones" and the latter two "uneven tones"; and there is an intricate pattern by which corresponding characters in adjacent lines have to be of opposite tone-groups, while yet of parallel syntax. A translator might conceivably divide the English vowels into two groups—a, e, i, and y on the one side and o and u on the other—and, opposing the vowels of the two groups in conformity with the pattern of opposed tones, arrive at an effect faintly akin to the music of the Chinese convention; but to translate three hundred poems in this manner would be a lifework. As to the parallel use of words of a similar nature, I am convinced that the result would monotonously offend the English ear, though I am not sure that a final translation may not be made a thousand years hence, faithfully following the Chinese order. In some of the four-line poems it is possible in 1921 to use the parallelism throughout and in some of the longer poems to use it now and then. For example here is a poem by Po Chü-yi, a slightly different version of which I have already published in *Asia*:

A Suggestion to My Friend Liu

There's a gleam of green in an old bottle,
There's a stir of red in the quiet stove,
There's a feeling of snow in the dusk outside—
What about a cup of wine inside?

I have in China, like two of the poets I quote, a friend named Liu—to whom I successfully sent this reminder.
    A poem by Liu Tsung-yüan shows the same method:

Snow on the River

A thousand mountains and no bird,
Ten thousand paths, without a footprint,

A little boat, a bamboo cloak,
An old man fishing in the cold river-snow . . .

Here you have the verbal parallelism, but nothing, of course, of the pattern of tone and rhyme.

I agree with Arthur Waley that a rhymed English version is treacherous ground. Let me give the carefully simple reading which Dr. Kiang has helped me make for the *Outlook* of Liu Fang-p'ing's

A Spring Heart-Break

With twilight passing her silken window,
She weeps alone in a chamber of gold;
For spring is departing from a desolate garden,
And a drift of pear-petals is closing a door.

And then the long-established version by Prof. Herbert A. Giles:

The Spinster

Dim twilight throws a deeper shade across the window-
screen;
Alone within a gilded hall her tear-drops flow unseen.
No sound the lonely court-yard stirs; the spring is all but
through;
Around the pear-blooms fade and fall—and no one comes
to woo.

When a Chinese poet wishes to present you with flat terms, whatever he may imply by them in the judgment of commentators, he speaks as Wang Chien does in

A Bride

On the third day, taking my place to cook,
Washing my hands to make the bridal soup,

I decide that not my mother-in-law
But my husband's young sister shall have the first taste.

But the heart of the poem, "A Sigh of Spring," beating forever in its last line, seems to have made on the eminent sinologue who was translating it as "The Spinster" either no impression at all or else too much of an impression.

The use of metaphor by the T'ang poets? In comparison with our use of it, they hardly use it at all. Their language is compact of it. But so, to a lesser degree, is ours. And it is surely as much an error in translating from the Chinese to drag out from an ideograph its radical metaphor as it would be in translating from the English to uproot the origins of our own idioms. It lands you in a limbo-language. If an English poet incidentally used the phrase, "at daybreak," and a translator made it appear to a Chinese reader that the phrase read, "when night was broken by the day," the relation of the phrase to whatever else the English poet might be saying would be distorted and the balance of his poem would be broken by what in itself is a valid and arresting image. But the image is now a commonplace. Hence it should be translated into an equivalent phrase in the Chinese and not dislocated by an unintended emphasis. Dr. Kiang once said to me of an English translation, "Three heavy words in a four-line poem? One would tip it over."

Unfortunately the English poet or reader who approaches a literature like the Chinese or the Greek is so accustomed to our lavish use of surface-images that he feels ashamed of the nudity he sees and hastens to clothe it. Gilbert Murray, even, says in one of his introductions that, if he should translate a play from the Greek in terms as simple as the original, the effect in English, a language naturally ornate, would be so plain as to be bald. That approach seems to me mistaken and a little insular, as though English literature had nothing to learn; and it has caused, on the part of many translators and through their work, a misunderstanding of the spirit and beauty of Chinese poetry. We Westerners are forever expressing things in terms of other things, exalting metaphor too often above truth. The triumph of the great Chinese poets is the art by which they express a thing in its own innermost terms. And it is that very art, concealing itself, which may make them seem to the casual observer persons of slight attainment, not "literary" enough. A friend remarked to me, on hearing some of Wêi Ying-wu's verse, "There's nothing in that. That's what everyone feels and anyone could say." I doubt not that Wêi Ying-wu, had he overheard, would have been comforted.

Restricting myself, in order to keep within bounds, to the four-line poems in which the words stop but the sense goes on, I choose from Wêi Ying-wu

An Autumn Night Message to Ch'iu

As I walk in the cool of the autumn night,
Thinking of you, singing my poem,
I hear a mountain pine-cone fall. . . .
You also seem to be awake.

The poet here selects an exact touch in natural happenings that starts alive a sense of the nearness of a friend—a moment mystic, but not too mystic to be real. He makes no surface metaphor of it by saying that the pine-cone fell like a footstep. His metaphor becomes one only through your own application of it. It is at the very heart of his mood and of his meaning, not on the surface. And it is only as you also are touched by the pulse of it, that you feel what the poet feels when an unexpected sound brings him acutely the sense of life, of motion, of change, and so of human relationship. It is only by your becoming the poet, by his humanly taking you into himself, that you feel the communion of the earth and the presence of his friend. So it is with the concluding suggestion of the petals in the poem of spring. The poet tells what is happening, which is enough in itself to make a charming and wistful picture of a lady and her garden. It is left for you to form, if you like, the metaphor of a drift of loves, of memories, of regrets, closing like petals the door of her youth.

Giles constantly elucidates and sacrifices the poetic suggestiveness of the original. L. Cranmer-Byng, in his *Lute of Jade* and *Feast of Lanterns*, overdecorates and thereby forfeits clean selectiveness. To be sure, he makes beautiful Tennysonian lines, such as

> Till she of the dark moth-eyebrows, lily-pale,
> Shines through tall avenues of spears to die.

But Dr. Kiang assures me that those lines are by Cranmer-Byng, and not by Po Chü-yi, who says, more simply,

> Till under their horses' hoofs they might trample those moth-eyebrows . . .

I cannot judge yet of the interesting translations by Florence Ayscough and Amy Lowell; but, from the few I have seen, I should say that these authors, also, tend to inflate the poems with too much pomp and color. The contemporary writer who is contributing most of all to spread an erroneous idea of the great Chinese lyrics is E. Powys Mathers in his popular books of translations from the Oriental verse of many countries. I suspect that he may be translating them through the French and that the French versions, like the charming paraphrases of Judith Gautier, may be partly to blame. At any rate, he uses, in his book, *Colored Stars*, the French name Thou-Sin-Yu for Chu Ch'ing-yü, giving from that poet a whimsical, rather droll little poem, which possibly but not necessarily refers to a telltale among the ladies. Here is the poem, with nothing added, a version accurately checked by Dr. Kiang:

A Song of the Palace

Now that the palace-gate has softly closed on its flowers,
Ladies file out to their pavilion of jade,

Abrim to the lips with imperial gossip
But not daring to breath it with a parrot among them.

Mathers translates this very simple poem as follows:

In the Palace

What rigorous calm! What almost holy silence!
    All the doors are shut, and the beds of flowers are giv-
    ing out scent; discreetly, of course . . .
Two women that lean against each other, stand to the
    balustrade of red marble on the edge of the terrace.
One of them wishes to speak, to confide to her friend the
    secret sorrow that is agonizing her heart.
She throws an anxious glance at the motionless leaves, and
    because of a paroquet with iridescent wings that
    perches on a branch, she sighs and is silent.

I make no comment—except that, fortunately, there is another
Englishman, Arthur Waley, whose honest translations are even
more popular.

    I am often asked whether, in making these translations, I
have learned any Chinese myself. No. Wandering through out-
of-the-way places in China, following at Si Wu and up through
the Yangtze Gorges the very footsteps of the poets in whose
work I was engrossed, I learned to ask in several dialects for a
few necessaries; but that is a very far cry from being able to
read. I learned that *shan* means mountain and that *shuêi* means
water and that *shan-shuêi* means landscape. I learned that
"mountain-water" paintings lack sometimes the mountain and
sometimes the water, and I learned to translate the word as
landscape. I am not even sure how to spell the word for water. I
am spelling it as it sounded when I added to it the word for hot,
which I herewith avoid spelling, and summoned, according to a
middle or an upper gesture, a hand-basin or a pot of tea. But
had I learned Chinese, I should not have fared much better as a

translator. I am assured that not even foreigners born in China and knowing the language from childhood are safe guides when it comes to Chinese poetry.

The Chinese themselves vary in their interpretations—not in a way that conflicts with basic and essential clarity, but in one that is only natural, considering the absence from the poems of such grammatical details as person, tense and number. Sometimes I would lay before Dr. Kiang divergent readings from several Chinese whom I had the pleasure of consulting. Dr. Hu Suh, an influential young modernist of Peking Government University and author of widely read poems in the so-called "vulgar tongue," was a patient listener. And World-of-Jade—otherwise Nieh Shih-chang—the young student and friend who piloted me on many trips, was constantly reading the poems and making helpful suggestions. I remember, too, the charm and delight with which Princess Der Ling, former lady-in-waiting to the Empress Dowager, would recite aloud with me instantaneous translations of the poems, which she knew by heart, as I read my versions. For the most part we would coincide. Now and then she would take issue. And when I would carry her challenges and those of the others to Dr. Kiang, he would make sure that I knew the literal meaning of the successive characters, explain his own preference, give me sometimes my choice of the various interpretations, or even let me make one of my own. It is due him, for better or worse, to say that I generally chose his.

Among the scholars I met in Peking was the queued and aged Dr. Ku Hung-ming, a conservative in both politics and literature, a monarchist and a classicist. Attendant long ago at the University of Edinburgh and familiar with five languages, he is a witty opponent of foreign influence and a doughty upholder of traditional Chinese culture. I cannot do better than to call him as witness in favor of some of my contentions as to T'ang poetry, by quoting a passage or two from *The Spirit of the Chinese People*, his naïvely brilliant and stalwart book, written in English but published as yet only in Peking.

"The *classica majora* Chinese is not difficult," says he, "because, like the spoken or colloquial Chinese, it is extremely simple . . . plain in words and style . . . simple in ideas . . . and yet how deep in thought, how deep in feeling it is!" Consequently, "Chinese is difficult because it is deep. It is difficult because it is a language for expressing deep feeling in simple words." Dr. Ku then gives a translation of his own of a rather long poem by Tu Fu, and comments, "The above version, I admit, is almost doggerel. . . . The Chinese text is not doggerel, but poetry—poetry simple to the verge of colloquialism, yet with a grace, dignity, pathos and nobleness which I cannot reproduce and which perhaps it is impossible to reproduce, in English, in such simple language." A passage from another essay of his may explain to us in wider terms the warm, live presence of the Chinese poets: "The wonderful peculiarity of the Chinese people is that, while living a life of the heart, the life of a child, they yet have a power of mind and rationality which you do not find in the Christian people of medieval Europe or in any other primitive people. . . . For a people who have lived so long as a grown-up nation, as a nation of adult reason, they are yet able to this day to live the life of a child—a life of the heart. Instead, therefore, of saying that the Chinese are a people of arrested development, one ought rather to say that the Chinese are a people who never grow old. The real Chinaman is a man who lives the life of a man of adult reason with the heart of a child: the head of a grown-up man and the heart of a child. The Chinese spirit, therefore, is a spirit of perpetual youth, the spirit of national immortality."

This quality which Dr. Ku describes in the Chinese spirit, this directness, this pulse of the heart, is the quality by which the T'ang poetry endures. Sinister and devious the Chinese are not, except to shield themselves from even more sinister and devious foreigners, or to outwit brutal exploitation. They are not to be judged from the depraved conduct of scheming eunuchs, of profligate monarchs and courtiers, nor from the debased callousness of generals and soldiers; they are not to be judged by a foreigner who arrogates to himself racial superiority. They are to be judged from the spirit of the people at large; they are to be judged evenly and honestly. And then will be found in them the deep simplicity of the T'ang poets.

The clothes of poetry change from age to age: fashion, manner, decoration. The body of poetry is the same a thousand years ago, a thousand years hence. Poetry that depends on its trappings dies; but poetry that is bare and vital and true is imperishable. There are many Chinese court pieces and poems of official adulation that are overloaded with artifice and ornament. As curiosities, they may survive to astonish the eye of the literary tourist: jade for the jaded. But the power that makes the best of the T'ang poetry permanent is the honest bareness of its beauty, relating it to the poetic hearts of any race or time.

As artist and as human being, I cherish my three years' labor and the hope that it will help to interpret for the West not only the perfected artistry of the Chinese but the spirit expressed through that artistry—a spirit as nobly simple and as nobly sad, after all, as the spirit we Westerners must find fundamental in ourselves whenever we have time to be alone with it. Before there can be political equity in the world, there must be human equity, an end of racial ignorance and snobbery on all sides, an end of the superstition that superficial differences of skin and mold mean fundamental differences of mind and spirit. East and West, there is only one human spirit in the world, though knaves and fools would keep it divided. And it is the nearest thing we know to what we confidently call the divine spirit. At its best it is the spirit of beauty, whether in nature, in art or in the conduct of man. And still, through the centuries, the poets are its heralds.

New poets from the West are now assembling, as well they may, in the spirit-house of Wêi Ying-wu at Su-chou, where he greets them as, long ago, he greeted other poets:

Entertaining Literary Men in My Official Residence on a Rainy Day

Outside are insignia, shown in state;
But here are sweet incense-clouds, quietly ours.

Wind and rain, coming in from sea,
Have cooled this pavilion over the lake
And driven the feverish heat away
From where my eminent guests are gathered.
. . . Ashamed though I am of my high position
While people lead unhappy lives,
Let us reasonably banish care
And just be friends, enjoying nature.
Though we have to go without fish and meat,
There are fruits and vegetables aplenty.
. . . We bow, we take our cups of wine,
We give our attention to beautiful poems.
When the mind is exalted, the body is lightened
And feels as if it could float in the wind.
. . . Su-chou is famed as a center of letters;
And all you writers, coming here,
Prove that the name of a great land
Is made by better things than wealth.

—*Asia*, December 1921

New Wicks
for Old Lanterns

· ❧❁❧ ·

Are you thinking of a trip to China? If so, I have found a delightful and useful book for you, a book that gives in public print much of the information I have had to give over and over again in private letters. It is a book called *Swinging Lanterns*, by Elizabeth Crump Enders (D. Appleton & Company), and the route followed in her narrative is so nearly identical with the northern and eastern part of my own travels in China that I am venturing to add, as a sort of supplement for you to slip into her volume, a few comments and a few additional directions.

It is apparent that Mrs. Enders had not been to the Orient before, and the novelty of her experience had given an effective freshness and zest to her note-taking. On page after page, as I renew, through her reminders, my own Oriental experiences, I marvel at her far-seeing eye, her remembering mind, and her minutely recording hand.

Being a woman, Mrs. Enders is a constant guide to fashion. She excels particularly in description of accoutrements and accessories: the clothes of men and women, the style and fittings of their houses, the detail of ceremonies, the aspects of street life, market, temple, riverway and countryside. Perhaps she is too much concerned with the surface of China and not enough with tokens of its inner life. Yet she makes that surface as crowded with motion as though she had cast her notes pictorially upon a moving picture screen. And she is not betrayed by her trip into imagining herself, after the easy way of many tourists, to be an immediate expert in Chinese character, a lightning initiate into Chinese philosophy. You may draw for yourself, as early as you like, your own conclusions as to spiritual China; but, headed for physical China, take *Swinging Lanterns* in your hand.

You had better choose autumn or spring for your visit. Chinese winters are unconscionably cold and the summers unconscionably hot. When Mrs. Enders tells of the early morning jade market in Peking, I remember prowling there among jade-laden street booths, standing first on one foot and then on the other, huddling my goose-flesh under bulky layers of wool and fur, and bargaining badly through the chatter of my teeth. When she tells of a night spent at a temple among the Western Hills, I remember how numbly I enjoyed the hospitality of monks at a similar temple and how long I waited, like a diver above icy water, before entering my bed. She fails, however, to complete her weather report; she fails to remind me, except by not reminding me, of the summer heat. There were long sleepless Shanghai and Hangchow nights through which an American poet and I, with no smile on our faces, spent hour upon hour of heavier heat than at midday, desperately fanning each other's naked bodies. If you must pass a summer in China, pass it either at Mokanshan, near Hangchow, or at Kuling, near Kiukiang. It is better to suffer relaxed missionaries than unrelaxed heat.

Now that I have given you these general warnings in advance, to be capped as to war and banditry by warnings from someone on the spot, I advise you to follow the trail Mrs. Enders describes; extending it, if possible, to Hongkong, Canton, Macao, and especially Foochow in the south, to Hankow, Wuchang and Changsha in central China and to the Yangtsze Gorges as far as Chungking in the west. Fascinated though you may be by Foochow or by Chungking, still, like less adventurous tourists, you may well spend a major portion of your time in Peking. Live there in a Chinese house, and conceive a grateful respect for Chinese servants. Let me, as an instance, briefly record my own respect for Hu Chi.

On my first trip to China, I accidentally encountered Hu Chi as a ricksha-boy. He spoke a little English and exercised not only a good body but a good mind—for instance, when I left

Peking in 1917, what he said he wanted most was my photograph. I gave him one. The war intervened; and I lost all trace of Hu Chi, who had gone with other Chinese coolies to France. In 1920 I was in Peking again; and on the second morning I found Hu Chi waiting at the hotel door, with my photograph in his hand and the same old smile on his face. Before long, when I moved into a Chinese house, I elevated him from ricksha-boy to house-boy—lower wages but higher dignity and perquisites. Soon he surprised me by turning his comparative leisure to the designing of minute wooden frames, mounts of cloud and water to hold pieces of jade. He had the designs carved for me. They are beautiful. One night in Peking, when I was going to dinner at a friend's, Hu Chi silently handed me a book which, months before and known only to my friend and me, I had borrowed and forgotten. My friend had forgotten it, too. But Hu Chi remembered; for the Chinese can always remember more than they know. At the end of my stay in Peking, not wishing to see my good servant demoted, I tried to secure him elsewhere a permanent position as house-boy. Within a few days he lost it. When I asked him why, he answered gaily, "I was too dirty." It must have been a temporary indulgence; for he was soon in another dignified post and not only is still there, but is now, on the outside, boss of several rickshas. I add these observations, because they are in the same vein as Mrs. Enders' wondering tributes to individuals, yes, and to a race.

Established in a Chinese house with Chinese servants, you should not fail, as for some reason Mrs. Enders failed, to follow the routine excursionist and to visit the Great Wall and the northern Ming Tombs. What Mrs. Enders had to say in praise of the Ming Tombs at Nanking might better be said about the Ming Tombs near Nankow, where the natural setting is larger and the sculpture far superior. (Was it here or at Nanking—I have forgotten—that when a Manchu emperor had decided to appropriate these sculptured guardians for his own tomb a Ming adherent damaged each of the figures slightly, knowing that the

Ming guardians would therefore and thereafter be left undisturbed in their loyal and reverential occupation?)

Mrs. Enders speaks of a delightful landlady at Nanking. There is no harm in my naming her as Mrs. W. A. Martin, of Bridge House Hotel, and recommending her friendly and invaluable services, and there may be much point in my wondering if she told Mrs. Enders about the Winged Tigers. Be sure to inquire about them. In Nanking none but Mrs. Martin seems to be aware of them and, even with directions, only a Chinese friend could help a foreigner to find them.

You take the "coolie-train" at six in the morning and travel about sixteen miles to a station near the Chi-hsia Shan Temple with its marble pagoda and its Hill of a Thousand Buddhas. Even there, you will be lucky if you find anyone who has heard of the finest pieces of sculpture in eastern China, ranking, indeed, among the noblest of ancient carvings anywhere. When a Chinese friend and I went seeking them, the priests knew nothing of them, nor did the pilgrims, nor the carpenters who were building new guest rooms in the temple, nor the little boys riding on water buffaloes. Farmer after farmer shook his head as we tramped along toward Nanking again, foot-sore but determined; until at last one farmer looked up from his labors long enough to say, "Yes, I have some animals," and to point casually towards his house. And there we found them: as high as the house; one of them close to it, with a donkey loafing in the shadow of a winged flank; the other, at a little distance, acting as a mighty support to a haystack. The Ming Tomb sculptures are individually lumpish and static. Not so the Winged Tigers. Carved a thousand years earlier, they are no sullen mourners in a dumb enduring row but are alive, as alive to the future as to the past. They dare the ages, they dare the intimate oblivion growing up about them. From their substantial stone mouths, or from their mouths insubstantially remembered, they roar, they shout, they create invincible vibrations of beauty and renewals of its power. These two are in an obscure dooryard; others are sunk to the haunches in rice paddies. Incomparable monsters of glory, they are ignored by Chinese scholars and artists, are known, among travelers, only to a few amazed archaeologists and are so lightly regarded by local republican tenants of imperial domain that any fine day the stone of ancient wonder may become the stone of modern use. In Japan they would have been planted about with decorous trees, they would be guarded by the government and revered by the inhabitants. They die in China. And yet, though they die in China, in China they never die. They are symbols of the isolated genius of beauty which, in Cathay more than anywhere, through all changes of time and space and through all the petty generations, roars from the cavern of silence its mysterious and unchangeable vibrancies. Therefore, beyond my other recommendations, make note of the Winged Tigers, if you would care to listen for whispers of secrets at which the Sphynx herself has barely guessed.

On your trip to Putoshan, which Mrs. Enders recommends, you will have an advantage over me, who have never been there. And very near Nanking, if you will stop at Chinkiang before you start south for Putoshan, you will have a similar advantage over Mrs. Enders. Be it said incidentally that every foreign resident will warn you, rightly, against Chinese hotels. But if you are a man and single, put up with the discomforts. Even at Nanking, though comforts were available, I lived at a Chinese inn, amid dirt and racket indescribable, with grimy quilts on unyielding beds, but with food beyond the food of Paradise (if you like the food of Paradise) and with various encounters and experiences not otherwise to be gained. In Chinkiang, you will have to live either at a native hotel or at a monastery. I can recommend one of the latter, a monastery on a bluff where the Yangtsze turns inland from the Grand Canal. High within the walls of this monastery, overlooking town, river and far country, is a nest of rooms where surely any foreigner would pause to consider how much of the world's good may be forfeited for the world's goods. On the whole, I found nowhere in China more beautiful and varied temples than these at Chinkiang: this monastery at which you must rest a while; and, at the other end of town, Golden Mountain (or "Island," as it was once called when it was an island) with its noble courts and pagoda; and, serenely risen in the very course of the Yangtsze, Silver Island, with a clambering monastery whose abbot loves poetry. On a wall backing the highest terrace of this island, I followed the example of countless Chinese before me: I inscribed a poem. Under the circumstances of that twilight, while I faced the long river, the far-floating blue of mountains and a line of wild geese floating faster, I could not help writing my one and only perfect poem; and, under those same circumstances, I could not help leaving it there on that high wall, unrecorded and forgotten.

I have mentioned Chinkiang because of its easy offers to the traveler who may follow Mrs. Enders' itinerary. By the same token, I should mention the two glories of Shantung: T'ai-shan and the Tomb of Confucius. It is to Mrs. Enders' credit, however, that not visiting these famous places, nor the Wall, nor the northern Tombs, she has adequately filled her book with moving pictures of Chinese life; and one forgives her, as one would forgive a Chinese traveler who might fail to visit monuments of our own nobler days, Bunker Hill and the Statue of Liberty.

Mrs. Enders pays her respects to a Manchu Princess with whom she was on easy terms. I, also, met charming and fortunate Manchus. But I wish I could forget the charming and unfortunate Manchu Prince who served me at table in Peking. The terms between us were not easy, either for him or for me. Now and then I would intercede with my friends who employed him and who lost patience; I pled for him, lest he starve on the five or six Chinese dollars doled him each year by the little Emperor. I wish I could forget the tall, handsome figure of superbly sad failure, the fine eyes looking beyond the potato dish, the fine hands failing to pass it. He tried once to buy me some railroad tickets, but came back without them, helpless. He was the conqueror conquered and, as always, without quite knowing why. So has Mrs. Enders been conquered—and without quite knowing why.

But go there, yourself. Go, see and be conquered. See if you can solve the Chinese secret, the secret of this ancient child at the heart of chaos, the child who has conquered Tartars, Manchus, Mrs. Enders and me, and who in the end will have conquered even missionaries, merchants and marines.

—*The New Orient*, May 1924

Do We Know the Chinese?

· ❧❈❂❈❧ ·

As a boy, I knew nothing about the Chinese other than that they were "Chinks," a more menial race than even Micks or Dagoes, that they were mostly laundrymen who wore pigtails, pushed wooden balls across framed wires, and gave out red tickets with black marks on them, were gibbering heathen (even worse than Catholics; I was bred near Boston), who spat on clothes to wet them for ironing, and who ate rats. Once I joined a juvenile gang which threw stones at laundry windows and then fled the monsters in holy terror. College likewise taught me nothing of the Orient, though there was Lafcadio Hearn, and there was *Madam Butterfly*; but gradually through the next fifteen years I came to know, or to think that I knew, a little about Japan, not only because they had long been experts at wood-block printing but because they were beginning to be experts at propaganda. It was not until 1917 that I had my initial glimpse of the two countries.

At first sight Japan bore out all that the prints had mirrored and that Lafcadio Hearn had written. It was a beautiful garden, tended by a race of perfectionists. Not only was there every evidence of loving respect for nature, crowds swarming to see cherry blossoms as we surged to see baseball games, great trees laboriously moved to better vantage by singing workmen with countless ropes and endless patience, plants and flowers tenderly and exquisitely shaped and trained, not only the clean beauty of the land, not only the clean charm and meticulous courtesy of the people: nowhere else had I seen so much appearance of loving respect for mankind, or what we call Christian living, of men seeming to treat their neighbors as themselves.

Later in Korea I became cognizant of the treatment Japanese accord people whom they do not consider their neighbors. How-

ever much they had tidied Korea, they had tidied it for themselves, for their own advantage, as is the way of Empire; and
they were treating Koreans with sickening brutality. At the
Seoul museum priceless celadon vases showed in repair the
slashes with which Japanese swords had beheaded them, as with
other instruments art-loving Nipponese had after Boxer times
beheaded many stone Buddhas on a stupa at the Yellow Temple
near Peking. It was later, I believe, that they burned the Royal
Palace in Seoul to remove reminder of Korean sovereignty and
that they opiumized and debauched the heir-apparent. They had
already appropriated all lucrative business, and in every way
they were disdaining and flouting the conquered race. My
Japanese ricksha-boy in Seoul (even such minor occupations had
been taken away from the natives) suddenly stopped, set down
the shafts of the ricksha, and running thirty or forty feet ahead
planted, for no reason but general contempt, a swift hard kick on
the rump of a well-dressed elderly Korean who was crossing the
square. Having knocked down the Korean, the Japanese returned
to a job from which some other Korean had been kicked out and
looked back at me over his shoulder with a grin of high satisfaction. A Japanese policeman smiled too.

•

Unhappily, the Nipponese, like the Teutons, regard themselves
as a chosen people and reserve their good behavior for use toward their own breed. Major Compton Pakenham has recalled an
incident of his boyhood in Japan concerning Prince Fuminaro
Konoye, who became Premier in 1937. The Prince had stolen an
Irish setter belonging to young Compton and had stoutly denied
taking it. When the theft was proved, the apologetic Japanese
explanation of falsehood was the mother's teaching, "To mis-
state to a foreigner is not to lie." We have been assured, though,
that Japanese industrialists and militarists exploit and impoverish
their own people—that the decency one sees from man to man
is only inside a class, and at that the humbler class.

Proceeding from Japan to China, one felt at first like proceeding from a proper bathtub into an open battering ocean. In China, which the later converted Arthur Davison Ficke had described, when he crossed to it from Japan in his boyhood, as "a vast, dirty, dreary, savage waste," one met no effect of sweetened order, no populace of model charm. Instead one entered a sprawling land, enormous and unkempt, and with a motley multitude of individuals who often seemed to one wilful, wayward, wicked, and yet usually warm and wise. But whether smiling rascals or dialectical scholars, they felt known to an American, kin to him. They could laugh with him from kindred bowels of amusement, whereas the Japanese titter had been from a nervous cerebral guess. He could be comfortable with them, whereas in Japan he had tried to be correct and had had misgivings.

On slight acquaintance with people or at a distance from them, one tends, I grant, to generalize about them—to idealize or the opposite. Persons who have been recently in the Orient know well that government officials and many others in China are no nearer the angels than are similar individuals anywhere. The Chinese are not all good nor the Japanese all bad. But underlying the individual deviations and temporary fluctuations, it is the basic spirit of a people which counts and endures. And I could quote agreement from many observers far more seasoned than I that, in contrast to the Japanese with their herd-instinct and their blind obedience to discipline, the Chinese, though proudly revering family and tradition, are primarily democratic individuals, many of whose faults are in the long run their virtues.

So are we Americans democratic individuals. The Chinese twenty-five years ago preferred commercial dealings with the British rather than with us. Whatever the personal and social attitude of the British, they were commercially punctilious, men of their word, as some of us were not. Chinese used to complain to me that the filling of their orders from America was often slipshod and inaccurate or indifferent: not the width of goods they had ordered, four-tine forks instead of three, and so on. We knew better than they what they wanted. And so it is today, I am told, in Central and South America, while we wonder why the British find an inside course. For all our technical skill, our psychology in business is inferior. An advertising campaign for a North American soft drink imported recently into Argentina bade the dapper citizens of Buenos Aires to "drink it out of the bottle," and the reaction was not favorable. But on deeper ground than business our faults are in the long run our virtues; and in spite of our racial conceit, our commercial inefficiency, and our infernal bad manners, we win personally in China with an easygoing amiability as democratic individuals.

•

As to Chinese individualism, I remember seeing a crowd in Hangchow ringed around a wall against which a woman crouched, with a man beating her. And while he wielded his stick, not a person in the crowd moved or spoke. Through an interpreter I asked why they did not interfere. "Because," answered a grave-looking fellow, "he may be right." As to Chinese respect for "family and tradition," I need not dwell on their love of children or on their deep-rooted reverence for age. The Japanese, equally or even more tender toward children, appeared to me tenderer toward age in a tree than in a person. Caste, rather than the wisdom of maturity, wins their deference; whereas, for the Chinese, caste varies only according to individual distinction. Age, on the other hand, is a dignity which comes to anyone who lives. Not even death can interfere with it, much less birth. When told that I am over sixty, a polite American will say to me, "You barely look fifty." When told that I was under forty, many a polite Chinese said to me, "You look fully fifty." The intent to be courteous is the same, the accent of the courtesy is different.

A Chinese custom strange to us, and connected with veneration of age, is ancestor-worship. And yet when we of the West inherit good qualities from a worthy forbear, we quite naturally venerate that forbear and try to keep his good qualities alive in ourselves. When we inherit unfortunate qualities from a weak forbear, we instinctively or deliberately try to offset them with increased consciousness of inheritance from stronger kin. Or else, even if we do not think of it just this way, we sometimes try in our own lives to propitiate the bad influence of a weak forbear by understanding him and, as his life goes on in us, to give him a wiser and a happier time. In either case, when we do our best to continue good inheritance and to bequeath it to descendants or when we understand poor inheritance and do our best to better it through comprehensive advantage, we are tending to make of ourselves ancestors worthy of worship by our children in a sort of rational immortality. Deploring my bachelor-hood, a young Chinese friend asked, "If you have no children, who are you?"—meaning, "What becomes of your existence?"

No, an American visitor to the Orient does not remember the Chinese as a race fundamentally different from us, strange, alien, or veneered like many Japanese with a lacquer he cannot scrape through to the natural wood, but as human beings very much like himself. He learns a difference between Japanese gaiety and Chinese content, Japanese veneer and Chinese bark, Japanese form and Chinese reality.

And yet, long before blindness of war supervened, we had been cursory and supercilious toward Japanese beliefs and customs. We had not appreciated the simple dignity of the great Shinto temple at Ise, burned down and rebuilt every twenty years to remind men that they might overvalue the work of their hands. Arrogant though any race may be which exclusively assumes divine origin, or is taught so to assume it, Japanese reverence for the wonder of existence was a deeply beautiful spirit as I felt it in that great bare log cabin with no trappings or fittings save the pure white curtain across one end of it, beyond which in no lesser image than the presence of nature and the imagination of man dwelt the source, the godhead. A Japanese nobleman is said once to have flouted even this much of what he deemed superstition by flipping aside an edge of the curtain with his cane to show that behind it there was nothing; and the worshipers present, though they were commoners, are said to have torn his rash body apart. Hara-kiri, sacrificial suicide among the Japanese, we have dismissed, as an uncouth and barbarous practice, forgetting that these victims are scapegoats and that the major religion of the West has come to be based on the idea of vicarious atonement, on the sacrificial suicide of a king's son for the salvation or purification of his father's subjects.

Many years ago I received a letter from Dr. Lucius Porter of Yenching University in Peking, a missionary-professor with whom I had become friends on my first trip. In it he wrote: "We are trying to help Westerners realize the flatness of their intellectual geography. Isn't it curious how we believe we are fully educated if we know something about the origin and development of movements of the stream of Western culture without realizing that the stream of Chinese culture has run through the history of mankind with strength and fullness and life-giving for many millions? I am trying to lead a few Westerners to venture with me on a sort of Columbus voyage, to discover that, after all, mankind lives spherically and not nationally or even hemispherically." A woman missionary had told me earlier that she despaired of possible growth in the West for the Kingdom of the real Christ, that the true soil for it was in China. I wonder if she meant that Laotzu and Confucius had already planted the spirit of Jesus and that there was no need of a Christian Empire. Many missionaries in the Orient have been doing double work, work in two directions, work for the East and work for the West. Dr. Porter was aware of the need of this a quarter-century ago. Pearl Buck, Lin Yutang, and others have followed him with realization that as much missionary work is due here as in the Orient, perhaps more.

In 1917 a Chinese student guided me around Hangchow and Lake Si Wu, where Marco Polo was once governor, where a bridge is still named for him, and where a gilded image of him sits among other saints in one of the temples, looking, like all of them, happier than our saints, though odd with his lush beard. Nieh Shih-chang was fairly far along in the study of English as well as in the wisdom of his race and when I said to him, "If you Chinese chose to organize and direct your manpower, your genius, your endurance, you could conquer the world," he replied, "We did it once. Why should we do it again?" He was right that they had done it once. Like Germany yesterday, China in the time of Genghis Khan had been a wind of fury on the earth, a blind power of destruction over territory far wider than Hitler's reach. "Genghis Khan," according to Henry Hart, "captured the Persian city of Termed, and left it a city of one million and a half corpses. At Nishapur not even domestic animals, cats, or dogs were spared. A mountain of skulls smoked into the sky. When he died in 1227 he ruled the largest empire in the world, no man a larger before or since, and left over eighteen million human corpses in Asia alone as a memorial. The Mongol flood washed the walls of Prague and looked toward a supine Europe." But in the minds of even its youngsters twenty-five years ago, China had learned.

Japan had not learned. Three years later, when Japan was making her infamous Twenty-one Demands on China, I exclaimed to another Chinese student, "If you don't take care, the Japanese will conquer you." "But if they do," said he, "in at most another thousand years we'll conquer them." George Santayana philosophizes: "Those who cannot remember the past are condemned to repeat it"; but I do not think my friend meant repetition of conquest in the manner of Genghis Khan.

•

Times have changed since a quarter-century ago. Though I doubt if the philosophy and practice upon which internationalism is bred can ever die in China, nationalism has lately been encouraged again by Chinese leaders as well as by Western influence. Nationalism has been forced upon her by overwhelming outer powers of evil against which, at least temporarily, it has had to be used as a defense for mere human and decent survival. Philosophy can face man better than it can face machines. And man for a while in the world is subdued to machines. They almost do his thinking. I do not believe, however, that machinery will fare any better in trying to conquer China than man has fared. And Chinese wisdom will survive these few Westernized decades as serenely as it has survived the preceding forty centuries.

In a poll taken in 1943, chiefly among young Chinese in West China, out of 11,262 replies 58.1 per cent were in favor of giving a beaten Japan a position of equality. Some of them may well have realized the successful dignity with which Japan had for years resisted Western intrusion in the Orient, may have appreciated the accomplishment of the one Eastern country which had been able to preserve its property from Western greed and its independence from Western trespass. When we are angered by Japan's recent course, which began as defensive and became offensive, which began as nationalistic and became imperialistic, we should not fail to remember that we of the West set the pattern. Rabindranath Tagore remarked twenty years ago, "You Westerners have made Japan over in your own image and now you are afraid of her." The Chinese are not finally afraid of her. Beyond this war, Chinese philosophy—bits of which I have quoted from the two students—will live profound in other students, perhaps in students from the West.

These students, my young Chinese friends, for example, were aware of their continuous participation in the past, the present, and the future. Though strongly individualistic, yet they felt connected with the whole growth of life, not only with their living kin but with their dead ancestors and with their unborn descendants as with a single stream. We Westerners try to get things done in a hurry, as though life were forever ending with the death of each of us. Another lesson the Chinese have learned is that to conquer a race with arms is less important than to conquer it with thought, with character, with humanness. They know also that before there can be lasting conquest of others, whether by arms or by character, there must be mastery of self. They know that they have not as yet mastered themselves. Too many of us in the West have even failed to consider whether or not we have lives worth mastering, we are so busy mastering machines.

Names, phrases, labels are of little significance—monarchy, democracy, republic, commune—as compared with the spirit of a people which, through any form of government, is what actually and finally governs. China might seem to us to have a chaotic civilization; but a chaotic civilization may, after all, be a higher reach of spirit than a mechanized civilization. This is what we of the West are a stubbornly long time in understanding. We impose mechanical benefits and expect thanks for displacing an imaginative life with a literal existence.

"That's all very well," you might say, "but something must be wrong with a people who continue in a state of cruel anarchy, with self-seeking warlords at the top and filthy ignorant beggars at the bottom." As to the doings of warlords or economic masters, can the Western world bring accusation? As to hygienic conditions and literacy, China has managed in the last decade, for all the heavy grind of war, a marked betterment. Dr. V. K. Wellington reports that "despite the lack of books and pens, some seventy million more people have learned to read and write during the war years." We might note, moreover, that a touch of earth does not in itself seem to a Chinese unclean. He might live longer and with more neighbors, if given wholesale sanitary improvements; he might also, in that event, seek room for his cleanliness in other countries and very scientifically soil the earth with blood.

In the present Western world, country after country presents the spectacle of the state overwhelming the individual, whether by pretended majority rule, by collective financial power, by military dictatorship, or by sheer lunacy. In China, even to this day, in spite of the invasion of machinery, materialistic education, foreign money, and a stress of nationalistic fervor necessitated by the moment, the individual survives.

Hitler had not learned, nor had Hirohito, that without free individuals there cannot be an enduring state. Social, cultural, and mechanical standardization in the Western world, at least for a while, gives less and less opportunity for individuals to maintain their individualism. The unreality we call "the state" interferes not only with their lives but with their thought. This mythical compulsion has always been active in Japan. In China, on the other hand, the reality of individualism has continually exposed the unreality of the state. Among the most distinguished figures in Chinese history, from earliest to latest times, have been men individual enough and brave enough to voice constructive complaint against the government. Such citizen-statesmen have often been officially punished; but they have counted and conquered, century after century, with the mass of individuals who compose the public.

•

In Shanghai I met Dr. Sun Yat-sen, better known then as Sun Wen. On entering his study I was at first struck with amusement to see him standing as with his back to a tailor's mirror. On the walls behind him and flanking him hung three huge chromos of himself. But I was quickly brought to attention by the impressive simplicity of the man who had selflessly renounced the presidency to Yüan Shih-k'ai; and then, as interpreters translated his hopes and plans for China, I was caught along by his eager gravity. Sun's initial role in the democratic development of his country had been political; but at this period, ten years after the Revolution, he was deeply concerned with the economic aspects of democracy's development. He drew me a diagram: more a poet's diagram than a painter's. It was a circular pattern spoked like a wheel but with hollow tubes. Up to the outer ends of the tubes came images of farmers, artisans, producers of all kinds, and—following his brush—each group poured its product into an appointed pipe. The hub of the wheel was a governmental clearing-house, an official concentration of all middlemen, where the products were assessed and where tokens were handed out, stamped as of this or that worth according to current values of supply and demand. Then the products were passed through the clearing-house into pipes spoking out on the opposite side, where tokens were to be presented by this or that group for the stamped value's worth of supplies brought by other groups. In this poetic diagram there was a good deal of terse prophecy.

But this was governmental management of products rather than of people. Sun's other plans, as far as I could gather in an afternoon call, were decidedly toward popular management of the state, government ascending from below rather than descending from above. While we of the West may still somewhat incline to build our national structures on sand which has given way under earlier Western edifices, the Chinese may still stay wise enough to choose for their foundation the rock of individual thought, on which their racial structure has withstood already as many assaults as it may have to withstand again.

Confucian codes have led foreigners to believe that China is a country of basic and strict formalism. In manners, yes, there are conventions, many if not most of which have served usefully, being ethically founded. Confucius may have overestimated the importance of coded conduct; but Laotzu is a deeper, more tacit element in Chinese character and conscience than Confucius, and in Confucius's own time, five hundred years before Jesus, Laotzu—in this saying, as in the other eighty—was making an immortal plea for each individual microcosm of the cosmos:

Rid of formalized wisdom and learning
People would be a hundredfold happier,
Rid of conventionalized duty and honor
People would find their families dear,
Rid of legalized profiteering
People would have no thieves to fear.
Those methods have failed, all three.
Here is the way, it seems to me:
Set people free,
As deep in their hearts they would like to be
From private greeds
And wanton needs.

Dr. Ku Hung-ming put his firm finger on the secret of apparently imperishable Chinese individualism when he said that his race had developed the head of a man without losing the heart of a child. I have also heard him remark in foreign houses where, for his character and wit, he was very popular: "China will not be well as long as you Westerners are doctoring her."

The Western physician has doctored Japan and will do its best to doctor China, to treat it to death. But, by much evidence, China will refuse to die. While European civilization declines we Americans remain, to considerable degree, civilized only with our hands: good surgeons for the body and perhaps for the body politic. For the spirit there are better mediciners in an older civilization still deeply extant.

—*The Saturday Review of Literature*, January 22, 1949

The Chinese Brush

· ❧❀❧ ·

I

Soon after my arrival in the Orient in 1917, I asked a Chinese friend why he preferred writings on his walls to paintings, of which he apparently owned none and this at a time when good originals, as well as almost equally desirable copies, were often found by a watchful seeker with small means. "In this one poem on my wall," he answered, "there are several paintings." He referred not only, as I thought then, to scenes or figures or actions visualized through the poem. I believe now that he referred quite as much, or even more, to details of brushwork combined, like parts of a painting, in the whole composition.

It is no wonder then that Chinese calligraphy—whether used merely for signature and date and place or more fully for record, comment, homily, poetry, philosophy—should have become an inherent part of paintings for its own sake, its own forms, its placing and brushwork, as well as to convey informational data or literary significance. In brush strokes almost always seeming to be part and parcel of the painting, there are countless such inscriptions as "Painted at his home, Three Friends, in the summertime." There are inscriptions also by copyists, disciples, admirers:

Lung Yu's brush was quick as a wind, flowing as a cloud—
I have had him in mind and tried to be like him.

Copied from the Sung painting, with a dragonfly added.

Bound into a book of small landscapes and fragments attributed to Wang Men are separate pages of script telling how that painter, like Lung Yu's follower, continued not slavishly but creatively the tradition and spirit of the predecessor:

> Wang Men studied with Li Kao-tze and drew trees as vigorous as spears in a camp, and rocks not dead but changing with life. Though Wang learned the ancient manner, he was able to adapt it, using only its virtues.

This reverence for the work of past masters by no means precluded new zest and new inspiration. On a four-panel screen of "Pines and Storks" Ch'ang Hsung, for example, has versified:

> Drunk with my subject, I have painted hard enough
> To shake the roots of the Five Sacred Mountains.

Such balance and fitness between painting and writing are not customary in the Occident. Here a signature is often a blemish. It rarely participates in the composition but seems to have been perfunctorily added, and in most cases badly written, at the lower corner of the canvas like a scrawl at the end of a business letter. Occasionally Western artists have used careful lettering, such as the Holbeins', or have signed their work with a decorative monogram, such as Dürer's. Whistler, under the spell of Japanese charm, used for signature his butterfly symbol—which, however, was an alighting decoration, a butterfly entering from outside rather than a bud stemming from the design or a bird echoing it.

Chinese custom is different and here is an extreme instance. In my private collection of paintings is a scroll attributed to Huang Shen (c.1720–1760). "Two Fishermen" is drawn with a minimum of broad, bold strokes. Above them the artist has affixed his brush name, Ying-piao, in strokes so similarly broad and bold that they less resemble writing than they do his wen and the gourd he always carried in his sash. The ideographs for wen and gourd, which were the actual characters of his painting name, are so roughened in this instance to conform with the style of the painting that they long baffled a Chinese friend who tried to decipher them for me and thought them possibly but a whimsical echo of strokes used in the figures of the fishermen.

One notes that in lama paintings, which crowd the space full of line and color, a signature—even if allowed by ecclesiastical regulation—could find no resting place, no perch, no air to breathe; and it is possible that in the usual solidity of Western painting not enough air is left for lettering.

Or does our difficulty arise from the nature of the letters themselves? Is it because our script, our print, is not beautiful? Unfamiliar letter-strokes seen apart from knowledge of their meaning may be more directly felt as design than familiar letter-strokes in which knowledge of meaning takes precedence. But that is not the point here. The Chinese, conscious of what their ideographs signify, are almost equally conscious of the graphic form with which the meaning comes through. Though Germany's Gothic type has its chunky charm, there is no doubt that in Oriental characters lines and spaces are more agreeably related for the aesthetic eye than in any pattern of Western lettering. The Chinese ideograph is within itself, like the Egyptian hieroglyph, a compounded pictorial design. Many of the radical strokes joined into Chinese characters originated as rough illustrations or symbols, so that a character which combines such radicals is a graphic composition beyond any likeness to Western script, is literally "significant form."

Lettering used by a Chinese artist is a part of his own skill: his signature and whatever else he inscribes on his scroll usually prove him to be as individual a creator in his handwriting as in his painting. He has not used a piece of type fixed by some other man; he has used personal calligraphy. I wonder again if our own artists might not also have been calligraphers had the forms of our script paralleled, as do Chinese characters, the directions of the creative brush, so that handwriting might have been in itself a worthy and highly esteemed art.

II

From the very beginning of Oriental calligraphy, when ideographs were so different from those now in use that only the most learned scholars can still read them, the Chinese have deeply reverenced the art. The eminent T'ang scholar, poet, and calligrapher Han Yü (768–824) was prompted to write his famous "A Poem on the Stone Drums" by an ink rubbing taken from one of the oldest known stone carvings in China, the ten stone drums which had been made and engraved with poems during the reign of the Chou Emperor Hsüan Wang (827–782 B.C.). Three of the drums still exist and were lately in the Confucian temple at Peking, together with replicas of the other seven. Han Yü tells the story:

> Chang handed me this tracing, from the stone drums,
> Beseeching me to write a poem on the stone drums.
> Tu Fu has gone. Li Po is dead.
> What can my poor talent do for the stone drums?

Then he tells of their origin, of the Emperor's great concourse and hunt which they celebrated, and continues:

> And the exploit was recorded, to inform new generations. . . .
> Cut out of jutting cliffs, these drums made of stone—
> On which poets and artisans, all of the first order,
> Had indited and chiselled—were set in the deep mountains. . . .
> Time has not yet vanquished the beauty of these letters—
> Looking like sharp daggers that pierce live crocodiles,
> Like phœnix-mates dancing, like angels hovering down,
> Like trees of jade and coral with interlocking branches,
> Like golden cord and iron chain tied together tight,
> Like incense-tripods flung in the sea, like dragons mounting heaven.

The poet laments the fact that

Historians, gathering ancient poems, forgot to gather these,

and recounts

> How a friend of mine, then at the western camp,
> Offered to assist me in removing these old relics.
> I bathed and changed, then made my plea to the college
> president
> And urged on him the rareness of these most precious
> things.
> They could be wrapped in rugs, be packed and sent in boxes
> And carried on only a few camels: ten stone drums. . . .
> We could scour the moss, pick out the dirt, restore the
> original surface,
> And lodge them in a fitting and secure place forever. . . .
> But government officials grow fixed in their ways
> And never will initiate beyond old precedent;
> So herd-boys strike the drums for fire, cows polish horns
> on them,
> With no one to handle them reverentially.
> Still ageing and decaying, soon they may be effaced. . . .
> But now, eight dynasties after the Chou, and all the wars
> over,
> Why should there be nobody caring for these drums?

Somebody eventually cared enough to save three of them, still fairly whole; and I judge that on the replicas of the other seven the fragmentary poems and the writing thereof were reproduced from old ink rubbings. Thus, for devout Orientals, the script which Han Yü admired nearly two thousand years after it had been written has sounded its drumbeat from stone, and the echo of it from paper, through another thousand years.

A slightly later T'ang poet, Li Shang-yin (813–858), in his poem "The Han Monument," tells a story about lettering on stone designed by this same Han Yü, who died when Li was eleven years old. Emperor Hsien-tsung's premier, P'ai Tu, had written an account of the overthrow of the Huai-hsi rebels, and Han Yü, who was P'ai Tu's secretary, was appointed to inscribe the exploit on a monument. After the monument had been installed, the Emperor, having sent envoys to India to import Buddhistic doctrines, was preparing to receive a relic, a bone of the Buddha. Han Yü, resisting imposition of a religion unsuited to China, maintained that, whatever virtue might have resided in the Buddha, there could be none in his bone—which, besides, might be really that of a dog or a sheep, whereupon the Emperor angrily exiled the protestant. The monument was then thrown down and another, with an inferior inscription, set up in its place.

Here, in part, is Li Shang-yin's account of the original inscription, its ordering, its accomplishment, its destruction:

And the Emperor said: "To you, Tu, should go the highest
    honor
And your secretary, Yü, should write a record of it."
When Yü had bowed his head, he leapt and danced, saying:
"Historical writings on stone and metal are my especial art;
And, since I know the finest brush-work of the old masters,
My duty in this instance is more than merely official,
And I should be at fault if I modestly declined."
The Emperor, on hearing this, nodded many times.
And Yü retired and fasted and, in a narrow work-room,
His great brush thick with ink as with drops of rain,
Chose characters like those in the *Canons of Yao and Hsun*,
And a style as in the ancient poems, *Ch'ing-miao* and
    Shêng-min.
And soon the description was ready, on a sheet of paper.
In the morning he laid it, with a bow, on the purple
    stairs. . . .
The tablet was thirty feet high, the characters large as
    dippers;
It was set on a sacred tortoise, its columns flanked with
    dragons. . . .

And jealousy entered and malice and reached the Emperor—
So that a rope a hundred feet long pulled the tablet down
And coarse sand and small stones ground away its face.
But literature endures, like the universal spirit,
And its breath becomes a part of the vitals of all men.
The T'ang plate, the Confucian tripod, are eternal things,
Not because of their forms, but because of their inscrip-
    tions. . . .

III

When I was in China the second time, twenty-five years ago, I
met several men whose skill in handwriting was an honored
distinction and whose scrolls of lettering were as treasured as
paintings. One of these men, a physician in the native city of
Shanghai, whose grandfather had been a calligrapher even more
noted, offered through an English-speaking son to show me
their family collection of paintings. After entering the house
and sitting to our tea, I could feel the shadows and hear the
breath of women who, though in other rooms, were yet present,
peering through some crevice while Dr. Liu Chen-tung unrolled
and hung landscapes, figure paintings, portraits. I remember
having brought with me a landscape I considered buying, and
asking him if it was good. "It is as good as you think it" was his
answer.

Later in the afternoon he showed me two small inscriptions
by his grandfather, Liu Wen-ch'ao, which took my breath. The
several characters on each scroll were like the changes of an
assured voice. Their meanings, when translated, did not especially catch me. "Ten thousand volumes lodged in the heart" was,
I believe, one of them. But I was held by the spell of sheer, pure
form. They had the remote closeness of stars fixed and yet moving in space. It was the first time I had thoroughly felt the dignity
and power of fine Chinese writing, and the doctor warmed to
my exclamation.

His own writing, which he then showed me, was of a

different order, microscopic, meticulous, admirable, but not bringing the quick whole unquestioning exhilarated "yes" plumped
out of me by the other. He presented me, however, with four
of his closely written pages, which the son later translated.

The first in verse and the second in prose may have been
the doctor's own composition, but I have forgotten:

> Under heaven are works of many kinds.
> You cannot realize that things are hard to do by seeing
>   others do them.
> The time comes when you have to face them and do them
>   yourself.

> Even if a man is a master at his work, he listens to what
> other men have to say and learns thereby. It is the ignora-
> mus who claims to know and thereby fails to learn from
> other men. However great or little his means, a man must
> not squander what he has but must put it to square use;
> and he should think less about how much a dollar counts
> than about a copper's doing a copper's worth of good to
> himself or to someone.

The third, signed by the doctor, was presumably his own neat
poem:

> Turn to all men your true face,
> Tell the truth to your own heart,
> Foresee the results of whatever you do,
> Be as helpful to the rich as to the poor.

And to the fourth was signed, in the doctor's hand, the name of
his distinguished grandfather, who must therefore have been its
author:

> To be contented with your means is to be happy.
> With such contentment you can often smile,

For you are trained to meet all circumstance,
To live above fame and to think above what happens.

The Liu family must have been well trained in Tao, well founded in Laotzu who said:

A man who knows how little he knows is well,
A man who knows how much he knows is sick;

A man's work, however finished it seem,
Continues as long as he live;

Content need never borrow;

and

Only he who contains content
Remains content.

Upon taking leave and being asked by Dr. Liu what I had liked best of all I had seen, I was candid in naming his grandfather's two scrolls. That evening, when I returned home late from a theater, the scrolls were in my room at the hotel.

The rest of the story may be digression and does me doubtful credit, but is worth telling. I knew the Oriental gesture of making a present of what is admired, but with little or no expectation of the gift's being finally accepted. I would be Oriental too. I told the doctor that I was going north and should be pleased if he would let me take the scrolls to hang in my rooms as I traveled, and presently to hang in my memory, but that I was borrowing them, not keeping them. On the other hand I should be happy to accept, if he would write it out for me, a copy of a four-line poem by Wang Wêi of which I was particularly fond. I showed him my Chinese calling card. Because I so admired this poet, Dr. Kiang Kang-hu had enjoyed translating my name, Witter, into Chinese characters which mean a devotee of Wêi. Fond himself of Wang Wêi both as painter and as poet, Dr. Liu told me which of the shorter poems was his own favorite. Before I left Shanghai he sent me, in his small perfect script, the lines I had asked for, "A Parting." Having found out meantime from young Liu that a metal ink box from Peking would be a gift acceptable to his father, I took one to an expert craftsman in the northern city and had him engrave on it Wang Wêi's "My Retreat at Mount Chung-nan," the doctor's favorite.

The day before I was to sail from Shanghai for America I went again with the son to call on the doctor, taking with me the ink box and the borrowed scrolls. The boy commended me for returning them, inasmuch as they were the only formal examples left in the family of his great-grandfather's writing, a fact I had not known till then. "The rest," he said, "were burned." And he added frankly and not, it seemed to me, quite Orientally— though politeness is an odd bird anywhere—"I am sure that my father would prefer their coming finally to me, so you are acting well to return them to my father."

When I handed them back to Dr. Liu I expressed my appreciation of his entrusting them to me awhile, especially since he had no others by his grandfather. "My son should not have told you that" was the severe answer, which I understood from his expression, even before the son dutifully interpreted. But the doctor laid the scrolls aside on a table and bowed. Then he took the ink box and, bowing again, read the Chung-nan poem aloud to me with a delicacy of intonation comparable to the delicacy of his script. He gave me a beautiful small landscape which I accepted. And as I bade him farewell, I felt that I had correctly and courteously met the delicacy of the situation.

The son had said little, walking back with me to the hotel. Next day when he came to see me off on the steamer, he handed me a package from his father.

"Here are the scrolls."

"But no," I exclaimed, "I can't take them."

"My father wishes it."

"No," I persevered, against a firm look in his eye. "They

were a present from him to me and now they are a present from me to you. There is no other way. And now, not later—now before I sail, I must leave them with you, lest they be lost in sending."

"It would not be right," he held his ground gravely.

"But tell me what would be right, what I can do."

"Nothing more," he concluded and then the quiet bomb, "because you did wrong."

I sailed with the scrolls and without being told how I had done wrong. Nor shall I ever quite know. The son and I corresponded for some years, but friends in Shanghai cannot tell me what has become of him or of his family. Perhaps he has been lost in the wars. Perhaps, if I had persuaded him to keep his great-grandfather's scrolls, they would have been lost too. When I look at them now, they are more than poised and beautiful abstractions. They are the presents and presence of friends to whom I innocently "did wrong."

—*The Atlantic Monthly*, **August 1949**

A 1921 Letter to an Inquiring Stranger

· ❧❦❧ ·

The editors of *The Literary Review* have suggested that there might be found in files carbons of some of my letters which would be of interest in print. At first I thought of a small group dating from my connection with *McClure's* magazine and Small, Maynard and Company between 1902 and 1909; but after several attempts, I think the possibility of this project had better be left to the future.

My secretary did, however, come across a copy of an excerpt from a letter written probably in 1921 to a correspondent whom I had never met and whose name is not even entered on the copy. Its beginning stirs me to amusing memories of Peking in 1920, when I spent several winter months there.

Bertrand Russell had arrived in China from an observant visit in Russia and taken a house in the Chinese capital. I remember well going to a lecture he gave concerning his trip. In a distinguished audience of Chinese and foreigners were many refugees from Russia who thought he would condemn the usurping revolutionists. He did. Through the hour of his talk, he went into detail concerning Russian errors of both accomplishment and intention. At the end of his talk, however, he threw a bomb into his audience by stating quietly: "And yet, in spite of these mistakes, in spite of my criticism, the Russian government of today I should judge to be the ablest in Europe."

Another episode I remember in connection with Russell is an evening's entertainment he and Dora Black gave at his house to a number of his Chinese students in company with a few foreigners. Most of the latter, noting the invitational hour as nine o'clock, thought that this meant the evening meal according to its usual hour in the foreign colony. The result was that after a lengthy period of Western games with which Russell entertained his young Chinese guests and the rest of us—such as charades and pinning the tail on the donkey—we foreigners were a hungry lot. We could see a table of tempting viands in a room adjoining the one in which we were being jovial, but not yet could we eat. Mr. Russell asked me to initiate a game. I think the name of the one I chose is "Menagerie." It purports to be a comical racket made when at a signal all present emit the various noises of animals and birds whose names have been whispered into the various ears by a master of ceremonies. What the latter regularly does is to tell all but one of the participants to remain silent and then to instruct the sole victim to make a noise like a pig. Youngsters in New England used to enjoy the result; but lest I might hurt the feelings of the Chinese boy I had picked as the butt of the pastime by assigning him the role of so ignominious a beast, I asked him to make a noise like a dog. He did so with sharp barking into the silence, after which he sank into sobs. It took much work on my part and our hosts' to assure the youngster that in the West what I had asked him to do would not have been an indignity, as apparently it was in China. Someone told me later that in that country the dog is held lower than the pig. The victim himself forgave me and continued to be a friend, but some of the other young guests were not so cordial to me later.

After this mistake, I made another. As soon as we were let into the dining room, I swallowed an entire piece of sponge cake —which is very good in Peking—before realizing that the inch thick frosting on it was pure lard, almost as unwelcome to my stomach as later my gift of butter proved to a Chinese stomach whose owner apologized for having to "unswallow" it.

Another Chinese memory is connected with the stray letter which I am prefacing. In those days foreigners in Peking usually had each his own "ricksha-boy," a misnomer since the boys were usually fairly grown men. Even visitors comparatively transient like myself became good friends with the pullers of their hired vehicles. Mine in 1917, Hu Chi, shortly after I left Peking that earlier year, had gone off to the European war with many other Chinese workers. By 1920, after his return to Peking with savings, Western clothing and a watch, he had opened a stand of ricksha-boys, employing a considerable number—he himself of course retired from active work. When I came out of the doorway of the Grand Hotel des Wagons-Lits the first morning of my return visit in 1920 and started toward the row of rickshas at the curb, one of the boys whom I had known in 1917 and sometimes employed as an alternate to Hu Chi ran forward to me with what I took to be the proffer of his service. Instead he indicated that I was to wait, which I did for four or five minutes. Then I saw approaching in ricksha garb with a torso menially bare, my old friend Hu Chi who insisted for that first day I use his own services as before. At the end of it, on a street corner, his friend and mine who had met me at the hotel door that morning, took over the shafts and Hu Chi climbed into another ricksha which was waiting. Then we all proceeded to Hu Chi's house where our host changed into his Western attire, watch included, and we all had tea.

It was his friend who, a few days later, drew me—alongside two others in their rickshas, Bertrand Russell and John Dewey, the latter being briefly a Peking visitor that winter—to a performance given especially for us at a school built and maintained entirely by ricksha-men for their children.

On one of the streets we rode through we were troubled to see an old man harshly beating an old woman. The latter ran miserably toward us and of course we did the only thing we could do—remonstrate with the fellow and give his companion generous handfuls of coppers. The woman's face immediately wreathing into a happy grin, she handed all the cash to the old boy, whose grin reflected hers while they dramatically embraced. It was a typical Chinese performance.

So, after our addresses at the school, was the performance of the ricksha-men's children giving us a concert of so-called

"Confucian music"—much softer and subtler than the theatrical clangor to which travelers in China are accustomed.

It is sad to remember during these current days of Red China that, in this school built by the hardest of workers, the walls of three rooms were hung with portraits of Washington, Jefferson and Lincoln. It is sad also, though in its way amusing, to recall that later the same winter an invitation was sent through the diplomatic quarter asking guests to attend at the American Legation an afternoon of *Confusion* music.

Shortly before this the American Minister had been a straight-cut unpretentious business man. Eminent Chinese, respecting him for his integrity, had made him gifts of valuable rarity. Then at his departure, so it was told, he held an auction in the Legation garden, and they sent agents who purchased back each gift for its donor. Still earlier, in the fine old temple where I in my time was to live awhile, and which had been the American Legation, with its pillared nave used as reception room, our Minister's wife, not liking the ancient red lacquer on columns and walls, had imported Western wallpaper to supplant it with a cover of purple violets.

And I remember dining one night at the Legation and being seated near an American admiral. At a pause in the conversation at his side of the table and catching a sentence on our side, he inquired, "Who was that?" When I answered that we had been debating the relative merits of Keats and Shelley, he continued, "Let's see now, which branch of the service are they in?"

By the literate world, Americans were not then considered a cultivated people.

These memories and more have been prompted by discovery of this excerpt saved in carbon, part of a letter I had written forty years ago to an inquiring stranger. I might remark that since then I have come nearer to the philosopher's views on religion than I was then.

. . . Bertrand Russell told me in Peking that the reason the Bolsheviki are bound to fail is their attempt to apply religion to politics, when only science can do the job. He called it the one genuine endeavor on record to apply the force of Christianity, as apart from the churches, governmentally. He says that wise men will be following stars someday to the birthplace of Lenin but that, meantime, Lenin's system will have disappeared from all but theoretical and hypocritical application like the present application of Christianity. Less emotion and more reason is Russell's prescription. I defended the ideal Christian. "But there'll never be one," he answered, "till Christianity is dead." He has, of course, little or no faith in the potency of Christianity—except as a pleasant drug for sentimentalists. I am not in agreement with him.

But then, I am not always in agreement with myself. Perhaps there should be only the scientific spirit in government. Balanced emotion may in the meantime be bringing about a happy condition in which what we think of as government will no longer be necessary. That idea would seem to make me an anarchist. But I think, instead, I am a reluctant socialist—one of those who will be despairing presently when our contribution will have helped to bring on something more than we intended. Some of us like the pendulum at the left, some of us like it at the right: probably the wisest of us will let time tell itself in its own way and find what beauty we can between the tickings—or on the tickings—or whatever. It's easier to refuse to do the wrong thing than to do the right; that's certain, though negative.

—*The Literary Review*, Spring 1960

Poets and Scholars

Robinson Jeffers

· ✹✿✹ ·

. . . If I had known him first and his work second, I might better have appreciated the work. He himself is a good old tree, yet his bark presses angrily, not against other trees, but against grass. In that, he is somewhat like D. H. Lawrence. Why ought the other lone trees to be denied, and the fact that they, after all, make the landscape? He is too young a soul to be so old, too tender to be so tough, too sweet to be sour.

Humanity happens to motivate openly and speak. If the rocks and trees and the beasts had reached that state, they would do no better than humanity. How can Jeffers be content with a dumb unfulfillment and think he has dodged his germ? The old fawn should come into the human world with a new patience. He should let the hair on his ears be trimmed a while. It will grow again. He is, after all, an element made into man, made into something more intricate than his gulls and his seaweed. It is part of his job to find this intricacy not only beautiful, but simple.

The incest he worries about, and at the same time likes, is nothing worse innerly than the members trying to belong to their membership. He should change his disgust into patience and become a real seer.

At seven o'clock last evening on the train a forlorn tooth in my head began ulcerating. The abcess pounded at my jaw and ear and mind all night but never succeeded in disgusting me with my head. Just now I had the tooth out. I have babied that tooth for a decade. I know its every crinkle. It is gone, but the head, for a while, remains, and something more than the head. This pulse actuates more than heads and nervous teeth.

Jeffers begins always like a preacher with a text, and the text is usually beautiful, and then he deteriorates into anathema against the human race as the pulpit deteriorates into dull beatitudes. He and the pulpit are no different, because neither will be tolerant of the fact that a happy heart and an abcessed tooth can exist in the same carcass, and need no heaven to arbitrate between them.

I am doubtless too gregarious a person for Jeffers. I am in some ways too gregarious a person for myself. But finding in persons the jaggedness of rocks, or the pulp of seaweed, or the emphatic greed of gulls, I refuse to entertain, as Jeffers and Lawrence do, a necessary difference between the human and the animal world, except in favor of the human.

If it is the earth Jeffers favors, the long, large, high, wide, giving and receiving earth, then I am with him. Therein lies my first value through these breathing seconds. But drawn into that value is the human value—and Jeffers, with his wife and boys, knows it far better than I, a bachelor.

Here is my preachment against his.

—*The Carmelite*, December 12, 1928

Vachel Lindsay

· ❧❀❧ ·

It was years and years ago that a note in some column in a Chicago newspaper called to my attention for the first time a man named then Nicholas Vachel Lindsay. The note said that Lindsay was printing privately a collection of poems which he had been reciting about the country as a vagabond, that the poems were notable and that the poet would be glad to send free copies to persons interested. I sent for the pamphlet and became acutely interested. In fact, I was sure that I had found, mingled with genial playful doggerel and a good deal of fanciful verse, a number of poems sprung from original imagination and promising that a new genius was at the horizon.

Out of my consequent letter to Lindsay and his response sprang a friendship which lasted and deepened with time. It was not long, of course, before the pioneers who had heard the vagabond readings or who had encountered the pamphlet became the nucleus of a legion of admirers. His poems on General Booth and Governor Altgeld, his "Congo," "Santa Fe Trail," and "Chinese Nightingale" bid fair to hold their own in American letters with poems by any of his contemporaries and by many of his illustrious precursors. The fact that his later poems were not so good nor so popular is, in my judgment, easily and rather sadly explicable.

From the beginning, Lindsay had a passion, and a unique gift, for reciting his poems. He once told me that he knew every one of them by heart. An evangelist of poetry, he personally carried his moral fervor and his contagious rhythms to thousands of audiences. He appeared to have endless energy and an untirable voice. Once when he and I both were reading in Madison, Wisconsin, he offered, during a period of several days, to perform gratis in any schools roundabout which wanted him. I asked him about his strength to carry such giving. He answered with a swaying shrug of his shoulders and a characteristic wave of his hand, as though to say, "Ask a river about its strength." Troubled myself by a voice fagged from overuse, I inquired if his voice never weakened. "No!" he boomed. "That's what comes from having hog-calling ancestors."

Anxious about him nonetheless, I wrote him within the year expostulating against his absorption by the platform. Now that people knew his rhythms and his delivery of them, I argued it was far more important for him to be devoting his time and energy to the creation of new poems. I pointed to numerous instances of poets whose work had been injured by the labor and subtle contamination of constant public appearance. I warned him, but without persuasion, that his apparently inexhaustible physical and nervous force would finally fail him and would leave him suddenly empty and, for awhile at least, helpless to work. That is what happened. He gave way. He broke physically and nervously. Though later he recovered and resumed both writing and reciting, he had not yet become at the time of his death the Vachel Lindsay of old. He may have been on the way to new and larger creativeness. At least he was happy again; and that must remain enough. He had done, moreover, what he wanted to do. Sometimes I think that, loving people more than he loved poetry, he deliberately sacrificed further great writing which might have come from him, sacrificed it in order to enjoy the trinity which he ardently and righteously loved: people, poetry and himself.

Besides all this, he had to live. And it remains a melancholy fact that American audiences, perhaps audiences everywhere, are readier to pay a poet for his presence than for his work. Vachel Lindsay's physical presence is to be had no more. He died young. But the best of his work remains to speak for him, in his own powerful innermost voice.

—Unpublished manuscript in the Houghton Library, Harvard University

The Whole Lindsay

· ❧❧❧ ·

It is difficult for me to write, as I have been asked to do, concerning Vachel Lindsay's child-poems. Perhaps the very difficulty makes the attempt worthwhile.

The trouble is that I have never much cared about Lindsay's poems written for children. I have understood and sympathized with his motive, and I have no doubt that many children enjoy the verses he set down for them. Such children as have heard him chant them must have been, with him, enchanted. The spell of his presence and voice could at times almost make his lesser poems sound as good as his masterpieces. Nevertheless one may regret that he indulged his genius too often in trivial exercises, that he was too often misled from magic to the mediocre.

There is definitely a kind of genius which can put nonsense into magical form—Lewis Carroll's, for instance. There is a talent, almost amounting to genius, which can do for children what Gilbert did for grown-ups—A. A. Milne's, for instance. And now and then there have been poets writing as admirably in one vein for the young as in another for the old. Robert Louis Stevenson was such a case, though the popularity of his *Child's Garden of Verses*, it seems to me, has obscured the superior quality of much of his other verse.

Lindsay was of quite other stuff than the stuff of these three men. From the beginning, he was a child and spoke to the child in the hearts of his hearers. His responses to life were those of a child unfrightened by growing up. The Golden City which he wished his town to become was a town laid out in toy-blocks by an imaginative child. The Negro, whom he felt and echoed in his "Congo," was the Negro a wise child would feel when brought under the spell of Negro rhythm, charm and fate. And his "Chinese Nightingale" sings forever, against growing maturity and consciousness, the dawn of romantic love. So does his earlier "General Booth" ascend to heaven in the eyes of a child listening from the curbstone to the impressive emotion and simple rhythm of the Salvation Army. Even his "Lincoln" is the Lincoln of a thoughtful schoolchild, as all his flesh and blood heroes—except perhaps Altgeldt—are the heroes of a boy dreaming in a schoolroom.

In no whit when I say these things do I disparage Vachel Lindsay.

I would to God there were more modern poets who could bring a childlike faith and fervor to their song of life. Despite a momentary fad, among critics and pretentious laymen, favoring hyper-sophistication in both poetic content and form, the time is small now compared with the time when Lindsay struck its note. All the intellectual conceits in the world, all the inwrought mannerisms, all the fundamental faithlessness of the men and women who have turned poetry into this or that school of empty complication, all the egotism and blind gush of those who have made of it a mere sexual noise, are a sad drop in poetry from the singing child-heart of Lindsay. And this is why I have not liked those poems of his which are intentionally and technically childish. It would have been better had he trusted that young children as well as grown-up children would have responded to him at his best and richest. Very early in a child of any imagination, of any rhythm, of any future, surely there must lie, toward Lindsay's best poems, an intuitive understanding of the sweetness in the poet's young response to life, as well as an ear-beat echoing the primitive rhythms.

Accounting for the weakness of Lindsay's later poems, I believe that he tried in his work to separate the child and the man. Impressed by harmfully intricate praise or dispraise of his quality as both poet and craftsman, he forsook himself. He divided himself into two Lindsays. The Lindsay who must be a thinker and must write importantly, who must be a technician of parts and must write subtly, he separated from the Lindsay who must be a playboy and who must romp with children like a

Father Goose; and he thereby left behind him the whole Lindsay who should have remained a heaven-sent child through all vicissitudes. Had Vachel lived longer, I think that he would have found the whole Lindsay again. If he died divided, he lives whole.

—*The Elementary English Review*, May 1932

"Ave Atque Vale"

· ❧❦❧ ·

It was thirty-three years before his death in November 1945 that Arthur Davison Ficke opened with a group of poems the first number of *Poetry*. Yet the period since then, despite all that has happened during it to persons and to the world they constitute, seems to me in our friendship hardly more than thirty-three minutes. And how few minutes had passed before 1912, after my first meeting with him when he came to Harvard in 1900? Though I was two college years his senior, as well as two actual years, we were at once kin when we met, and from that day to this we have so remained. The whole period rounds into an hour far too brief, a crowded hour.

It becomes then both difficult and easy for me to say a word about him. I cannot speak objectively. After college, good fortune kept us often together as housemates:—in his birth-town, Davenport, Iowa, then in Japan, in China, in California, in Florida, in New York, in New Mexico and in Old Mexico, through a proportionately spaced number of the forty-five years. Though the half-jest always continued of our not caring much for each other's poetic manners, our close companionship by converse or by letter never ceased. And I know that I speak for many others with whom he maintained lively, warming touch when I say that he was a man of attributes not sufficiently published.

In 1914 Ficke received, through publication of *Sonnets of a Portrait Painter*, recognition as a distinguished poet and as one of America's most expert sonneteers, a recognition widening with publication of later volumes. His books on Japanese prints were highly esteemed not only in the West but in fastidious Japan. His one published novel, *Mrs. Morton of Mexico*, is an acute and tender observation of life in the southern Republic, a book already cherished and more to be cherished as time goes on by visitors in that country. His final absorption in the beauty of Chinese painting and the philosophy behind it should still yield from unpublished material notes of surpassing value.

With all his love for the aesthetic aspects of life, Ficke steadfastly served by word and deed the human needs and causes which give man his right to enjoy what is pleasant and beautiful. Someday, I hope, there will be a volume of his letters. I am not sure but that his generous communication with intimates contains his most potent and poignant writing, his warmest and wisest exampling to his fellows. Unguarded gaieties abound in his letters and so does hurt outcry. Both were requisite for his spirit and for the sharing of it. And I am confident that in due time, even more through his letters than through his professionally published writings, many who did not know him will feel that they do know him and will take his stalwart fellowship to their hearts.

There was satire too, a keen sense of it, as who should know better than I, particularly from our experience in putting *Spectra* together. Our pitch was such, in writing those poems, that we would not sleep nor eat and were at last banished by his rightly exasperated wife from the house in Davenport, finishing them at a hotel across the river in Moline. In this book for once we wholly liked each other's verse. Nor was the caprice without its own firm integrity. The story will someday be told of how we conscientiously had to exclude from the Spectric School five or six of America's better known poets who, under oath of secrecy, experimented for participation in the hoax.

At the risk of being too personal, I cannot help mentioning the fact that in his last illness when any exertion was extremely difficult Ficke, liking finally some poems of mine, or poems of Laotzu's through me, overcame his scruple against praising a friend in print and wrote a review of *The Way of Life According to Laotzu* for *Poetry*. After many months of harsh ill-health, he had known long before it came that death faced him; and he wrote to his friends letters of farewell which carried all that the word means, fondness for them and for life, no repining, no resentment, but appreciation of all that had been of good and all that would be of good. Those friends know and should prove that it was an annunciation of his being born again, at least in this life.

—*Poetry*, April 1946

Alice and I

· ❧❦❧ ·

In tireder or wiser age one abstains both from giving and from attending lectures. In my comparative youth, the date being 1922, I arrived in Santa Fe to give one. The town was off my professional beat; but I had asked a reluctant agent to swing me here, unprofitably, between Oklahoma and Colorado and to let me have a week's respite besides. Because of influenza, in one of those years when influenza was not just a cold, I took more than the week's respite, had to stay in Santa Fe six weeks to recover and have been recuperating here ever since. The person who was to blame for all this is Alice Corbin.

In an earlier year of lecturing—1916 I think—I had been heckled from the floor at Chicago. My subject was "Contemporary American Poetry"; and, before the secret had broken that Arthur Davison Ficke and I were respectively Anne Knish and Emanuel Morgan, founders and wielders of the Spectric School of Poetry, I was telling my audience how superior Spectric verse was to Imagist verse. I was advancing the Spectric theory. The poet is imbued with a subject or faces one suddenly. Instead of emotionalizing or intellectualizing his approach to it, he blanks his conscious heart, his deliberate mind, and lets the subject submerge him both from inside and from outside. He acts as a medium and records the force and range of his theme in a mode seemingly beyond his control. It might have been called the Ouija School of Poetry; but on a brash platform I was taking our "school" more solemnly than my conscience should have permitted. I was preferring the specter to the image and probably confusing image with imagery, when an interruption came from the audience. A woman's voice gave us the Imagists' insistence that an image was not a mere figure of speech but a clearly seen picture of an idea. In a sharp but friendly interchange between auditor and lecturer, was the former unwittingly siding with earlier artists who would nowadays be called representational, and the latter unwittingly siding with present-day artists who believe the inner consciousness chooses better pictures than the outer consciousness? Brittle though our talk was, each of us was thinking he had the better of the tilt, a liking sparked between us; and after the lecture Alice Corbin and I shook hands and planned to join again. We did join shortly afterwards at the Hendersons' studio in Chicago, where I met Alice's painter-husband, William Penhallow Henderson, and their diminutive daughter.

I was wandering in those days, still young, still lecturing, the commercialized troubadour, and from time to time I saw the Hendersons in Chicago. Some years later I heard that Alice was ill, that she was in Santa Fe for her health, and I wrote her. In answering she proposed that I come to Santa Fe on one of my tours. And so I came.

It had not occurred to me that she was seriously ill. I had thought merely that Santa Fe was a better climate for her. And so, when I stepped off the primitive car which a spur track brought from Lamy into a town of nine thousand, I thought I was greeting with a kiss the Alice I had sparred with in Chicago and thought I was giving my luggage to a broad-hatted cowboy hand from some frontier hotel. Not until we had almost reached the sanitarium did I realize that the Alice alongside me was the diminutive daughter, now grown to fifteen, that the cowboy hand in the front seat with my luggage, who had not till now said a word, was William Penhallow Henderson and that the elder Alice was a bedded invalid.

Though it troubled me at first to stay in a building which was half hotel, half sanitarium for tuberculars, I was soon persuaded that I was safer at Sunmount than in a New York trolley car and I remained beyond the six weeks needed for recovery from influenza. Alice Corbin's room, perhaps purposely, was opposite the doctor's office. She was not only a bed-patient but under strict watch as to rest and diet. Doctors, nurses, servants, and patients were all, in those years, easy comrades and so were such guests as lived long enough in the haphazard hotel section to become fellow Santa Feans. Waitresses would bring coffee for groups in this or that private room instead of serving it at this or that table in the long dining hall. Later Alice brewed her own coffee, and we would gather nightly in her room for gay, swift talk and forbidden cigarettes. Now and then we would enjoy in our coffee cups a fill or two of Taos Lightning, that fiery corn whiskey which we keg-rolled in the backs of our cars. Willy would be there, Little Alice would be there, a nurse would be there. Finally even the head doctor would be there and almost grant that these trespasses upon rule were doing his patient good.

In spite or because of such trespass, Alice presently emerged from the sanitarium, well enough to move to the little house on Camino del Monte Sol which her fifteen-year-old daughter and Nella, their canny Spanish-American maid, had been running with the authority of Mothers Superior. Amusing moments ensued when neither of them wished to yield any of that authority to the lay mother; but soon life continued around Big Alice very much as it had done farther up the hill: intimate gatherings, tea, coffee, cigarettes, white mule, and talk, talk, talk. At the sanitarium, we had often read poetry to one another, poetry established and poetry our own. Now, with mainly practitioners present, poetry and painting took fuller sway.

It was a small, pleasant, primitive adobe house, with an outdoor privy and with horses corralled alongside. I remember well when little Starlight was foaled on a cold night. Visitors would come across distances which now demand motoring; but we came on horseback then by day or at night on foot with lanterns and would kick snow off our overshoes in the welcoming glow of the room with its corner adobe fireplace. Painters from nearby houses on the Camino would be there, Applegate, Bakos, Shuster, Nash, sometimes Sloan and Davey from streets farther away, often Indian painters like Awa Tsireh from the Pueblos and occasionally a visiting writer, Lindsay with his chants, Sandburg with his guitar, Frost with his wit, Lummis with a red bandanna round his gray temples, or neighboring Jack Thorpe with his brother.

The Hendersons and I attended many Pueblo ceremonials together in those days; but we liked to watch singly and to absorb the dances, or to be absorbed by them, rather than to make them the social occasions they are now; and when the Easter dance or the August dance came at Santo Domingo, each lasting three days, we would last the three days with them, sleeping on the schoolhouse floor, and be up at dawn to see the first Koshare, with Alice Corbin as alert and hardy as any of us. Sometimes we were the only white watchers. Sometimes we took with us a visiting writer like Bliss Carman or Edna Millay, or a composer like Ernest Bloch.

Resident writers in 1923 were few. Elizabeth Shepley Sergeant was here, telling in *Harper's* about her "mud house"— whence dated, I think, the local dubbing of us painters and writers as "mud-hut nuts." Manuel Chavez was here, but not yet called Fray Angelico. Mabel Sterne was in Taos but not yet known for her memoirs. Erna Fergusson was in Albuquerque but was conducting tourists to the Indian country, not yet a courier in print. Ruth Laughlin's pen was not yet notably busy. Mary Austin, Haniel Long, Lynn Riggs, Ernest Seton, Oliver La Farge, Alfred Kreymborg, Paul Rosenfeld, Arthur Davison Ficke, Raymond Holden, Louise Bogan, Clifton Fadiman, John Gould Fletcher, and others came later to settle or sojourn in Santa Fe. But Spud Johnson shared my house in 1922, and it was then that the D. H. Lawrences made their first Santa Fe visit. Mabel Sterne, now Mabel Luhan, was bringing them through town from Lamy on their way to visit her in Taos, but it was too late for them to undertake what used to be a long and tough drive. At quick notice she could find no Santa Fe roof for them but mine, although at that time it covered only three small rooms, porous to the wind.

But what a sudden warmth we whipped together—Lorenzo and Frieda, Mabel and Tony Luhan, Alice Corbin, Willy Henderson and Little Alice, Spud and I. Mabel and Tony left early; but the rest of us talked by the fireplace into the snuggest of the small hours, all of us bobbing at Alice as children bob at apples on Halloween. She looked like an apple, with her round, rosy cheeks. And Willy was drawling his narratives of earlier Western days. And Little Alice was correcting both parents at intervals. The Lawrences, tired after their journey from the Coast but relieved to find a simple household, were soon recounting global adventures and they were as much like children as were the rest of us. With the Hendersons' help we gave them a late supper, and Spud and I were up early next morning to wash the dishes and feed our guests; but the Lawrences, let me record, were up before us and every dish was either clean or holding part of a good, hot breakfast which they had prepared and exactly timed for their hosts.

Later, when other writers and multiplying summer visitors came to Santa Fe, Alice Corbin was a main organizer of the annual Poets' Round-Up, to raise funds for Indian causes; and, in closer bound and bond, she brought a small group of us residents together to read and criticize one another's poems and to stimulate new writing: Spud Johnson, Haniel Long, Clifford McCarthy, Lynn Riggs, Robert Hunt and me, with others occasionally joining. Sometimes there would be personal poems betwixt us, a challenge and an answer; and, since Alice Corbin is not to know beforehand that we offer her herewith a garland of respectful affection and therefore cannot be asked to grant me the right to print a sonnet of hers, I venture, without her permission to enter a brace of exchange which dates from those poetry meetings. Alice wrote:

El Conquistador

You are so much to every casual friend—
The butcher and the baker and the rest,
And anyone who has a mood to spend
May spend it in the hollow of your breast:
Lowitsky has a share in you and all,

All, all possess you—and I only groan
To see you thus made common carnival,
And nothing left for me to call my own!

O Hal, O Hell—what is the use to sue
The insubstantial, evanescent you!
Harlot of sympathies although you be,
I search and hope and never may be sure
If what you give me differs from the lure
That holds Lowitsky and that maddens me!

I replied at the next session of our group:

*To One Who Exclaims at My Friendship with a Second-
Hand Dealer*

("You always like anyone.")

Lowitsky breathes his portion of the sky,
He too a curious vessel in the sun,
Of bright afflatus and opinion,
With as good veins to hold them in as I.
Why then pretend that he can only buy
And sell mean objects and perforce be done
With other thinking and with other fun?
Man has a second hand if the first die.

All men are made of earth to comprehend
Sun, moon and stars and thoughts: diameters
Crossing the wheel. Circumference encloses
You, me, Lowitsky too. Unto one end
We move together, while the circle stirs
With all its knowledge and with all its noses.

This sort of interchange was good teasing, good questioning,
good fun. I wish it had continued longer. Alice's sonnet, femi-

ninely playful, and mine, masculinely pontifical, were not, for others, of any special import in content or expression but for us, in personal and literary stimulus, they were of timely import; and that sort of give and take enlivened our enjoyment and experiment. It was good for us; and Alice managed continuance of our meetings as long as she could. It was not her fault that they ceased, nor was it ours. Towns grow too large. Nor should this particular verse exchange have ended where it did. My pulpit sonnet was not fair. Alice's understanding of every sort of person, her sympathetic entrance into the feelings and reasons of others, have been a lifelong characteristic. Years ago, as everyone knows, she was Associate Editor, with Harriet Monroe as Editor, of *Poetry: a Magazine of Verse*—in fact she was cofounder of it. And in that golden period of American poetry her vivid, sympathetic spirit meant much to most of the poets who made it golden, as it has meant much to all of us who have encountered her in poetry or in life.

Among my letters through the years from Ezra Pound I have found a pertinent passage:

"Alice was only intelligent element (in that frying pan) 1911–12 or whenever—only means of getting an idea into dear ole 'Arriet's hickory block. In short Alice my only comfort during that struggle. Blessings upon her."

Blessings upon her, say we all.

—*The New Mexico Quarterly*, Spring 1949

On Translating a Classic

· ❧❧❧ ·

It might be wondered, when what little Greek I had learned at college was forgotten, why and how I came to venture a version in English of a Euripidean play.

In 1914, Isadora Duncan with her six dancers had for some time been bringing Greek figures and friezes to life on the stages of several nations. Almost everyone connected in those days with any of the arts knew Isadora; and when she had been given use of the New Theater near Columbus Circle in New York, later called the Century Theater, we often heard her wish for a "right translation" of a Greek play to produce there. She had removed orchestra seats to make a deep-aproned stage on which she offered almost daily, at public performances, her rehearsals and experiments in dance and drama. Charging dearly for what lower seats were left but only ten cents for a gallery seat, she attracted substantial and ardent audiences to an exciting laboratory unique in American history. After her production of *Oedipus Rex*—the lead well played by her brother, Augustin—she kept begging me to try my hand at a version of *Iphigenia in Tauris*, which, she said from some knowledge or other, "though superbly simple in the original, had never been humanly translated into English, but always with stilted inversions and scholarly heaviness, and the sense subjected to the sound."

She made me try it, the choruses first. Scenes of the play were to follow and be combined into growing length for performance, as fast as I could write them. We had put on the stage all of the choruses, for Margherita Duncan and Helen Freeman, besides the six girls and herself, before someone discovered and reported that by living in the theater's large, luxurious dressing rooms Isadora and her group were breaking New York's fire regulations. So the whole experiment ended. But I finished the play, which was published as a single volume in 1915 and again, as part of my *Book of Plays*, in 1922. Both times, forgetting that we had omitted certain sections of the choruses which Isadora had thought too remotely allusive to be understood or effective, I neglected to restore them for print. They are included, however, in the present volume. I must add that in making the text for Isadora I relied only on close study of all English versions available. In revising it through the past two years, I have kept the choruses more or less as they were, a sort of musical accompaniment to the drama, but have otherwise written and discarded some seven manuscripts, with the devoted intent that what I could do for it might become ever simpler, clearer, and worthier of the humanist who wrote it. . . .

—Prefatory note to Witter Bynner's translation of *Iphigenia in Tauris* included in the introduction by Richmond Lattimore, *The Complete Greek Tragedies, Euripides II*, edited by David Grene and Richmond Lattimore, Chicago: The University of Chicago Press, 1956

Ezra Pound

· ❧❧❧ ·

My bit of memory and comment may properly find place in one of the letters. Here it is. A year or so after 1902 when I went to work for *McClure's* magazine, "the Chief" gave me free hand as poetry editor. My main exploit in that capacity was the introducing to an American public poems from A. E. Housman's *Shropshire Lad*. I did, however, print a few poems of my own, the first example of which proved to be half plagiarism. A Harvard classmate who had happened along while I was at verse manuscripts in Cambridge had quoted from somewhere two lines which he liked. I had absently entered them among my own lines and eventually they appeared in *McClure's* as part of a quatrain purporting to be mine, whereas the two lines were Dante Gabriel Rossetti's English, part of a sonnet he had translated from Michelangelo. For some years only the classmate, who reminded me, and Mr. McClure, whom I told, shared my unhappy realization of what I had done. This quatrain, half of it very good, may have been the principal poem of mine which several years later had sufficiently recommended itself to a citizen of, I think, Pennsylvania that he sent his son to me with poems.

Since all of it happened fifty years ago, details blur; but I vividly remember the youth who came to me in New York, who was not on that occasion "soft-spoken," as he has been remembered by others, but firm-spoken and confident. "Would I look at these poems and see if I thought they warranted his being sent abroad for stimulus and study." Not only was my ready answer, "Yes, if that was what he greatly wished," but it developed later into arrangement that Small, Maynard and Company of Boston, who had published my own first book in 1907, should publish three books by Pound: *Provença, Sonnets and Ballate of Guido Cavalcanti*, and *Ripostes*.

My memory of Pound, at that first meeting when he read his poems to me, is the eager face, voice and insistent spirit behind them and then a sense of his being an even more happily cuckoo troubadour than the young Vachel Lindsay. But never have I seen Lindsay attired for it as Pound was. I should say that his jacket, trousers and vest had each a brave color, with a main effect of purple and yellow, that one shoe was tan, the other blue and that on a shiny straw hat the ribbon was white with red polka dots. I liked both the poet and his poetry and have often regretted that our connection, through the years which followed his sailing in 1910, could be only by correspondence.

When I saw him again, after his detention at St. Elizabeths in Washington, it was the same great, booming boy, or so he seemed, who clutched me with a bear-hug and cried out, "After forty years!" Time and the beard had made little change for me in his presence; and he seemed quite as sane as he had seemed at the turn of the century or in letters after that.

And yet I wish that Pound would stop blaming me for the dissolution of Small, Maynard and Company, as though I had the little publishing house in hiding somewhere and would not produce it. But after all I enjoy the vehemence—when I can decipher it. Or his vehemence against my preferring Laotzu to Confucius for final import. And I enjoy Pound's poetry—when I can decipher it. I do not agree with Wallace Stevens that "poetry is the scholar's art" nor with the young scholar Ezra that Rihaku was ever the English way to spell Li Po. In the ponderings of the *Cantos* I grant that for me there is too much ponderous ore; but I maintain that in Pound's poetry when the veins are pure they are as pure as any. And on the hill of his poetry the child rides high, still daring to indulge his importunate self.

—*The Ezra Pound Newsletter,* April 10, 1956

D. H. Lawrence

· ❧❦❧ ·

Edward Nehls's three-volume biography is compositely and objectively built of quotations from D. H. Lawrence, and from others concerning him, with no direct opinions added by the compiling editor. However, choice of excerpts is more or less indicative of opinion, and in at least this part of an exhaustive and valuable work, which is all I have had time to read before contributing a few prefatory paragraphs to the second volume, I could not at first help one misgiving: perhaps Frieda Lawrence's basic dignity in her husband's as well as her own life, and her creative influence on his work, are understressed or not understood. Among the books which have become a small library on Lawrence, the men's are not so spitefully telling as the women's; but they, too, like the women's, incline to overlook the power, sometimes explosive but mainly steadying, with which she measured, admired, and guided her husband and his writing: a maturer, more grounded power than the young, tenderly devoted influence of Jessie Chambers had been on the living and writing of *Sons and Lovers*.

However, I have often wondered since the issue of my *Journey with Genius*—and am glad of this chance to say so— if I may have overdone a wish not to use hindsight ahead of its time and if I failed to enter early enough in the book, for casual readers, my later realization of the fact that, sick though Lawrence was, he had never given me any evidence of his illness by complaint in words or faltering in spirit but only by bursts and acts of temper. Perhaps I have not appreciated how fairly Mr. Nehls keeps the order and proportioning of record, round wife as well as husband, and gives a true chronological transcript.

In this volume I have relived the time when I watched Lawrence write *The Plumed Serpent*, extolling the noble savage in print while he dreaded or disliked him in person. Two years later he could still state, in regard to the book which I still consider his least discerning or important: "My Quetzalcoatl novel lies nearer my heart than any other work of mine," and a month after that he could write, "We had an Indian and his wife to do for us, till last week; then we sent them away. Savages are a burden." Fear had given place to irritation. And the growing irritation was not only with savages. "I feel so weary of *people*— people, people, people," he wrote, and again, "The world gives me the gruesomes, the more I see of it. That is, the world of people," or "I don't feel so easy in my skin."

The truth of the matter was that people of any sort anywhere could depress him almost to a pitch of madness because he was sick and unknowingly blamed them for the way he felt. It was as simple as that. Under it all and from the start he was oppressed by the wooden voodoo of caste and yet as bound and impressed by a sense of its sanctity as Jane Austen was, or Thackeray or Meredith or almost any recorder of human doings. At the same time, his lifelong struggle was to prove that somehow, somewhere the natural peasant, though not necessarily The Noble Savage, is truly and powerfully the aristocrat,—and to bluster away his own physical and social shyness and the almost painful purity of philandering's sternest foe by verbal precocity as to the physical acts, like a small boy leading his playmates, his followers, his potential cult. And in somewhat the same way he never really wanted to outgrow a small boy's delicious faithful terror of the dark.

Finally, despite often hysterical sharpness against people, he loved them well enough to want to lead them out of desolation. And toward the natural world he remained one of the tenderest lovers of all time. In particular he loved the beauty of New Mexico with magic ardor. On his small ranch near Taos his life nearly came true. But his illness felled him in Europe and he could not flee again.

In Mr. Nehls's concluding volume, I anticipate further aptly assembled evidence of Lawrence's essential devotions, as well as of his suffering the fate of the average man, helplessness against ego, against mankind, and against death.

—The Foreword to *D. H. Lawrence: A Composite Biography*, edited by Edward Nehls, vol. II, 1919–1925, Madison: The University of Wisconsin Press, 1958

Edgar Lee Masters

· ❧❀❀❧ ·

Spoon River Anthology, first published in 1914 as by a very modern poet named Webster Ford in the St. Louis *Reedy's Mirror*, and the next year a resounding success in book form by Edgar Lee Masters, has now been issued in a stately edition by the Macmillan Company ($7.50) together with "The Unfinished Spooniad" which had better not have been begun and an equally negligible "Epilogue," both in clumsily regular verse. One feels in reading them that Masters, somehow ill at ease with the main text, was trying to creep back to the conventional style of his earlier writing. About that stubborn nostalgia of his there is a tale to be told, and I should like to tell a part of it as I remember following it from my own vantage.

As early as the summer of 1909, I had met and admired a Midwestern editor, William Marion Reedy, whose *Reedy's Mirror* had not only a local circulation in St. Louis, where he lived and edited, but was followed by enthusiasts all over the country. It had begun earlier as a scandal sheet, digging up untoward tales about Missouri citizens and Reedy after buying it continued it at first as partially a gossip sheet through which he entered the publishing world as a lusty advocate of Henry George's single tax plan advanced in *Progress and Poverty*. Single tax had made converts of many Midwesterners besides Reedy. Mayor Johnson of Cleveland was one, Brand Whitlock another. The latter I first knew through Reedy as mayor of Toledo. Whitlock later was wartime ambassador to Belgium, but always maintained his literary interests. There were two other single taxers of this period—a white-haired old fellow and his wife who in Chicago edited together a small Henry George sheet like Reedy's in St. Louis. Their names and that of their journal have gone from me, but their gentle faces come to light in my memories of both Reedy and Masters. It's too bad they cannot all be in a Kennedy Cabinet!

Little by little Reedy changed the color of his journal not only from mischievous gossip to single tax, but from local to national quality, largely by printing the work of emergent poets whom he chose to encourage. Among them besides Masters were Vachel Lindsay, Sara Teasdale, Rose O'Neill, Robinson Jeffers, Edna St. Vincent Millay, Arthur Davison Ficke, and myself.

Within the past several years, after having given a sheaf of Reedy's letters to the Missouri Historical Society, I gave to the Houghton Library at Harvard not only the issues of the *Mirror* containing Masters' masterpiece as it ran serially, but pages carrying the best sequence I yet know of Millay's sonnets, and my own "Songs of the Unknown Lover" later published in 1919 as a book: *The Beloved Stranger.*

The date of my first meeting with Masters was perhaps in 1914. At any rate, on August 4, 1914, he wrote me the following:

". . . This is me—Webster Ford of Spoon River, also the Loop. Many thanks for your hearty word of encouragement. I know your work and the work of all the boys around here and across the water. You're doing things all right. So is Lindsay. Glad if I can add a bit to the circle. Will you join the philosophers' union? Quarters in Chicago to consist of the most barren room we can find—a few tables and chairs where men drop in to reflect and speak occasionally. . . .

"Well here's to you ever. . ."

Thereafter, with him and Reedy though I don't remember the "philosophers' union" as such, I do remember that besides our eager discussions of single tax, there was much discussion of American letters. Masters himself, even in his earlier days, more resembled a judge than a minstrel, but the eyes were alive and the heart active. There had not then come into him the troubled look which resulted from the success of only one of his books, to which he felt that some of the others were definitely superior. In later years, he often seemed to me to be feeling ill at ease—not only with the world but with himself.

Reedy, although he had published some of Masters' early verse, most of it conventional, reproached the poet for dead classicism and urged him to try his hand at writing more like Burns and Wordsworth,—in other words, about real people he had known in the town where he was brought up—a quick straightforward diary of village lives.

Just at what point it was I cannot remember, but I recall seeing some of the contributions Masters sent in for the *Mirror* under the pseudonym Webster Ford and I remember the editor's kindling ardor over their nature and quality. I should say that Reedy's enthusiasm surprised Masters, who had begun in a spirit of parody,—"I suppose this is the sort of thing you want." Reedy persisted however in his fervor and at once offered to publish the series. My memory is that Masters continued with new installments after Reedy had begun publication of those which had come earlier. Although Reedy seemed to have made a convert in his poet, Masters never again was the success he had been in his new manner. Indeed, if I remember correctly, it was because he reverted to the old manner and during later years was a perplexed and saddened man—as if there had been a mistake on his own part as well as on that of the public.

This situation as it had developed in 1939 was recounted to me in a letter from Arthur Davison Ficke dated January 1st of that year:

". . . I am seeing a great deal of Masters nowadays. He clings to me with the clasp of a drowning man: sometimes I think that I am the only person left in the world whom he likes and trusts. His bitterness against everything else is a tragic thing to watch. You and I, whose lives have been so rich in many beautiful friendships that still exist in actuality or in memory, can hardly visualize the picture of a man whose own inner bitterness of spirit has made him now feel that he has never had a friend. . . . It is very sad. . . ."

And yet in an earlier letter (November 15, 1936), Ficke quoted to me from Masters' latest book:

> . . . I have become
> A part of something whole, I have been taken,
> Mixed and absorbed and saved as if in sleep.

As one reads *Spoon River* in this fine Macmillan dress, it is revealing to note how over and over again lines occur in it edging back to conventionally poetic expression. The straightforward expression yields here and there to old poetic words and phrases. The straight talk with natural cadences is broken into by traditional literary expression. Here are instances:

> My flowering side you never saw!
> Ye loving ones, ye are fools indeed
> Who do not know the ways of the wind
>
> For many times with the laughing girls and boys
> Played I along the road and over the hills
>
> Why did Albert Schirding kill himself . . .
> Ere he was sixty?

And here is an instance where a mannered ending almost undoes the fine simplicity of what precedes it:

> This is life's sorrow:
> That one can be happy only where two are;
> And that our hearts are drawn to stars
> Which want us not.

Masters loved to be literary and in the sure sense he often was —in spite of himself.

In this new edition, I found myself drawn ahead by one page after another so that even with poor eyesight, I had in three evenings reread the book. Midway in the *Anthology* though, I felt the brief biographies swerve a bit from honesty into contrivance. The book would now seem to me to have been better shorter. But perhaps the next reader, feeling this or that passage strike into his life, would find true poetic echo in lines seeming to me artificial.

In any event, the book remains a vivid and absorbing document, dramatic in its human contents and for the most part straightforward in its expression. And I have much enjoyed renewing my acquaintance—or more than acquaintance—with its originality. It is true that the Greeks wrote elegies. These geographic obituaries are Greek as well as American.

Here lies
WEBSTER FORD
Or rather
Tells the truth

—*The Santa Fe New Mexican*, April 21, 1963

The Mirrored Self

Do Poets Work?

· ❧❧❧❧❧ ·

If it is self-revelation you ask, I suppose first of all I must confess my original aversion to poetry and the apparently accidental manner of my initiation to it. In 1897 there was no such kind attitude toward poets as has slowly come about since then; and, as editor of a high school paper in Brookline, Mass., I shared the general prejudice. We had poets writing for *The Sagamore*, but only as the professional magazines had poets writing for them. We younger editors and our business managers were tempted, like our elders, to put out the poets; but we had a kind of super-stitious tradition about them and let them stay fiddling, much as the housewife annoyedly lets the cricket fiddle on the hearth. Then one month there was no verse in the till. The obscure little strays who usually contributed verse were more than usually shy. None of the other editors would make the sacrifice. It was up to the editor-in-chief. So I wrote a poem on Peace. Rereading it, I don't wonder I was ashamed to be writing poetry, though at the time I thought that, as poems went, it was a pretty good one. At any rate it had no effect whatever on anybody but me. The virus had entered. I continued verse writing. With a sense of humiliation at joining the poets, nonetheless I went on till the time came when habit had conquered prejudice. I rejected prose, I accepted verse—as under the tropic pressure of a Cuban sum-mer I once found myself going without fish and meat and living on mameyapple and pigna fria. Little by little at college I ceased as a story writer, though I hung my head a bit by signing my verse in the Harvard *Advocate* not Hal Bynner but W. Bynner. It so happened that Wallace Stevens, then editor of the *Advocate*, signing his delicate lyrics W. Stevens, tyrannically objected to another W. in the index and imposed on me my middle name in full; so that not only my profession but the name I use in it came to me through editorial exigencies.

The layman little dreams of the patience of love's labor which goes into a poet's work. No eight hours for us. We couldn't stop with eight if we wanted to. The pity of it is that we often seem idle when engrossedly busy and are therefore interrupted. You musn't expect a wireless apparatus to go round like a windmill. But many of you do expect it—especially you tired businessmen! That's why, like my "official enemy," Amy Lowell, I have had to resort to night writing. Many's the night I have put in my eight hours without stirring from my seat, without a bite of bread or sip of water, holding in my lips for long intervals an unlighted and forgotten cigarette and in my mind the teasing differences between half a dozen words, differences that seem trifling and yet seem tremendous.

Much has been said in the press of the "Spectric hoax." It has even been charged by Arthur J. Eddy and others that Spectra, which Arthur Davison Ficke and I advanced under the pseudonyms Anne Knish and Emanuel Morgan, was a Freudian case of "self-revelation." That may be true. All we intended in our deceit was a puncturing of the pretense and pedagogic bombast with which certain of the "new poets" have prescribed and circumscribed work of theirs, some of which has been good in itself. And I acknowledge that in the freedom of disguise Ficke and I found a lyric enjoyment. Haven't poets often done well with larks? Why shouldn't we do well with ours?—a lark which flew beyond almost everyone's sight but our own for nearly two years! Some of my friends deplore the fact that, with the joke exploded, Morgan goes on writing. But Emanuel feels at last relieved to have the joke out of his system, cherishes his new book and relishes its approaching candid publication. After all, the more facets a joke has the better the joke. Emanuel Morgan is going his own way now and Witter Bynner his, and you may take your choice. For *Songs of the Beloved Stranger*, Morgan's new volume, I accept no responsibility. I am not quite sure that it is mine. But for *Grenstone Poems*, *The New World*, *Young Harvard* and the plays I accept responsibility, as a careful parent should. I know about Witter Bynner, his conviction that beauty is a comrade of kindness, his intentions, his shortcomings, his perseverance.

—*The Chicago News*, October 16, 1918

Over 65

First of all let me say that since I was 65 I have discovered with no warning that I am almost 75. The speed of these later years is a phenomenon. The giddy, golden days and nights of youth did not travel nearly so fast. The main reason for the speed in my own case is realization that I have left undone until now a great amount of writing for which I have always thought there would be plenty of time.

Age of course brings or increases physical troubles. Mine, except for blindness in one eye, are familiar because of earlier experience. I almost would not know what to do without them and have learned that when one can manage it, hard work is good medicine in that it takes the mind away from trouble. Since reaching 70 I have taken two six-month trips to Europe, realizing in 1952 that I had not been there in 50 years. I had, however, been abroad in Asia only 30 years ago and since then had found Mexico an excellent and handy substitute for countries farther away.

Also I have each year gone abroad in my garden. It is just as well perhaps that I cannot do that any more if I wish to progress with my writing, but somehow I do not regret the long hours of gardening—of touching earth, which took me away from trying to touch visions on paper.

As for a philosophy to alleviate supposed decrepitude, but really for facing not so much one's own death as the death of others, I have found that it is happiness to accept the wonder of life without any narrow creed and to realize that somehow the two currents—positive and negative—life and death—make light.

Friends, of course, are ever a source of happiness. A few of them may be a plague on a leaf, but there are ever other leaves;

and the good life force moves unshaken by trifles. Happiness consists in moving with it and at the same time realizing that life
forces and death forces are one.

—Publication and date unknown

Autobiography in the Shape of a Book Review

· ✂✂✂ ·

Once upon a time there was a young poet who thought he knew what was best for him. He had managed his way through Harvard and on Commencement Day was assured that he should accept the post offered him of being presently an instructor in the English Department after his twenty-first birthday, August 10, 1902. His family, however, plotted against him and when they divulged the plot, he capitulated. The agreement was that he should accept the terms of his mother and stepfather: immediately on graduation in June, he was to receive from them a trip abroad lasting until October, after which he was to take for only a year a post they would find him in some New York publishing house. Upon his return from the journey, he found himself indentured—practically as an office-boy at ten dollars a week—to Mr. S. S. McClure, editor of *McClure's* magazine. . . .

*   *   *

Despite the ability active on the *McClure* staff, the assistant editors had all seemed to me somewhat hypnotized into following him as a sort of sure shepherd. When he would briskly enter his office in the morning sixty years ago, the editorial group would be on the quick for summons and sit around him like a group at busy ease with a great man. Then out of his briefcase he would pluck pages of notes attached to newspaper clippings from all over the country. He would start reading aloud first a clipping, then a jotting and, fixing an excitedly sagacious eye closely on this or that member of the staff, he would say: "This is for you, Steffens," or to Ida Tarbell: "Will you report to us on this one?" or: "Your stuff, Baker." The following week the report would be made, each editor giving reasons for further report by himself or one of the others, or recommending no further attention in the matter, McClure himself being the final judge.

It was this way that the Standard Oil story had been written by Ida Tarbell whose only weakness would be toward use of such material as a bill for board which she told me she had in her possession, but refrained from using. A school friend of Mrs. John D. Rockefeller's had been invited for a Saturday and Sunday stay. After she had overstayed through Monday, she received from her host a bill for one day's board and lodging, promptly paid and receipted.

Ray Stannard Baker was a man and writer of tender virtue and I remember his being sent to investigate the Californian group under the leadership of a Mrs. Tingley, called the "Purple Mother." A former Cabinet member in Washington—Treasury, I think—and rich, was lodged there and Mr. McClure thought that the colony might be a racket. Baker's report on returning was that the institution was a society of idealists and the life in the colony such that he would like it for his own retirement.

Lincoln Steffens was the only staff member who to me appeared at base skeptical over the McClure crusades. He told me that, though he would write what he was paid to write, he felt that on the whole the miscreants were far more enjoyable company than their attackers and that if he had his choice it would be Tammany rather than Christian associations. I find a pertinent note I made at the time about him: "Steffens was always after that extra height which men who are short sometimes reach for with assertion, vivacity, or assumed humor."

Mr. McClure, though always thinking himself right, was never self-righteous.

When extraordinary material was brought by Georgine Milmine concerning the life of Mary Baker Eddy, Ida Tarbell was the first to undertake its presentation as a series for *McClure's*, but soon withdrew in favor of a newcomer to the office, an ex-schoolteacher from Pittsburgh named Willa Cather, one of whose stories in manuscript had greatly impressed Mc-Clure. I well remember businesslike Miss Cather working away at the tangled heap of manuscript for a considerable period before its exciting appearance in the magazine. I believe that Miss Cather years later helped Mr. McClure compile his own autobiography. I also remember his asking me to cut hundreds of words from Miss Cather's story "The Sculptor's Funeral." I explained to him that it would have to be cut bit by bit—words here and words there—rather than lose small sections or even paragraphs. He agreed and I did not know that the author was unaware of the process until the story was shown her in proof. I can still hear her explosion in his office and see her enraged expression toward me when Mr. McClure pretended that the cutting had been entirely my own idea. I had to let her believe him.

However, the only other time he interfered with my clear sailing at the office was when he interposed in my control of verse in the magazine by dictating acceptance of some very bad lines by a most incompetent young lady, writing the acceptance message himself and even asking me as a favor to deliver with his note a box of flowers. Peter Lyon in his book gives this episode and its consequences their due.

I need not more than remark the fact that I remained with McClure beyond the first year. I was having a very good time. My pay had gone up fifty per cent to fifteen dollars a week and I had begun judging and reporting on manuscripts from unknown authors, meantime sending a daily valise of work from familiar authors to our outstanding reader Viola Roseboro' at her home office. Although she paid less attention to muckraking, which the others of *McClure's* had initiated in the magazine world, she exercised even to the point of genius recognition of imaginative writing—a fine result in *McClure's* where the standard of story-telling steadily added to the magazine's pre-eminent popularity.

Before my arrival in the office, *McClure's* magazine had been printing contributors like Rudyard Kipling, Robert Louis

Stevenson, Sir Arthur Conan Doyle, Booth Tarkington, Stephen Crane and Jack London.

One day I had taken a shine to a manuscript called "Tobin's Palm" by a new author, O. Henry. I sent it along to Miss Roseboro', saying I thought it extremely good. When it did not come back to the office with her recommendation or question, I inquired by phone and found that this time she had followed her rare practice of returning it direct to the author with handwritten comments. Taking the case to Mr. McClure, I told him that the author, according to his address, lived nearby and that I considered the manuscript the best which had come to the office during my time. With quick challenge, he asked if I would stake my judgment on it. I answered: "Yes. Will you accept it on my say-so?" When he said: "Yes," I bounded across to the Lion d'Or restaurant and, in a bleak room overhead, found O. Henry —like a Western Buddha—occupying an unpadded rocker and on a trunk nearby I saw a sealed envelope. "Tobin's Palm?" I asked. "Yes," he said. "Accepted," said I, grandly and with young pride.

Mr. Lyon in *Success Story* says that the McClure group was already acquainted with the author through their newspaper Syndicate which had published him, but I am certain that nobody in the office recognized his authorship or his hand in "Tobin's Palm." Perhaps he had used his own name, Sidney Porter, for the Syndicate as he did in earlier writing. I don't know, but I do know that "Tobin's Palm" was O. Henry's first marked success in the literary world and that we continued publishing his stories to widening acclaim. I also remember that from the Klondike a youngster who had been reading O. Henry wrote Mr. McClure that if that was the kind of story we liked, he could do plenty of them himself. His name was Rex Beach and we continued printing him too. I remember wishing, incidentally, that John S. Phillips, head of our publishing house, had not substituted "The Spoilers" for Beach's original title "Loot."

Through this period in the office, I had taken over the greater part of Mr. McClure's correspondence with his authors and learned an accurate and authorized forgery of his signature. In one instance, I ventured amusement in having Mr. McClure mimic in correspondence the author's own style. I remember my conviction that I did extremely well in the instance of Henry James, but even when the latter and I became friends later, neither of us ever mentioned my impertinence. Before James arrived in this country, I was introduced to him by a letter from Henry Harland; and the following passages from letters Henry James sent me are amusingly pertinent to my efforts for *Mc-Clure's:* the first in answer to my request that he let us see his impressions of the United States after twenty years' absence and the second his response to Willa Cather's *Troll Garden* which I sent him with my recommendation:

(January 8, 1904)

. . . as my last visit was no less than twenty-one years ago, the expectation of "impressions" is, naturally, not other than strong within me. . . . I desire to vibrate as intensely, as frequently and as responsively as possible—and all in the interest of vivid literature! . . .

and the other excerpt:

(February 1, 1906)

I have your graceful letter about *The Troll Garden* . . . and if I brazenly confess that I not only haven't yet read it, but haven't even been meaning to (till your words about it thus arrive), I do no more than register the sacred truth. That sacred truth is that, being now almost in my 100th year, with a long and weary experience of such matters behind me, promiscuous fiction has become abhorrent to me, and I find it the hardest thing in the world to read almost any new novel. Any is hard enough, but the hardest from the innocent hands of young females, young American females perhaps above all. This is a subject—my battered, cynical, all-too-expert outliving of such possibilities—on which I could be eloquent; but I haven't time, and I will be more vivid and complete some other day. I've only time now to say that I will then (in spite of these professions) do my best for Miss Cather so as not to be shamed by your so doing yours. . . .

Possibly my outstanding service to the magazine was the printing of poems from A. E. Housman's *Shropshire Lad.* The book had not been copyrighted nor known in the United States, wherefore we might have published from it what we pleased without permission; but Mr. McClure let me not only republish poems already contained in a published volume, but to pay for them at a higher rate than most verse in those days received. Incidentally, Mr. Housman returned the first check and received none further because of his statement to me that he never took payment for his verse.

Probably with the idea of training me for increased activity among his authors, McClure took me with him on a trip to Louisville where we visited his popular contributor Mrs. George Madden Martin of the "Emmy Lou" stories. I remember our all driving for dinner to the house of Alice Hegan Rice, author of *Mrs. Wiggs of the Cabbage Patch,* and her husband the poet Cale Young Rice. The car ahead of us was driven by another of the guests whose name escapes me, an unmarried unassuming Southern lady who was also a quietly impressive local literary critic. Suddenly her car swerved off the road and head-on struck a barn door which threw the driver so violently forward that she was seriously injured. Her only comment, spoken softly, was that her glasses hadn't broken. It is characteristic of Mr. McClure that, at least until she recovered some months later, he helped by printing several literary essays from her.

In Louisville, where Mr. McClure delighted me by vigorously unmusical songs in the bathtub, he tried me on a case. As I remember it, a Governor had been killed by a shot through his office window in the Kentucky State House and a defeated candidate for the Lieutenant Governorship had been suspected and jailed for the crime. Mr. McClure had a feeling from newspaper accounts that the man was innocent and sent me to jail for an interview. I agreed with the McClure judgment and we sent Ray Stannard Baker to see the fellow, whose release was brought about by a subsequent Baker article in the magazine.

These were things that McClure did along the way. I think he also wanted to test me as a possible prose writer but no, that did not happen. I was not prompted to undertake that kind of task, although I did continue friendship with the young politician who was afterward elected to Congress as a Kentucky Representative.

The most vivid and the saddest memory I have of Mr. McClure remains his face on the grim day (May 10, 1906) when almost his entire staff left him. I always felt that his mild peccadillo and the editorial court martial of him in the office was the beginning of their defection. I had been planning to leave *McClure's* for reasons of my own general direction; but when he looked up haggard and tearful and said: "Bynner, are you leaving me too?" I couldn't forsake him but stayed with loyal Viola Roseboro' and Willa Cather.

To me, the main explanation from those who withdrew was that they could not continue longer toward the bankruptcy for which he was heading them all and they would shake their heads over the fact that he was a very weak man—bound to ruin them all with wild expenditures. In one instance when his offer for a Kipling serial, *Kim*, was $15,000 and a rival editor offered $16,000, Mr. McClure concluded the deal on the spot by making it $25,000 which in those days was unheard of.

He made me managing editor and I was misled for several days by the importance of such a position for one so young, so that I was jolted when Will Irwin soon turned up to take over what I had thought my desk, with Mr. McClure saying: "But I thought you liked the other post better—with authors and all that." I know now that he was right, but a warning would have been pleasanter treatment.

I stayed at least until autumn, still fond of McClure and

enjoying my work with him and yet persistently tempted to try the life of a free-lance. My final complete resignation from the office was later that year, after I had received the following in a letter from a friend and counselor:

> Dublin, New Hampshire
> Oct. 5–06

Dear Poet:

You have certainly done right—for several good reasons; at least, of them, I can name two: 1. With your reputation you can have your freedom and yet earn your living. 2. If you fall short of succeeding to your wish your reputation will provide you another job. And so, in high approval I suppress the scolding and give you the saintly and fatherly pat instead. . . .

> Yours ever,
>
> Mark Twain

I did not see Mr. McClure again until some seven years later when he looked me up in Tokyo and went with me to the Kabuki Theater. I took him behind scenes to meet one of the foremost actors of the time in the latter's dressing room. The actor kept us waiting while he passed to and fro through the room naked behind a silk robe in the hands of attendants and steaming from his bath. This meant a considerable wait for us on our knees so that, fifteen minutes later, Mr. McClure could stand it no longer and without good-bye to any of us crawled on all fours out of the room. Years later, when he was in his seventies, I had dinner with him again and after that I was saddened to hear that members of the Union League Club were begrudging him a corner in their library which he was reserving more or less as an office of his own for his papers. I can only hope that he never realized their attitude.

Mr. Lyon makes clear how it became practically impossible for the staff to sustain McClure's financial vagaries—none of the latter being so much for his own benefit as for that of them all.

On the other hand, he did become more and more impatient and difficult personally; and despite most of their leaving him in a business way, none of them lost an essential tenderness toward him and their new editorial venture, *The American Magazine*, failed to prosper.

But what I have written sounds more like autobiography than like a review of Peter Lyon's *Success Story*. And the reason is clear—at least for me. I have been supplying this or that detail of observation on the spot which Mr. Lyon could not help omitting from his vivid and penetrative account of S. S. McClure's life and times. And yet I feel as though Mr. Lyon had actually been in the offices with us, going from one editor to another and I were challenged to come back at him with a few paragraphs he had skipped, overlooked, or not known about. I can hear the figures he portrays speaking with amazing accuracy.

Mr. Lyon wrote me several years ago that as a young man he had known S. S. McClure and found him "a garrulous old bore," as any young man might. In this mature book, however, he makes him anything but that and seems to have grown rightly sensible and fond by these latter years of careful study.

Being probably the only survivor of the McClure editorial staff from any of its periods, I have naturally concentrated on the brief bit I experienced of Mr. McClure's career and the biographer's record of it. But, in vouching for the accuracy with which Mr. Lyon records those several years, I can only feel assured that the rest of the book is as accurate, including Mc-Clure's picturesque and harsh childhood in Ireland, his visions ahead of what he wanted in the literary and journalistic world, his achievement of those hopes rather than of material reward. If he had been a more average American, he would have had far more of such gain to show for his consistent and popular success as editor and publisher. *McClure's* magazine was not only the most popular in its day, but set an example for journalism of the following half-century. Not only was McClure foremost of editors as muckraking crusader, but he had an unerring sense of direction. He was a divining rod for characters, for abilities and for decent interesting righteousness. And Peter Lyon with sympathy, admiration and able writing brings him alive.

—Reminiscence occasioned by reviewing *Success Story: The Life and Times of S. S. McClure*, by Peter Lyon, New York: Charles Scribner's Sons. Published in *The Santa Fe New Mexican*, November 3, 1963, and *The Harvard Alumni Bulletin*, February 1, 1964

REVIEWS

· ❧✦❧ ·

Poetry from the Trenches

· ❧❧❧❧❧ ·

Robert W. Service has been a poetic phenomenon. More or less ignored by the critics, he has won a vast following. And it seems to me time for a fellow craftsman to protest that in this case the public is right. During these years while *The Spell of the Yukon* has accumulated a staggering sale of five hundred thousand copies and while the wells of Kipling have been growing muddy or dry, the professors of poetry and the dilettanti have been paying attention to Imagists and Spectrists, leaving Service —they thought—to schoolboys. But the popularity of this poet need not have hurt him in the eyes of the discerning nor need his debt to Kipling have injured him in their ears.

It happens that I had just read and reviewed *Spectra*, the latest expression of "the new verse," and been struck with it as a strange phosphorescent crest of impressionism, when there came into my hands the volume by Service, *Rhymes of a Red Cross Man*, two hundred pages of sturdy sentimental realism. And I started up with a gasp. Here was "the old verse." Here was something actual, intimate, human, alive.

I will grant at the outset, to such as incline to disagree with my estimate, an occasional familiar crudeness in the book and the mawkishness of poems like "Our Hero," "Son," and "The Convalescent." But the crudeness is the kind you grasp hands with heartily and the mawkishness is the kind you look away from respectfully, and what's left, by far the greater part, you thrill and laugh over like a boy.

Here, as in the earlier poems, is an implicit acknowledgment of the debt to Kipling. It reaches even to free use of the phrase, "thin red line of 'eroes'" or to the refrain, "For I'm goin' 'ome to Blighty in the mawnin' " echoing the refrain of "Danny Deever." But such echoes are the proper salute of kinship; for this latest book confirms Service not as Kipling's imitator only but as his successor. The *Ballads of a Cheechako* and *Rhymes of a Rolling Stone* were a disappointment to those who suspected their author of a true and important gift; for they contained nothing of the caliber of "The Spell of the Yukon," that big poem which distinguished his first volume, *Songs of a Sourdough,* and has become the title-poem of its later editions. Nor did the general contents of his two intermediate volumes bear out the general promise of the first or prepare one for the vigor and sweep and human emotion of these poems of the War. The poems are dedicated to Service's brother, "killed in action, August 1916," but the emotion in them is not melancholy or bitter. It is not *against*; it is *for*. And it is not for a kingdom on earth or in heaven, but for your home and your fellows; and there's a recurrent feeling that your fellows may, after all, be Germans.

The best of the poems are long narratives in dialect, Cockney or Scottish. There are "The Odyssey of 'Erbert 'Iggins," "The Whistle of Sandy McGraw," "Bill the Bomber," "The Haggis of Private McPhee," "The Coward," "Only a Boche," "My Bay'nit," and "My Mate." Fragments are unsatisfactory, but one stanza from "The Red Retreat" shows how the Tommies set out and hints at days and nights that followed.

> A-singin' " 'Oo's Yer Lady Friend?" we started out from
> 'Arver,
> A-singin' till our froats was dry—we didn't care a 'ang;
> The Frenchies 'ow they lined the way, and slung us their
> palaver,
> And all we knowed to arnser was the one word "vang";
> They gave us booze and caporal, and cheered for us like
> crazy,
> And all the pretty gels was out to kiss us as we passed;
> And 'ow they all went dotty when we 'owled the Marcel-
> aisey!
> Oh, Gawd! Them was the happy days, the days too good to
> last.

Perhaps in "The Song of the Pacifist" Service is expressing his own judgment that the establishment of "justice and truth and love" and of Right against Might, can only be a lesser victory, in fact will be "a vast defeat," unless our children's children "in the name of the Dead" conquer War itself. But the book is not in its best element a commentary or a conclusion, it is an emotion; and therein, in emotion and in action, lies its strength. It is what Kipling might have made of the War, had his genius still been young. Though the master would have written with surer artistry and less sentiment, the pupil has an advantage or two. Kipling showed what discernment genius could give an imperialist; Service shows what discernment sympathy can give a democrat. And where the Englishman used technical terms with an impressive proficiency sometimes confusing to the layman, the Scotsman uses the slang of the trench so casually and fitly that the picture and the action is on the instant clear-cut and unmistakable. Detail after detail of life at the front takes its place in the various narratives, adding touches of excitement, pathos, terror, tenderness, or humor, and in the end imbuing this particular reader with a closer sense of life in the Great War than any correspondent, novelist, or poet has yet given him— making it so natural, straightforward, first-hand, vibrant, that if you are like me you will close the book with the painful silence in the ears that follows great sound and the flush in the head that comes from the sight of broken bodies and the squeeze in the throat that comes in the presence of honest human emotion. It is not a criticism from without, but a cry from within—dignifying even "Tipperary." We have been inquiring for the poetry of the War. In my judgment, here it is.

—Review of *Rhymes of a Red Cross Man*, by Robert W. Service, New York: Barse and Hopkins. Published in *The Dial*, December 14, 1916

Dragon-Drama

· ❧❦❧ ·

Though it is not free from errors, there is considerable truth in the first book to be circulated in America concerning Chinese drama*; and Miss Kate Buss also deserves thanks for seriously bringing her subject to the attention of Westerners. When, however, she prefaces her slim *Studies in the Chinese Drama* with a Chinese proverb that anticipates and denies Christian Science, "Without error there could be no such thing as truth," she invites us to apply the aphorism. What does she mean, for instance, by saying of Chinese actors, "Their faces are painted in delicate or exaggerated imitation of the infrequent sex"? Why does she risk offending people whom she evidently admires by speaking of one of them as "a Chinaman"? How can she so confuse the profound teachings of Laotzu with the degenerate confusion of modern Taoism as to say that "Taoism is based on superstition"? (Would she say that Christianity, with its degenerate ways, is based on superstition?) How can she use spelling so "elabourate" as "emperour," "interiour" and, three times on one page, "villian"? And how can she use villainous English like "Symbols—as is the god of war—may vary in name to accord with the three doctrines of China"? Is she sacrificing to her proverb?

While the Chinese, with their incomparable poetry and painting, have neither considered nor developed their drama as a fine art, it has rewards for study: better rewards than Miss Buss has received, for better study than she has given. Since her book is not scholarly in substance or form, but rather a popular handbook, one wonders why she did not relieve it of a

---

* *The Chinese Theatre*, by Chu-Chia-Chien, translated from the French by J. A. Graham, London: John Lane Co.

spectacled or at least a monocled manner by quickening her assembled facts and opinions with more of her own direct human observations. She bares herself to the suspicion that what has attracted her to the imperial theater of China is not so much the human qualities of it—the human qualities which are the core of any permanent art—but the brocaded surface of it, the artifice, the convention, the exotic formalities. In her otherwise promising preface, she stresses not simplicity and penetration as the qualities of art that engage her, but "splendour" and "magnificence." But at least a romantic deference like this, which is typically American, helps to remove the sting from the following accusation, translated from a recent issue of the *Mercure de France*: "There are probably not ten people in the whole Occident to whom the words 'Chinese theatre' call up any image save a whirl of outlandish costumes amid a deafening clangour of gongs and cymbals."

In dealing with the origins of drama in China—the music dates from 5400 B.C., the religious dances from 2205 B.C.— Miss Buss quotes, from the "Chou Ritual classic written several centuries before the time of Confucius," a passage concerning six ceremonial dances "in vogue at that early period":

> In the first, wands with whole feathers were waved—in the worship of the spirits of agriculture; in the second, wands with divided feathers were used—in the ancestral temples; in the third, feather caps were worn on the head, and the upper garments were adorned with kingfisher feathers—in blessing the four quarters of the realm; in the fourth, yak tails were used—in ceremonial for the promotion of harmony; in the fifth, shields were manipulated—to celebrate military merit; in the sixth, the bare hands were waved—in homage to the stars and constellations.

Anyone who has lived among the red Indians may well wonder, from such evidence, whether the origins of Chinese drama ought not to be studied in the Western States of America. Though I cannot answer for an exactly parallel application of ceremonial instruments, I can vouch for their obviously Chinese use among Hopi and Pueblo Indians in many of the dances I have watched during the past two years; and I can wish that there were some scholar, versed in the beliefs and observances of both peoples, who might forge, from these rituals, a new and golden link between the past of America and the past of Asia. The Smithsonian Institution, or some of those commendable associations that have newly arisen for the appreciation and defense of American tribal culture, should promptly enlist native Chinese scholars to study our Indians and explain them to us—now that America has begun to realize her need of all the beauty, dignity and antiquity she can preserve. A generous Chinese traveler told me once that he thought his people were the offspring of America. The usual theory is that the first Americans were immigrants from China, possibly across the Bering Strait, where in winter they might have walked the ice. Others believe there was only one continent, with no Pacific. Whatever happened, it is certain that, among the most native Americans "the origins of Chinese drama" remain today a living phenomenon of almost unsullied imagination and beauty; and the investigator would discover in many details a development similar to that of the Asiatic.

In recording the growth of the Chinese drama, in noting the types of plays and actors, in considering the integral music, the imagined scenery and the solid "costumery," Miss Buss is more successful than in conveying a sense of inner vitality in the art she presents; whether it be the art of the playwright, the art of the actor or the art of the audience. "Although nearly all Chinese plays in contemporary use," she writes, "date from one of the three prolific periods of the country, the T'ang Dynasty, A.D. 720–905, the Sung Dynasty, A.D. 969–1277 and the Yüan Dynasty, A.D. 1277–1368,* it is agreed they lack the literary value of the poetry and the novels written during the same

* These dates are more properly 618–907, 907–1280 and 1280–1368.—W.B.

epochs." She quotes at the head of a chapter: "The art of the actor cuts the sinews of all earnest government." But when, as a reason for the drama's literary poverty, she remarks, "The actor is so despised in China that he has not had the association of scholars, and the playwright has suffered for the actor's stigma," she forgets possibilities amid parallel conditions, the magnificent emergence of Marlowe, Shakespeare and their crew above all social prejudice and constraint. Perhaps China's great dramatists are due today, since her drama is at about the same stage of development that English drama had reached in the sixteenth century.

It is notable that Miss Buss fails to impress on her reader a single memorable theme from Chinese drama. That this is an unnecessary omission I can testify from experience in at least one Chinese playhouse. In China, and in Japan as well, dramatic themes have usually seemed to me exaggerated and strained, even trivial, just as our love-themes seem to an Oriental; blind loyalty-devotion being as silly a procedure as blind love-devotion. But I have seen one traditional Chinese drama of great force and beauty. It was a story of Chu-kê Liang, an eminent sage, statesman and general of the third century, and a frequent subject, by the way, in T'ang poetry. It concerned his treatment of a notorious rebel, called the "Pheasant Chieftain." When the rebel was captured, Chu-kê Liang set him free. This crazy generosity, to the consternation and despair of the loyal staff, was repeated six times. Each liberation was carefully enacted—the same thing over and over—without lessening the regard of the most patient people on earth. Variety was obtained by the methods of capturing the rebel: acrobatic battles, an ingenious ambush, an individual exploit, a stealthy seizure. One of the captures was managed through the aid of wine, woman and song. The women-spies were led by an actor well-known for his English library and for his familiarity with English songs. The drama had been presented strictly according to tradition; but, suddenly, at the side of the stage, a pale Swede with a brass band in uniform displaced the Chinese orchestra. Then entered the seductive women in low-necked, short-skirted gowns of green tulle, with green silk stockings and high-heeled satin slippers. Their coiffures were American, as was their dance; a ragtime cakewalk, performed by these men with a spirit and feminine grace that would have thrilled an American city. Anachronistic? Certainly. But anachronism is not anachronism unless you know it. Chu-kê Liang's period was remote from the Chinese audience. So were the manners, costumes and dances of Broadway. So was the song! The leading siren advanced, mincing; the band struck up a tune that whacked me in the vitals; and a falsetto voice sang, in fair English, "It's a Long Way to Tipperary." I must have been humming it myself unawares. Before I knew what had happened, I, the sole foreigner in the great theater, had been heaved to my feet by the Chinese around me, and was singing a duet with a famous Chinese prima donna. Only after the shouts of "Hao! Hao!" and the encore, did I realize how strange it all was, and yet how simple and human and natural. In a few minutes these actors, who had tolerated me and my interruption, were celebrating the final voluntary surrender of the Pheasant Chieftain and were singing in unison to a mountain-god a hymn of praise so exultantly beautiful and so thrillingly voiced and sustained that I prickled with goose-flesh and understood the ecstatic audience. Miss Buss is right when she says, "Although a dissimilar sense perception renders Chinese music unpleasant to the average Western ear, an occasional Occidental agrees with the Chinese to find it passionate, provocative, submissive, commanding, or sentimental, in accord with the action of the play, and of an inherent and singular beauty." I acknowledge that my taste for Chinese music had to be acquired; but I maintain that in Western grand opera I have never heard anything "grander" than this Chinese chorus of praise. Nor have I ever seen in Western drama anything nobler than the climax which occasioned the chorus. The Pheasant Chieftain, set free for the seventh time, refused the proffered liberty, ardently yielded himself and his services to Chu-kê Liang, and joined with the others in musical thanksgiving for a change of heart complete and jubilant. Then came Chu-kê Liang's quiet comment: "You may capture a man's body six times; but you cannot capture the man until you have captured his spirit."

If Miss Buss had seen this play, surely she would have told us about it. But are there no others as fine?

A partisan of imperial drama, Miss Buss dismisses modern experiments in the Chinese theater as unimportant: "Recent deviations in a few minor theaters are as yet transitory and without focus." It seems incredible that she can say this, if she has visited Mr. Shaha's theater in Shanghai and seen any of his superb productions. Though she may deplore his adoption of Japanese and Occidental methods, she owes him at least a mention of his extraordinary scenic and mechanical achievements, which outshine those of Mr. Belasco and the Hippodrome. I have seen on his stage the entire façade of a Shanghai hotel with its incandescent lights and the pedestrians, rickshas, carriages and motorcars in the street before it. I have seen a canal of real water in which a miscreant tried to escape by swimming. I have seen a sensationally popular drama in which Mr. Shaha presented, within a few months of the actual occurrences, a front-page murder story. A Christian Chinese, in a motorcar borrowed from an American friend, had taken a celebrated sing-song girl out into the country and strangled her for her jewelry. He needed money to keep pace with his foreign companions at the racecourse and elsewhere. The murder baffled both Chinese and foreign detectives. Finally the girl appeared to her mother in a dream, revealing the secret. A Catholic priest, hiding the fugitive, drew angry roars from the audience. The culprit was finally overtaken in a boat on the canal which I have already mentioned. All the characters involved in the real episode, both Chinese and foreign, were represented in the play by their own names. A hint for New York! Whether or not such drama is "transitory" in China, it is interestingly transitional. In this particular play there was an acute blend of realistic and heroic presentation. The Chinese playwright, management, actors and audience are afraid neither of the real nor of the heroic; and many of their "deviations," from the imperial theater of China and from the republican theater of the West, are both impressive and prophetic.

On the general subject of drama, Miss Buss concludes: "At this hour in the Chinese theater the disturbing and vital question is whether or no a republican government will corrupt the Imperial drama to destroy such unparalleled stage tradition." Let me call to her attention and to that of her readers the following opinion of Dr. Hu Shih, "unchallenged leader of the 'literary revolution' " in China:

> The present conservatism in regard to the reform of the Chinese theater is largely due to a failure to see that the Chinese drama as it stands today is precisely a case of long-arrested development. The singing and acrobatic feats, the unnatural voice and gesture, the symbolic movements to take the place of changing scenery, and many other defects of the Chinese drama must be regarded as vestiges which have survived their usefulness, and certainly not as culminating points beyond which no further improvement is necessary or desirable.

Is it not likely that Miss Buss is more concerned with the imperial gloss of Chinese drama, and Dr. Hu Shih with its human glow? A good deal that to Miss Buss is as alluring and novel as the nonsense of Miss Gertrude Stein is to Dr. Hu Shih as flat and stale as the nonsense of *Way Down East*. But, in spite of their diverse approaches, let us hope that Miss Kate Buss and Dr. Hu Shih may join forces in resisting the imminent American invasion of the field of Chinese drama, an invasion that is being planned with the assistance of a benighted ex-Premier, Chou Tsu-chi. According to the papers, the Dragon

Film Company is to "establish two thousand movies throughout China within the next year" and to carry, even into the remote interior, "American society films, Wild West thrills, serials and comedies, as portrayed by Hollywood."

—Review of *Studies in the Chinese Drama*, by Kate Buss,
Boston: The Four Seas Company. Published in *The Freeman*,
October 3, 1923

Edna St. Vincent Millay

· ✤✤✤ ·

In the first place, what a name! Except for Walther von der Vogelweide, was ever lyric poet so sung into being by the very syllables of baptism!—Unless Avis Linnell of Hyannis wrote poems to the Massachusetts clergyman who murdered her long since.

Frederick Pinney Earle and Mitchell Kennerley, who between them published in 1912 an anthology called *The Lyric Year*, noticed in the collection not only a singing name but a poem that sang with it, "Renascence." Fully armed from the head of Jove, had sprung a new miracle. Where there had been nothing, no whisper of her, stood a whole poet. Few were aware, but how aware were those few! Millay became at once a name for them to conjure with, a wand, a touchstone. The faithful remained faithful; but for nearly ten years, and even after a book was issued in which "Renascence," the title-poem, was combined with briefer sorceries, only an increasing few realized what had happened. Among most poets, as among most editors and critics, a Millay zealot encountered little more than faint agreement or sympathetic doubt; until in 1921 came *Second April*, a volume not so surprising as the first, and Edna St. Vincent Millay awoke on many mornings to find herself each morning more famous. And now *The Harp-Weaver* has won a Pulitzer Prize.

Prizes had gone to poems in *The Lyric Year*, but none of them to "Renascence," except the prize of life. Though the poem was as good then as it is now, literary authorities were at first languid, tolerant; it won attention mainly as a good sustained effort by a girl in her teens. Perhaps, as we are told, it won the poet a patron who, with the best intentions, sent her to a girls' college. Perhaps it won her admirers who afterwards, with whatever intentions, attracted her to Greenwich Village. Perhaps, as in the British cases of A. E. Housman and Moira O'Neill, it won her appreciative laymen, inconspicuous and quiet but numerous, whose ground swell has rippled finally with critics.

There have now been printed six Millay volumes. In the book, *Renascence*, I for one would gladly dispense with the two long, rather callow poems, "Interim" and "The Suicide"; and I am sorry that the admirable English edition called *Poems*, includes from *Second April*, "The Blue Flag in the Bog" (which, bravely intended, yet drags along lamely) and "Ode to Silence" (which is the sort of moldy Elizabethan stuff still affected by many of the Georgians). "Renascence," though long, is lyrical. These other four poems, beyond passages, are not. "Ode to Silence," like the drama, *The Lamp and the Bell*, is written not in water, but on a college blackboard. And yet the play, unlike the poem, emerges from classical stiffness and becomes finally an expanded lyric. The artificial, the imitative are sloughed off. In her own words:

> You may be sure 'tis nothing more than the thimble
> Of the matter she's forgotten. I never knew her
> Mislay the thread or the needle of a thing.

Or again, in the same play, she might be saying of herself,

> Who does not run
> As fast as I run shall be left behind me.

Aria da Capo, another lyric in dramatic form, is timely proof, like the later *Harp-Weaver*, that for a poet there is no gulf fixed between the lyric and so-called propaganda. Into this decade of timorous aesthetics has come a poet not afraid of something to say, whether it be the pang of second birth or the pang of first death, whether it be the truth about love or the truth about war. College has not taken away her native Shakespearean gift of making poetry seem natural speech; Greenwich Village, instead of affording her a Freudian God in her own image, has quickened her humor, as in *A Few Figs from Thistles*; and *Vanity Fair* has not as yet soured her humor to mere wit. She has survived her experiences.

The Harp-Weaver and Other Poems, her latest volume, contains as much poetry as any of the books but might better have been as slim as the others. It is a transitional book. For my taste the intellectual is here interfering too clumsily with the emotional. At times there is neither sandal nor stone. In the lyrics that continue her earlier vein, she is straining her youth; and in the maturer pieces, her wisdom is less intuitive and less wise than her younger wisdom. Perhaps only Housman, of our time, can be wisely young forever. The ballad from which the latest book is named is very deft and fundamentally moving, but I wish she had been able to quiet just a whisper of sentimentality; and, in my judgment, "Sonnets from an Ungrafted Tree," the concluding section of *The Harp-Weaver*, though dexterous enough in a new manner, are less genuinely hers, bear more signs of fabrication than any of her other achievements, sound more like some of her less lyrical contemporaries, contain even a note of ill-health quite different from the earlier gay pessimism. But the Millay humor, freshly growing from the great earth, is too well-rooted to be displaced by noxious weeds.

Says a critic in the *Chicago Times*:

Her poems play with the griefs that come as the obituaries of love. And they contain an ironical sadness peculiarly masculine. . . . They are the half-humorous apologies offered for the failures of emotions. And they are a more promising, if unfortunate, symptom of the feminine emancipation from illusions than twelve birth clinics and a score of suffrage rallies.

Is this "ironical sadness" peculiarly masculine, or is it honestly feminine? With open eyes, Miss Millay sees her own sex and the other. She sees her time. She sees herself. Now and then, when she sees out of proportion, she knows it. And, on the whole, with the aforesaid deepening sense of humor, she sees not only others but herself in proportion to the airy universe. In this respect, however well she may have adhered to traditional technique, she goes contrary to the usual spirit of English poetry and is one of the Occidental singers to subdue personal emotions to the larger motion of the earth. Being a woman, she is sadder in the process than Wordsworth was, but being human, she enjoys her melancholy. The pomps of this wicked world do not deceive her, and she puts the vanities eventually into their proper place. Like Emily Dickinson, she knows her hermitage in the heart of nature; but unlike Emily Dickinson, who retired to a garden, she carries her hermitage with her.

Reverting for a moment to the question of form, the fact is noteworthy that in her limpid stanzas and in those clear-flowing sonnets discovered and printed by William Marion Reedy, indubitably the most important of American sonnets, she has so infused her new spirit into old forms that her stanzas and sonnets seem fresher than all the technical variations of the experimentalists. She has proved that renovation can be innovation. Alongside "Renascence," "The Waste Land" with its careful capers grows stale and unprofitable.

Twelve years have passed since the appearance of "Renascence"; and, as much for the importance of that poem as for anything she has written since, Edna St. Vincent Millay holds a secure place in American letters, a securer place, I imagine, than any of her contemporaries. Remembering how slowly recognition came to her in the beginning of our poetic revival, it is pertinent and interesting to consider the recognition accorded newcomers in the year of poetic grace, 1924. Poetry, during the decade, has increased in vogue. Poetic schools have come and, when methods and trickeries were lifted for the moment above substance and truth, have gone. Poetry magazines and societies have flourished, and the lecture platform has resounded with verse. Editors and critics have been on the generous lookout for arrivals and, eager to discover, have in many cases accorded grotesque acclaim to mediocre or merely clever performances. The result is that poets who might have been genuine are petted into foppery, and that many little journalists are vaunting the laurel in their smart lapels. Would fresh verse hold its quality better if watchers like myself were not so impatient for the public to become aware?

Perhaps, sometimes away from us all, not touted in Chicago by *Poetry*, in New York by *The Measure*, in Philadelphia by *Contemporary Verse* or in limbo by *The Dial*, not even presented anonymously in Mexico by *Palms*, an important American poet may be creating an important American poem, another "Renascence," to miss a prize and win a permanence. If so, the slow-moving public will become aware again, in its own good time.

—Review article published in *The New Republic*, December 10, 1924

"The Tale of Genji"

· ❧❧❧ ·

1 · A JAPANESE GALLANT

From the union of a Japanese Emperor with a favored gentle-woman of the wardrobe came a beautiful son—an epic for epicures.

The Tale of Genji begins, as far as I know, with a device new in literature. A group of young courtiers sit about, in the second chapter, comparing notes as to their amorous adventures, each instancing the experience which seems to him most extraordinary. Genji, the Shining One, who has been born, bred and betrothed in the first chapter, and is described as "so lovely that one might have wished he were a girl," listens with apparent deference and with no report of his own and then proceeds, through this first volume of the six-volume story of his life, to outdistance, on almost any night he chooses, the exploits of his fellows. Whether the "anecdotes and reflections" of the others were romantic, audacious, ignoble, pathetic, poetic or grotesque, the story he tells, by living it, tops them all in every illumined particular.

This structural device is new to us of the West only because for a thousand years there has been no Arthur Waley sufficiently discerning, sufficiently accomplished and sufficiently industrious, to translate for us, from the Japanese of Lady Murasaki Shikibu, a tale which, "already a classic in the year 1022," remains, according to Mr. Waley, "by far the greatest novel of the East" and, "even if compared with the fiction of Europe, takes its place as one of the dozen greatest masterpieces of the world."

On the night of the story telling, Genji, already married, heard himself warned against women:

Beware of caressing manners and soft, entangling ways. For if you are so rash as to let them lead you astray you will soon find yourself cutting a very silly figure.

Nevertheless, Genji "had in his heart of hearts been thinking of one person only." Nor was this person his noble wife. Nor was it another person whom he encountered the very next night at the house of one of his gentlemen-in-waiting and whom he carried off to his room with a delightful minimum of ceremony. The subject of his thoughts was his host's young stepmother, who, be it recorded in wonder, resisted Genji's further attentions, with all the fluttered and scrupulous pertinacity of a Victorian heroine, the difference being that she was governed less by moral scruples than by scruples of caste. Not to those days can we trace the origin of the cryptic answer: "the higher the fewer." "Noblesse oblige" had gayer interpretations than in later times: sexual favors were then a part of the graceful duties of high rank. The young wife's resistance, however, served only to lend an occasional sweet sting of sadness to Genji's other amours. He allowed himself little time and, after all, had little need for vain regrets, except as they soothed with shadow the bright light of his conquests.

Not only Genji's own impulses, his heart-breaking comeliness and his moving mastery as poet and ceremonial dancer, but the devoted vigilance of his attendants and the curious favor of the moon, were of the utmost use to him in varying his diversions. A certain servant, for example, was "touched at his own magnanimity in surrendering to his master a prize which he might well have kept for himself." Even Genji's father-in-law melted toward the boy's waywardness. One night Genji and his brother-in-law, Chujo, returned together from secret expeditions.

They did not send for torchbearers to see them in at the gates, but creeping in very quietly, stole to a portico where they could not be seen and had their ordinary clothes brought to them there. Having changed, they entered the house merrily blowing their flutes as though they had just come back from the Palace. Chujo's father, who usually pretended not to hear them when they returned late at night, on this occasion brought out his flageolet, which was his favorite instrument, and began to play very agreeably.

With but two exceptions the ladies also were more than warm to the innuendo of his poetic messages, not only patrician ladies whose complaisance was expected, but ladies of the stricter caste.

Even those who seemed bent on showing by the prim stiffness of their answers that they placed virtue high above sensibility, and who at first appeared hardly conversant with the usages of polite society, would suddenly collapse into the wildest intimacy which would continue until their marriage with some commonplace husband cut short the correspondence.

Turning from these anonymous ladies to those others whom the chronicler distinguishes with names and importance, we find attached to Genji a prodigious network of intrigue. First came Fujitsubo who, succeeding to the affections of the Emperor after the death of Genji's mother, might in spite of her youth be called Genji's stepmother; then the stepmother and next the sister of the aforementioned gentleman-in-waiting; then his brother-in-law Chujo's lost mistress, Yugao, and finally Fujitsubo's niece, the ten-year-old Murasaki (not to be confused with Murasaki, the chronicler). At intervals moreover, during this four-year-period beginning when he was seventeen, he consorted with Lady Rokujo, widow of the Emperor's brother. In other words, he was lover, in part successively, in part simultaneously, to his stepmother, to his brother-in-law's former mistress, to his own uncle's widow and to his stepmother's niece. He also paid occasional attention to his own wife who, at the end of the first volume, dies bearing him a son while his stepmother lives in fearful anguish lest the Emperor recognize in a son born to her the features of Genji.

But I put a charming tale badly.

In a way it is worthwhile to strip from the beautiful bold bad figure of Genji his poetic ways and means, the glamour of his courtly associations and all the suavities of Japanese courtship, in order to realize that "the quest of the golden girl" was a more rapid and radical business in the days recorded by Lady Murasaki than in the days recorded by Cellini, Casanova, Fielding or LeGallienne. When Genji and his friends were only doing what everyone did and was expected to do, it may seem strange that they made so careful a pretense of secrecy. There can have been no real need of hypocritic deception or timid concealment. And yet it is not so strange. Might Romeo and Juliet have loved so well without their stealth? When in the world's history has open love been so tingling a joy as secret love? Perhaps delight rather than fear has been the mainspring of hypocrisy in England, as of poetry in Japan.

Returning from the moral isle to the poetic it is important to note that all of Genji's love-taking was done in more or less delicate verse. So also was his leave-taking. He seldom lacked the wisdom of the Emperor's dictum:

> Affairs of this kind must be managed so that the woman, no matter who she is, need not feel that she has been brought into a humiliating position or treated in a cynical or off-hand way. Forget this rule, and she will soon make you feel the unpleasant consequences of her resentment.

In one of his escapades, when Genji had spent much time courting a certain Princess because of imagined charms, he finally gained her presence.

What an absurd mistake he had made! She was certainly very tall, as was shown by the length of her back when she took her seat; he could hardly believe that such a back could belong to a woman. A moment afterward he suddenly became aware of her main defect. It was her nose. He could not help looking at it. . . . Not only was it amazingly prominent, but (strangest of all) the tip which drooped downward a little was tinged with pink, contrasting in the oddest manner with the rest of her complexion which was of a whiteness that would have put snow to shame.

Yet even to this stupid and ridiculous woman, who reminded him of Samantabhadra's white elephant, with its red trunk, he sent a poem:

Scarcely had the evening mist lifted and revealed the prospect to my sight, when the night rain closed gloomily about me.

And he added in a letter:

I shall watch with impatience for a sign that the clouds are breaking.

Here is one of his poems to the very different Lady Fujitsubo:

Now that at last we have met, would that we might vanish forever into the dream we dreamed tonight.

And here is one which, after the funeral of his much-neglected wife, he whispered into the ear of his father-in-law:

Because of all the mists that wreathe the autumn sky, I know not which ascended from my lady's bier, henceforth upon the country of the clouds from pole to pole I gaze with love.

Not only his verses but his writing of both Japanese and Chinese characters and various other little touches of breeding cogently affected the feminine heart. For instance, he knew how to impress the nun in whose care he found ten-year-old Murasaki; he knew how to pave the way toward adopting the child for his own purposes. Writing a poem to Murasaki he inclosed it in a letter to the nun.

Though she had long passed the zenith of her years, the nun could not but be pleased and flattered by the elegance of the note; for it was not only written in an exquisite hand, but was folded with a careless dexterity which she greatly admired.

Nonetheless she parried, writing for the child the following shrewd poem:

For as long as the cherry blossoms remain unscattered upon the shores of Onoe where wild storms blow—so long have you till now been constant.

Genji was the perfect philanderer. There were always more fish in the sea. In spite of the wide difference between his story and that of *Tom Jones*; in spite of all the perfume on Genji's sleeve and all the murmurings of his writing-brush, I find Murasaki's narrative persistently reminding me of Fielding's *Tom Jones*, with music by Debussy. The constant use of poetry, for epistolary and even conversational exchange among characters, is the main element that makes the Japanese narrative for us quaint and faraway; for in spite of occasional mists in the telling the story is vigorously alive. Its petals drift on eternal flesh and blood.

In what is to me the most memorable chapter of the book, the account of Genji's taking the mysterious Yugao away from her exposed and humble quarters to a sort of House of Usher, of her death there by his side and his remorseful visit to the mountain priest, Lady Murasaki exhibits something of the power of that later woman writer Emily Brontë in *Wuthering Heights*. The fox-spirits and the involuntary spell wrought by Lady Rokujo are no stranger than such Christian superstitions as ghosts and devils or such fell powers as Mrs. Eddy's malicious animal magnetism. Certainly nothing written in England before the twelfth century, and very little written in the eighteenth, begins to come as near America in the twentieth as does the essence of *The Tale of Genji*. Something of this modernity may be due to Mr. Waley's limpidly human translation, but most of it must inhere in the original.

Arthur Waley, with an already proven taste for Oriental masterpieces and a proven skill in bringing them vividly to English readers, has so translated *The Tale of Genji* that it reads like the wind. Only once was I halted, against my will, by this sentence:

> Was it being four years older than him that made her so unapproachable, so exasperatingly well regulated?

I quote the whole sentence, in order that I may praise even while I question. I should like to quote many other passages, such as

> The crowds flashed by him like the hurrying images that a stream catches and breaks. . . .

> The Emperor's envoys thronged thick as the feet of the raindrops.

or

> Among the leaves were white flowers with petals half unfolded like the lips of people smiling at their own thoughts.

Thanks to Lady Murasaki and to Mr. Waley, many a lady in the Western world will be taking Genji into her heart and many a gentleman will understand why. As the Shining One passes by in the rich procession of these volumes it will be pertinent to remember a sentence from the last chapter of the first volume:

> If even these strangers were in such a taking, it may be imagined with what excitement, scattered here and there among the crowd, those with whom Genji was in secret communication watched the procession go by and with how many hidden sighs their bosoms heaved.

—Review of *The Tale of Genji*, by Lady Murasaki, translated from the Japanese by Arthur Waley, Boston: Houghton Mifflin Company. Published in *The New York Herald Tribune Books*, September 27, 1925

2 · THE TREE OF KNOWLEDGE

The Sacred Tree is not so much a book as a sorcery. Remote as these tenth century Japanese manners are, these exquisite ceremonious approaches to love and to life, ennobled as this Genji is by his imperial birth, by his surpassing beauty, by his arts as poet, musician, painter and lover, by his generous graces of personality (and, doubtless, by his biographer), he seems a cavalier not only more distinguished and ingratiating than Cellini or Casanova, but closer to us than Lord Byron, more credible and even more modern.

On the whole, the second volume of *Genji* is more suavely potent than the first. These two volumes taken together, and the others taken on expectant trust, are enough to convince me that Mr. Waley is right in calling *Genji* one of the few literary masterpieces of all time. This is a tale that can enrich anyone's memories, anyone's imagination. It is a tale not only of the air, but of the ground; and it needs no heavy boots to stay on the ground. It is there lightly, but surely. Lady Murasaki breathes, in her upper caste, the same human air that Sherwood Anderson or Theodore Dreiser breathe, but not, like them, catarrhally. She finds her way through the life of a person, while they still grope and fumble. Social problems are not hers, nor, in the final analysis, theirs either. It is a person's relation to other persons or to himself, rather than to groups, that makes the substance of lasting literature. That is one reason why Murasaki is fadeless. Although at times Genji seems but a wild blood, the human spirit behind all his escapades and attachments is the very same spirit that prompts a man today to be as happy as he may be, to be in love as much as he may be, to be as kind as he can be; and when Genji errs, when he offends his own conscience, he errs without pretense, without humbug, without psychological formula, without self-flagellation, without fury, without cowardice. He errs serenely. He can smile the smile that cures. In this second volume of his adventures, though still alert for love, he is mellower with his maturing youth: not gaunt and hard and hectic like a latter-day sinner. Soberer, graver toward his ladies than he was in his boyhood, he is also surer than before of other rewards in the world, those rewards which the beauties of nature and art may afford to a sensitive spirit. Into his being something of the soul may have passed, even as we know it, but without its maladies. Soul or no soul, created he stands shining.

As to the divinely creative hand that formed him from her own Japanese rib, she was sheerly a genius. Mr. Waley in his introduction offers interesting suggestions as to the workings of her genius. In taking somewhat to task the critics of the first volume, for failing to probe the depth of her art, Mr. Waley has them at an unfair advantage. While they have known but a fragment of the novel, he has known the whole, its scope, its cumulation, its proportions, its deepening spell. Steeped in the book as he is, he expects that its beginning will forecast for others what it meant to him when he went back over it as translator. Perhaps he refers to reviewers in England. Surely in America there was a chorus of delighted appreciation, a proper impulse to accept and enjoy that first volume and to let analysis wait. Were we to chloroform the butterfly before it fluttered half a day?

Although "Murasaki, like the novelist of today, is not principally interested in the events of the story, but rather in the effect which these events may have upon the minds of her characters," Mr. Waley asks:

> How, finally, does Murasaki achieve the extraordinary reality, the almost "historical" character with which she succeeds in investing her scenes? Many readers have agreed with me that some of the episodes . . . become, after one reading, a permanent accession to the world as one knows it, are things which have "happened" as much as the most vivid piece of personal experience. This sense of reality . . . is not the result of realism in any ordinary sense. It is not the outcome of those clever pieces of small observation by which the modern novelist strives to attain the same effect. Still less is it due to solid character building; for Murasaki's characters are mere embodiments of some dominant characteristic. . . . It is due rather, I think, to a narrative gift of a kind that is absolutely extinct in Europe. To analyze such a gift would require pages of quotation. What does it in the last resort consist in save a preeminent capacity for saying the most relevant things in the most effective order? Yet, simple as this sounds, I believe that in it rests, unperceived by the eye of the Western critic, more than half the secret of Murasaki's art. Her construction is, in fact, classical; elegance, symmetry, restraint—these are the qualities which she can set in the scale against the interesting irregularities of European fiction. That such qualities should not be easily recognized in the West is but natural; for here the novel has always been Gothic through and through.

Would Mr. Waley, I wonder, consider Jane Austen's novels Gothic? Might he not see between the art of the Western woman and that of the Eastern woman some kinship, despite the apparent gulf between their choices of material and the real gulf between the domestic range of the one and the epic sweep of the other? And, surely, to indicate the art of Jane Austen by brief quotation would be as difficult as it is to point with chosen passages the art of Murasaki.

It is easy, but not convincing, to set down a few of the poems which these deft Japanese men and women improvise for one another in moments of either good or bad behavior.

Let me quote a passage containing two, rather better translated than the majority, and showing the responsive use made of them in the narrative. Genji is leaving a provincial lady who has eased his exile in the country.

> To the traveling cloak which had been specially designed for that day's journey the lady of Akashi attached the poem: "That this cloak of travel, cut and folded by the salt seashore, should bear a stain or two of spray, you will not take amiss!" Despite the noise and confusion of departure, he found a moment in which to write the answer: "Though for a while I must wear it in remembrance, yet soon as certain days and months are safely passed, once more no garment shall divide us."

This give and take of poems is not so forgotten a custom as it sounds, when we read of it in connection with Genji, his ladies, his friends, his attendants, even his servants. The old Japanese custom of tears, on the other hand, tears for every occasion, seems in our age to have vanished. There are enough shed on the first few pages of this volume to wash away many sins.

In his palace during an evening of essays and songs, as Genji sat

> flushed with the excitement of the party and wearing only an unlined shirt of thin gauze that showed the delicate texture of his skin beneath the old doctors of literature stared at him with delight and amazement from the distant

part of the room where they had respectfully taken up their stand; and many of them shed tears of wonder and delight.

Confessing that I have seen landscapes which brought tears to my eyes, I rack my memory in vain to recall weeping over the noble appearance of president or prince, actress or archbishop. This is not saying that I shouldn't. For Lady Murasaki I went that far toward tears over beauty; and I cannot remember rendering a like tribute anywhere to the art of Jane Austen.

And note how even artistry in handwriting was intermingled long ago with the love of life and the life of love. Genji, at home with the wife whom he loved in his fashion, was reading half aloud to himself a letter from the provincial lady, when his wife murmured a song implying reproach. Genji responded:

"It would be much better if you simply pretended not to hear. But here is the letter." He held it out to her, but in such a way that she could only see the outer fold upon which the address was written. . . . She saw at once that it was a flawless hand, such as the greatest lady in the land would have had no cause to disown. From that moment she knew what was in store for her; this would assuredly prove no fleeting fancy.

Where are such subtleties of culture in any land of telegrams?

Politics, religion, economics, ceremonious manners may change; but the heart of man seems to beat now very much as it beat in the beginning, beats now, and ever shall beat. It is because Lady Murasaki deals primarily and simply with that inner heart that her writing remains so modern.

She did not have to wait for an age of democracy to be able to say:

I have noticed that people of quite common origin who have risen in the world can in a very short time achieve a perfect imitation of aristocratic importance. And similarly, if through some accident an aristocrat falls into low company, he generally exhibits a meanness so thoroughgoing that it is hard to believe he has been at pains to acquire it.

She did not have to learn a certain kind of cynicism from a generation of youth after a world war.

That poet was a fool who prayed that he might know what happened to his mistress after he was gone. He cannot have cared much about her, or he would certainly rather not have known.

And listen to these passages between Genji and his lovable wife in regard to a patent triangle. The triangle connected with the handwriting I have already instanced had become in fact a quadrangle. Says Genji:

"I had far rather that this had not happened. It is all the more irritating because I have for so long been hoping that you would have a child; and that, now the child has come, it should be someone else's is very provoking. . . . She is of course very charming, but I think my feeling for her had a good deal to do with the place and circumstances." He began to describe how exquisitely the smoke from the salt-kilns had tapered across the evening sky; he spoke of the poems which they had exchanged, of his first glimpse of her by night, of her delightful playing on the zithern. Murasaki [his second wife bore the same name as the author] while she listened could not but remember how particularly unhappy she had been just at the very time when the episodes which Genji was now recalling with such relish were taking place in Akashi. Even if this affair were, as he represented it to be, a mere pastime of the moment, it was clear that he had been singularly successful in his search for distraction. "Come," he said at last, "I am doing my best to show you that I am fond of you. You had best be quick, if you are ever going to forgive me at all; life does not last forever. Here am I trying so hard not to give you the slightest cause for one speck of jealousy or suspicion. And now just because of this unfortunate affair." So saying he sent for his large zithern and tried to persuade her to play it with him as they used to do. But Murasaki could not help remembering his enthusiasm for the playing of the Lady of Akashi. With such virtuosity she did not care to compete, and say what he would he could not persuade her to play a note.

Was Genji, after all, merely a profligate, as these passages might suggest? Not at all. He lived well the wider truth of Prince Sochi no Miya's aphorism, when they discussed painting:

I know, of course, that mere industry will not carry one far in any art; his heart must be in the matter.

And it is because Genji's heart was in the matter, whether the matter was love or art or life itself, that this book about him, overlaid by millions of intervening books, will continue to gain for him, faithless though he was, persistent admirers. Whether the tree of knowledge were sacred or profane, he tasted of it to the full, hearing no serpent and blaming no Eve.

—Review of *The Sacred Tree: Being the Second Part of The Tale of Genji*, by Lady Murasaki, translated from the Japanese by Arthur Waley, Boston: Houghton Mifflin Company. Published in *The New York Herald Tribune Books*, April 11, 1926

3 · GENJI RELAXES

This, the third of six volumes, is very different in mood and content from the two volumes preceding it.

In the first volume, *The Tale of Genji*, the tenth century

Japanese authoress established her hero as a brilliant boy, preco-
cious in the arts of life and the graces of love. It was a lacquered
as well as a checkered career. Even the one tragic episode seemed
eerily painted on a fan or a screen, rather than cut into a heart or
a character.

In the second volume, *The Sacred Tree*, Genji continued his
seductive course. While the dark days of his exile brought him
a more serious sense of life and a growing dependence on the
beauties of the natural world he was not too dispirited to find
other beauties available and to add them to his heart's entourage.
It appeared for a while that "the soul with all its maladies" might
have crept into his being and might have begun to shape the
amateur into something of a philosopher; but in part three, just
issued under the title *A Wreath of Cloud*, we find Genji restored
not only to favor at court but to the life of a relaxed dilettante.

Preeminent now in the state, he delegates to others the more
onerous duties of his position, and he sets his house in order by
bringing his various ladies into the various wings of his new
palace, much as one might set out in a meticulously arranged
garden this or that favorite tree or flower. The third volume,
taken separately, is less beguiling than the first two. Fully half
of it is concerned with this landscape gardening, by a man in his
thirties, of *affaires* which have quieted down. For the rest, Genji,
grown a bit sententious, his gay poetic epigrams opening into
polished homilies, devotes himself to the education of his son, a
course of much stricter discipline than he himself would have
enjoyed as a boy, and takes a mature satisfaction in his wife and
in her wise and winsome tolerance of the ladies in the other
wings. It is the wife, Murasaki, rather than Genji, the husband,
who lends to this volume the interest of unfolding character. He
says himself, "Now that I have a grown-up child of my own I
feel that henceforward he will every day grow more intelligent
and I more stupid."

Midway in *A Wreath of Cloud* the scene shifts abruptly
from Genji and court life to a remote and barbarous island. After
all the elegance of life in the capital, described more in diary

fashion than in story fashion, we are suddenly in the midst of a simple, clear, forthright and exciting narrative about persons new to us. We knew in the first volume that a baby girl, daughter of a mistress of Genji's by a former lover, had disappeared with a nurse after the mother's death. Always tender toward the mother's memory, Genji had tried in vain to trace the child. Here she is at last revealed to the reader, a young woman of beauty and innate distinction, whom the nurse has reverently nurtured. To save the girl from a crude and lusty official on the far island the nurse's family flees back to Kyoto. The story of the flight and of the fugitives' final encounter with Genji is told somewhat as Homer might have told it and is a vivid, swift interlude between the slower passages before and after it.

One of the bits of subtle magic in the book is the reader's instant sense, from the moment when the girl appears on the island, that she is destined to be Genji's new love. Though she is in quest of her father, a high official at court, one feels a pulse in the stars above her stronger than her human pulses. Heretofore Genji has gone deliberately toward his ladies. This time a lady is bound unconsciously toward him. And the tempo of the stars is slower than Genji's former tempo. In the earlier volumes there has been a rapid succession of pursuits and intimacies; but this volume ends, after three hundred pages, with Tamakatsura installed in Genji's palace under a pretext of being a daughter of his own and very gradually succumbing to his charm. His fingers have touched hers as yet only on a zithern. But there's another volume coming. And meanwhile, to be sure, Genji's son has discovered himself madly in love with his stepmother, Genji's wife.

Though this volume is less interesting in itself than what has preceded it, it would follow with precise artistic relation if the whole work were read as a unit. It joins and varies a pattern of perfect artistry. Incidentally, it is translated by our benefactor, Arthur Waley, into smoother and more beautiful English than he used in the earlier portions. These are not artificial flowers of translation: they are perfumed from the very earth. Which of the many poems that star the long story has he worded in better English than this?

The light leaf scatters in the wind, and of the vaunted spring no tinge is left us, save where the pine tree grips its ledge of stone.

Can it be that when Genji loses his zest for amorous adventure the reader loses his zest for Genji? Has his story been no more important than the story of some modern young prince with loves along the Riviera, some prince who in middle age settles down, tired and stodgy, to a conventional life? Having said at the outset that a tragic episode in Genji's youth seemed to be pictured on a fan rather than deeply felt in a heart, I must be careful not to leave a wrong impression. It is true that during Genji's intrigues he has often seemed to be occupied merely with an indulgence or a decorative episode or with fantastic bravado. Modern Western novelists, telling this sort of story, lend exaggerated emotional importance to a hero's pastimes and so isolate him in a given absorption that he may be as selfishly cruel as he chooses to a wife or anyone at all except the object of his passion. Orientals take a saner view of physical love. Genji, in love, does not grovel nor tyrannize nor forsake. He enjoys, he respects, he cherishes. Once an intimate, he remains a friend— not necessarily with physical constancy but with personal constancy. And there may be more heart in this sort of devotion than in the blinder ardors of the West. Think of the sullen lovers we write about! Think how we analyze their egotistic stupidities into emotion! Genji was an egotist too, in his happier way—"but Genji had a peculiar gift of sympathy, which enabled him to penetrate the most obstinate gloom, the most imperturbable gravity."

Genji's modern idea of a novel, spoken undoubtedly for the author, is not so remote from our modern idea a thousand years later.

I have a theory of my own about what this art of the novel is and how it came into being. To begin with, it does not simply consist in the author's telling a story about the adventures of some other person. On the contrary, it happens because the story teller's own experience of men and things, whether for good or ill—not only what he has passed through himself, but even events which he has only witnessed or been told of—has moved him to an emotion so passionate that he can no longer keep it shut up in his heart. Again and again something in his own life or in that around him will seem to the writer so important that he cannot bear to let it pass into oblivion. There must never come a time, he feels, when men do not know about it.

The stuff of Lady Murasaki's novel was a life of ease and richness led by persons who could afford to decorate their existence with every material glamour. She notes once, "The ordering of the procession was not so elaborate as might have been expected, for it seemed likely at the moment that too lavish a display might try the temper of the common people." And yet when she delineates some of the "common people," she enters as naturally and sympathetically into their lives and doings as most of the time she enters into the lives and doings of the socially favored. If her own experience had been among the poor, I do not doubt that her art would have made of their actual world and "mundane life" a world of realizable enchantment and a life worth leading happily. With any material she would have been a great novelist.

—Review of *A Wreath of Cloud: Being the Third Part of The Tale of Genji*, by Lady Murasaki, translated from the Japanese by Arthur Waley, Boston: Houghton Mifflin Company. Published in *The New York Herald Tribune Books*, April 24, 1927

4 · THE PASSING OF GENJI

A symphony has been playing for four years—one of its movements each year. And a certain attuned audience has been listening. In the program which we saw at the outset something was said about six movements—and I, for one, had the contented idea that for six years I should be listening to *The Tale of Genji*. Now, suddenly, after the first three volumes of this incomparable romance, incomparably translated—*The Tale of Genji, The Sacred Tree,* and *A Wreath of Cloud*—comes the fourth part, *Blue Trousers*, announcing itself from the publisher as the last part and yet ending with a footnote on the final page, "The next chapter begins with the words: 'After Prince Genji's death.'" Perhaps the translator and the publisher have wisely agreed that the death of Genji is the death of the book. On the other hand the spirit of Genji may have so subtly survived in the succeeding volumes as to warrant a suspicion that the tenth century authoress knew what she was doing when she continued the tale. In my own library, unless the magician-translator be persuaded to wield his wand again and materialize two more living books, there will always be on my bookshelf a ghostly space alongside these four volumes, like the empty chair at tables told about.

In *A Wreath of Cloud* a reader who in the two earlier volumes had shared, toward life and love and art, the tremors of the young Genji began to regret a little that the Prince's middle age and the subsidence of his various passions and appreciations had to be recorded. It was a phase of human experience, to be sure, as rightly reflected by this amazing tenth century novelist, Lady Murasaki, as the eagerer phases of youth, but it was not a phase to which our contemporary Western novelists accustom us —it was a phase at which they usually stop. Now and then one of them dares to record youth, middle age and death; but not in the proportions of this little great book. And what proportions they are! Here was Genji, through two volumes, Genji the beloved, Genji the Shining One, riding on butterfly wings, on dragonfly wings, on bluebird wings, now and then on bat wings, but always riding through an air above earth. Here was a drop of dew that no sun could melt, that no black night could freeze, that no time could end. Love after love had come to him as strangely and sweetly as blossoms and blossoms come to a bough. And each new blossoming and each twig from which a petal had fallen combined to make against the sky as chosen and complete a design of beauty as the loveliest of cherry boughs an unending spring might show. Spring ends, though. And so with Genji. The summer came—the fullness of his love for the lady he liked best. It became a familiar love. The excitement of curiosity was gone, but not the excitement of wonder and devotion. Instead of a youth with nothing to do but to woo the wind and the voices it might bring, Genji had become a man with a moon in his own garden, but with a garden after all to tend. It was a little tedious, this gardening; but the tediousness was not so tedious as too much wandering might have been. Before the third volume ended, telling how Genji ordered and sobered his life, an honest reader knew that Genji was still shining somewhere behind the necessary rain.

And now in the fourth volume come autumn and the snowy chill of winter. Don Juan becomes Priam and watches the fall of Troy. May not Priam also have been a glittering youth? It would seem so, from his progeny. Genji, for his part, had few children and found the fact lamentable. When at last his closest love was taken from him, "day and night Genji wept, till it seemed that a veil of tears hung between him and the world. A thousand times he asked himself what use they had ever been to him—this beauty, of which so much had been said, these talents that were supposed to raise him above all his peers?" And yet, in the realness of the narrative, as in the realness of the life of any of us, Genji's acceptance of the loss of his beloved and of his own approaching end blends breathless love with breathless death.

"How high-minded were Genji's principles, and how unsuccessful he was in applying them!" So muses the authoress, when Genji encounters in his estimable and conscientious son sudden evidence of a graceful failing comparable to that of the father. She seems to moralize. But the wisest of tongues is in the wisest of cheeks. Even in the midst of Genji's melancholy, when he considers himself an old man, betrayed by a friend in the manner in which he himself had betrayed his own father and even when he is deprived finally of the person dearer to him than any person on earth, so that only religious consolations are left to his grief and disillusion, his biographer obviously sympathizes with a momentary weakness on his declining part toward a negligible lady of his household. And though the biographer lays away his beloved and even Genji himself, she is already turning the light of her imagination on the rewards this curious earth can give his son and his grandchildren for having been born. Sweet through the darkness of a winter night, she feels the breath of another spring, of a spring which in its turn shall pass into summer and autumn and winter—and then into spring again.

—Review of *Blue Trousers: Being the Fourth Part of the Tale of Genji*, by Lady Murasaki, translated from the Japanese by Arthur Waley, Boston: Houghton Mifflin Company. Published in *The New York Herald Tribune Books*, August 12, 1928

The West—Lorgnette View

· ❧✗✄✗❧ ·

For many years impressionistic books on the United States, written by cursory foreigners, have conveyed to sensitive American readers a more or less polite sense of snobbery. To a resolute resident of the Far West, or let me say New Mexico, Mrs. Katherine Fullerton Gerould's *The Aristocratic West* conveys something of the same sense. She brings to bear, on certain sections of the Far West, a friendly lorgnette.

A San Franciscan might promptly resent any remark, so disarming is Mrs. Gerould's romantic ardor over San Francisco; but I might introduce my friend from the coast to persons in Manhattan among whom he would hear a similar sort of romantic ardor expressed toward Harlem. It is one thing to kindle envy toward Westerners or Negroes, because of a rhythm in their lives freer than the rhythm of New England or New Jersey. It is another thing to like certain Westerners or certain Negroes because of human qualities we should like equally well in certain Easterners or certain Chinese. It is still another thing to set a theatrical stage in Harlem or in the aristocratic West and to spend an evening or a vacation visiting and watching and applauding.

Stage Set Engagingly

At the outset, Mrs. Gerould sets her stage so engagingly as to make it seem sufficient answer to my preliminary strictures:

Between the Missouri River and the Pacific Ocean there sprang into being in the nineteenth century a more original, a more vital and romantic social code—or civilization if you prefer—than any our country has seen since Colonial days.

We are very near to losing it, as we are losing the conditions that nurtured it, and the homogeneous, picked breed of men who created it. But it was perhaps America's most original contribution to social history. As we all become more alike, it tends to fade and merge in the chaotic American democracy. Yet by just so much as it still shapes and colors the Far Western attitude to life is the Far Western attitude admirable, interesting, superior.

She proceeds to admire the cowboy and "the code of the cattle country"—disregard of non-essentials, absence of affectation, presence of courage, "dignity, self-respect, and generous consideration of other people's feelings." She notes "sunburned eyes, the firm lips, the tall leanness, the wrist of steel." And then she says, to one's consternation,

On the screen, only William S. Hart, apparently, can give with subtlety and precision the human aspect of that West about which we have been talking. . . . for conviction through the visual medium watch William S. Hart and him alone.

An Exaggerated Westerner

At this point in the book, my suspicion began that Mrs. Gerould, though uttering much sound sense, was, after all and in spite of herself, a grown-up schoolgirl sighing over a theatrical hero. Surely, of all the Western actors, William S. Hart is the least human, the least simple, the least Western, the most affected, the most exaggerated, the most Eastern. Just as Londoners have always admired the picturesquely exaggerated American, so does Mrs. Gerould through her pages exalt the picturesquely exaggerated Westerner; and in exalting the exaggerated and deprecating mere normal stature, the voice is the voice of praise but the smile is the smile of self-content. The lorgnette tips up and with it the nose.

Toward the scenic West Mrs. Gerould has simpler responses.

She notes that "the Westerner—no more sensitive or aesthetic, originally, than you or I—must have plenty of landscape." Like Rebecca West, she is amazed by the superb and unadvertised beauty of Salt Lake City, she admires the northwestern states; and yet her chapters on Utah, Oregon and Washington are, for some reason, dull reading, casual, diffuse, even trivial. When she comes to San Francisco, her tune is different; and to one who shares, as I do, her feeling that San Francisco, like no other American city but New York, is "one of the capitals of civilization" and "correctly speaking, more cosmopolitan even than New York," there is delight on every page of this eager chapter —except the page where she records the grievous project for bridging the Golden Gate. One must hope with her, "for the credit of San Francisco that the project will never be put through."

Santa Fe

Not knowing Reno, I cannot defend the Nevada town against the amusing and desolating chapter which concludes:

> Curious little Reno! So pretty, so uneventful, so isolated— so very "small-town"—and yet so manifestly linked to a brilliant and lawless past; and bearing for all eyes in the broad light of day the light flotsam of divorcees, the heavy jetsam of shifty, broken men.

I leave Reno to the Nevadans. I turn to the major cause of my obvious annoyance with Mrs. Gerould's book: her chapter on New Mexico. Knowing New Mexico even better than I know California, being in fact a householder in Santa Fe (without the accent she gives it), I am staggered not only by the acerbity with which our traveler approaches the little capital, but by the thick succession of inaccuracies with which she has indulged her bad temper. Apart from the fact that, for no reason but choice, I myself have forgone San Francisco as a dwelling place and pre-ferred the more genuinely Western life in what she calls a "tragic and tawdry city," I resent her unjust and absurd allusions to crime and "riotous living"; her sneers at a few examples of experimental architecture, not so bad as her Victorianism thinks and not so different from the "Hopi architecture" which is redeeming from too much ugliness the rooftops of New York; her disregard of a general architecture which belongs simply and naturally to the earth it is made of, instead of tugging stupidly away from it; her glorification (at Santa Fe's expense) of the typically Middle Western Albuquerque; her intimation of a snobbish aristocracy of Spanish blood holding aloof from inferior neighbors; her evident ignorance concerning the malodorous Bursum Bill; her jibes at the disinterested groups that killed it, etc., etc. Granting that Mrs. Gerould's basic attitude toward the Indians is intelligent and well expressed, agreeing with her that we should trespass as little as possible on the Pueblo character, I am puzzled by her vagary, her apparent willingness that we should have trespassed as much as possible on Pueblo lands.

The Appeal of Santa Fe

My bewilderment over this and other mistakes as to New Mexico, even a little thing like "cinque centavos," was considerably enlightened by a pertinent discovery. Part of the discovery is Mrs. Gerould's acknowledgment that she has visited Santa Fe only once; the rest of the discovery is information I received through Mary Austin that Mrs. Gerould "had been in Santa Fe but a few hours, and in the whole state but a few days, and that her pages of discussion of the Pueblos and their problem was based on a short call at Laguana and a few hours at Acoma." If our recording tourist had taken into Santa Fe a little more "dignity, self-respect, and generous consideration of other people's feelings," she might not have had so ill a time there. I suspect that her trip was nearing its end when she reached New Mexico, and that she had grown a little tired of the aristocratic West.

As an adopted Westerner, let me reconsider a moment. Let me remember that I had been in Santa Fe a month before I began to realize its quiet, deep, and abiding spell, and that since then I have lived there four years without feeling qualified to explain, in answer to editorial inquiries, its curiously Oriental poise between past and future. Let us forgive a poor tourist, a poor journalist, who rushed in and out again and trusted her incredibly hasty judgments. After all, she has said herself,

> The wide spaces give every man room to breathe; and what that means in moral poise is most sharply felt by the confirmed haunter of cities.

She has said herself, "I would far rather live in the Far West than in the East." If she means it, if she means the real West she has described in her introduction and not just a William S. Hart West, she may live someday in Santa Fe. As she has said herself, "Mountain and desert alter very little."

—Review of *The Aristocratic West*, by Katherine Fullerton Gerould, New York: Harper & Brothers. Published in *The Christian Science Monitor*, March 3, 1926

"A Person with a Pen"

· ❧❦❧ ·

"A person with a pen" he calls himself in the first of these eight essays.

D. H. Lawrence is always a "person." Whatever he may be saying comes from the mind or middle of an acutely sensitive individual; and it is sometimes a pity that he will let his pen record too many sensibilities, not distinguishing, apparently, between the trivial and the significant sensations, between the pettily personal and the deeply personal emotions. His pen is so subject to his moods that it can make a pin-prick read like a lightning bolt. In this latest book, happily enough, pen and person are in more temperate accord.

To anyone who has read *The Plumed Serpent*, with its incomparably fine descriptions of Mexican places and characters, especially to one, like myself, who has lived in the very places and known the very characters, it is a disappointment to come upon them again in the first essays of this book, seen now with a tired squint and told about infirmly. Even his parrot and dog, on the early pages, lack life. You cannot hear them stir and breathe as you have heard the stirring and breathing of Lawrence's other birds and beasts. In fact, the first essay is dispiriting to a reader who expects of Lawrence miraculously observant writing about animals, or else, through his intuitive study of them, some arresting revelation of himself. When D.H. writes of persons, you remember little of them but much of the first person, D.H., pared into interesting contradictory parts. He is forever fighting with himself or patting himself on the back, in the guise of this or that man or woman in his books. He puts himself as he is into them instead of taking them as they are into himself. Lesser characters who concern him only as an impersonal observer he will describe in vivider, closer-fitting terms than are at the command of any other writer alive. He cages them securely and labels them correctly in his zoo. But as soon as he goes beyond their animal actions and engages in their motivating thoughts and emotions, he either wrangles his wit into a temper or muddles his nerves into some mystical half-angry ecstasy. If only the unspoilt artist might oftener discipline the spoilt child! Heretofore he has at times been able to exorcise his disturbed spirit and to replace it with the calmer spirit of some natural and easy-going animal. Seldom has he used the intuitive magic of accepting inside himself the spirit of other persons, not infecting it with his own fret. At last, in this book, he has done the trick; he has imbued himself with persons other than himself, as they are rather than as he is—unless D. H. Lawrence be, at heart, himself an Indian.

His title is pardonably misleading. Only the first and weaker half of the book deals with old Mexico, Mexico proper. And into the Indians of old Mexico he for some reason projects his own irritations; he visits his nerves upon them unto the third and fourth generations. He is by turns querulous, timorous, resentful, wistful and superstitious; and so he makes them. In New Mexico, on the contrary, the peak of the volcano has cooled. He is a different mountain. By no means a dead mountain. But a mountain aware rather of growth than of destruction.

Read the fifth, sixth and seventh essays in this book and you will know more of the Southwest than you could discover by taking an "Indian Detour." At any rate, read them before you see the so-called "dances." Allow Lawrence his discrepancies, his self-contradictions, let him be as inconsistent as Walt Whitman. He tells about a song of a man coming home from the bear-hunt. "The man coming home from the bear-hunt is any man, all men, the bear is any bear, every bear, all bear. There is no individual, isolated experience. . . . The experience is generic, non-individual. It is an experience of the human bloodstream. . . . Hence the strange blind unanimity of the Indian men's voices. The experience is one experience, tribal, of the bloodstream." He tells about the Hopi snake dance, the Indians' "animistic religion." "There is no oneness, no sympathetic identifying oneself with the rest. The law of isolation is heavy on every creature." Inconsistent as Walt Whitman, yes, but like him, this time, in other ways, too. Lawrence among the Pueblos more nearly escapes the heaviness of the law of isolation than he has ever done; he more sympathetically identifies himself with these Indians of the Southwest than he has ever done with persons of any other race. He is "any Pueblo, every Pueblo, all Pueblo." And the result is as always when Lawrence's passion for life outweighs his intellectual or neurological insistences. He describes Indian ceremonies with a greater degree of essential truth than has been dealt them by any other writer, whether or not that other writer may have been technically more accurate or archaeologically better informed.

The Pueblos are reported to have given Lawrence the name, "Lone Wolf." They might well adopt him by some other name. He might prove to be less lonely and less wolfish, more Lawrence and more man. The "person with a pen" has, at any rate, adopted the Pueblos.

—Review of *Mornings in Mexico*, by D. H. Lawrence, New York: Alfred A. Knopf. Published in *The New Republic*, October 12, 1927

Translating the Orient

One eagerly picks up Eunice Tietjens's selection of translated *Poetry of the Orient*—the Orient meaning this time Arabia, Persia, Japan, China and India. One reads thirty-four pages of excellent introduction and two hundred and eighty-five pages of verse. Coming at last to fourteen appended pages of bibliography, one marvels after all more at the editor's patience than at the genius of the poets she has assembled. Out of half a world comes a pittance of poetry. It is not her fault. By dint of long and close watching she has doubtless felt, despite the clumsiness of translators, the power or validity of the originals. Related to one section of her book, the Chinese, I have myself read many volumes of translation; and, knowing from association with a Chinese scholar the value of the originals, I have sighed at the paucity of what comes through to us in English from a golden source. The best translations available of Oriental poetry are probably from the Chinese, as she herself says. What painful tedium must she have gone through in English volumes from the other countries, before she could offer us this winnowing! She deserves no end of praise for her hard work.

The only honest approach to a volume like this is to the translators and not to the original poets. One can imagine Shakespeare mauled beyond belief by a translator into the Sanskrit and Eddie Guest made sublime. Miss Tietjens properly indicates in each section those poets whom their own countrymen hold in highest esteem; but she cannot indicate, through the translators at her disposal for evidence, the reasons therefor. Interestingly enough, the essence of greatness does not come through. Perhaps those critics are right who hold that the substance of human thinking is very much the same in all countries and all times and only of outstanding importance in accordance with the degree of art in language controlled by the expressor. A book of this sort most certainly weighs on the side of the contender for form as the more important half of literary matter. Again and again, in reading these classics from old literature, written originally in language beyond our ken, one is aware of noble enough human matter even through ignoble expression in our own language. Will a thorough reading of the book bear us out in this surmise? Let us read and see.

Imru-al-Kais does not emerge in translation as, concededly, the greatest of the earlier Arabs. His poems in fact make dull English, even the one suspended with six by other authors as the "Seven Golden Poems" in the temple at Mecca. So do the other six, in so far as we are allowed to know them. None of the Arabian poems written before the time of Mohammed, though we have our editor's word for their simple virility, conveys much in English. We feel the horses and camels slightly, but not the poetry. After Mohammed, when the wild, free spirit had given way in literary Arabia to a moralistic consciousness, we find this translation by Henry Baerlein from Abu'l-Atahiya of the eighth century:

> Full is my sorrow now that you are dead,
> And I have thrown the dust upon your head.
> In other days I preached unendingly,
> But now, my little boy, you preach to me.

J. D. Carlyle translates from a Syrian Arab, Ibn al-Rumi (died A.D. 894) this proof that Mohammed had not banished wit:

> So careful is Isa and anxious to last,
> So afraid of himself is he grown,
> He swears thro' two nostrils the breath goes too fast,
> And he's trying to breathe thro' but one.

Baerlein again proves from Ibn al-Rebii of the seventh century that there were Menckens against even Mohammed:

Traditions have been handed down to me
That would have had importance, would have had
But for my powers of credulity,
Which are so bad.

Edward William Lane translates from the *Arabian Nights* an "Admonition" written six centuries later, an aphorism sufficiently impressive in the present century to be used by Miss Tietjens on her graceful dedicatory page:

> There is no writer that shall not perish; but what his hand hath written endureth forever.
> Write, therefore, nothing but what will please thee when thou shalt see it on the day of judgment.

From the same book comes a gayer bit, "On Wine," the English by Edward Powys Mathers, known to me through his translations from the Chinese to be a flagrant and often wanton embroiderer on smothered texts but in this case deft enough to warrant his probable license:

> There's nothing like the blood of grapes
> To give escapes
> From care's infesting, festering apes.
> To set the wit upon probation,
> To give an edge to conversation,
> To make a friend of a relation,
> There's nothing like the blood of grapes.

Miss Tietjens calls the poetry of Persia the poetry of "world sophistication." Edward Fitzgerald bears out her contention in his quatrains from Omar Khayyam, and Richard LeGallienne is not far behind as a translator. Here, however, as with the Arabs, the great poets suffer through translation, Omar being, to the Persian mind, "a first-rate astronomer, but not even a third-rate poet." Firdausi of the ninth century seems unimportant in

English. So do Mu'izzi of the eleventh century, Nizami of the twelfth, Hafiz of the thirteenth and Saadi of the thirteenth— though the latter has Sir Edwin Arnold to thank for two couplets:

I

The counsels of the wise may go awry,
The fool may hit his mark at the first try.

II

What could he know of sky and stars, of heaven's all-hidden life,
Who did not see in his own house the knave that kissed his wife?

Ralph T. H. Griffith happens to conclude a negligible translation from Jami of the fifteenth century with these two lines:

If on the eye of a lover she stepped,
Her foot would float on the tear he wept.

And so Persia goes by.

In one of her notably compact and yet comprehensive individual prefaces to the five sections of her book, Miss Tietjens prepares the reader for the characteristic brevity and suggestiveness of Japanese poetry, in which the poet's imagination plays chess with the reader's. Anyone knowing Japanese poetry through translation, knows Basil Hall Chamberlain's famous *hokku* from the eighteenth-century painter-poet, Buson:

Granted this dew-drop world is but
A dew-drop world—this granted, yet. . . .

When one has read through the Japanese section of this anthology, one has found nothing more memorable, more characteristic and more poignant. Hitomaro, "the greatest of the older poets of Japan," in spite of earnest efforts by Arthur Waley,

Curtis Hidden Page and Clara A. Walsh, takes on no stature in English, not even the stature of a dwarf-pine. Waley gives grace to a *tanka* by an unknown author:

> Even for the space of a flash
> Of lightning
> That flashes over the corn-ears
> Of an autumn-field—
> Can I forget you?

Yone Noguchi, despite the unhappy inversion in his last line, cannot destroy the fifteenth-century Arakida Moritake's *hokku*:

> I thought I saw the fallen leaves
> Returning to their branches:
> Alas, butterflies were they.

Somebody else, perhaps Lafcadio Hearn, has made a better translation of the eighteenth-century Lady Kaga no Chiyo's "On Her Dead Child" than Chamberlain's lines:

> Today, how far may he have wandered,
> The brave hunter of dragon-flies?

Certainly no one could improve on Hearn's twelfth-century folk-song:

> All things change, we are told, in this world of change and
>   sorrow;
> But love's way never changes of promising never to change.

After one has ploughed through Fenollosa's dull translation of Motokiyo's dull Nō play, *Nishikigi*, and wondered again why Nō plays are so solemnly impressive to Japanese intellectuals, one returns through this section of the anthology to Hearn, Waley, Chamberlain, Page and, above all of them perhaps except

Hearn, to the less known collaborators, Shotaro Kimura and
Charlotte M. A. Peake, who are best represented by "Reminiscence," from the priest Sosei:

> Passionate music of the nightingale,
> Not joy you bring me but a strange regret,
> A memory of nothingness, the pale
> Face of a lover I have never met.

The Chinese section has the advantage which Miss Tietjens
points out, at least for readers during this generation, of having
a greater number of contemporary translators than have been
interested in the literature of the other countries represented.
She notes the kinship between the "objectivity" in Chinese
poetry and ours. She observes the influence of Confucius, "with
his practical wisdom," over the poetry of the Chinese as over
their lives—neglecting, it seems to me, the mystical influence of
Laotzu. She foresees a coloring of English poetry in the future
by Chinese poetry, "just as our poetry of an older day was influenced by the poetry of Persia and Arabia." And in this case,
when she presents to us some of the oldest classics, she is
fortunate in a translator, Helen Waddell, who, through conventional rhymed English stanzas, makes the three-thousand-
year-old folk-songs as fresh and alive as though they had been
written yesterday. Note, for instance, these three stanzas out of
four from "Baroness Muh of Heu Complains," written by an unknown pioneer feminist of the sixth century B.C.:

> I would have gone to my lord in his need,
> Have galloped there all the way,
> But this is a matter concerns the state,
> And I, being a woman, must stay. . . .
>
> I may walk in the garden and gather
> Lilies of mother-of-pearl.

I had a plan would have saved the state.
—But mine are the thoughts of a girl.

The Elder Statesmen sit on the mats,
And wrangle through half a day;
A hundred plans they have drafted and dropped,
And mine was the only way.

James Legge suffers by exhibition of his prosaic versions of the Odes. Herbert A. Giles is represented by one of the very few translations in which he has not made Chinese poetry ridiculous. Louise Strong Hammond is shown setting down English syllables which convey the meaning of the original into our language and at the same time allow it to follow the musical song-pattern of the Chinese characters. Florence Ayscough and Amy Lowell are present, uprooting the Chinese characters into lopsided prominence as against the colloquial intention of their authors and yet gaining something valuable through a sense of quaintness and color. Edward Powys Mathers is let in for his lusciousness. Arthur Waley is eminent, as usual, in any showing of translations from the Chinese, for his homely and straightforward vigor. Shigeyoshi Obata follows him in the same spirit; and so, I hope, do Kiang Kang-hu and I. Gertrude Laughlin Joerissen surprises me, as a translator whom I had not heretofore discovered. I quote her admirable version of Li Po's "White Heron":

That great flake of snow which has just floated over the lake
was a white heron.
Motionless, at the end of a sand bank, the white heron
watches the winter.

So much Chinese poetry has been printed lately from various translators that it will be enough to quote further out of this section only Arthur Waley's "What Should a Man Want?" from Wang Chi (about A.D. 700), as characteristic of the sane temper dominant among the Chinese poets:

"Tell me now, what should a man want
But to sit alone sipping his cup of wine?"
I should like to have visitors come to discuss philosophy
And not to have tax-collectors coming to collect taxes;
My three sons married into good families,
My five daughters provided with steady husbands;
Then I could jog through a happy five score years,
Craving no cloud-ascent, no resurrection.

Oddly, in view of Ezra Pound's latter-day pedantries, the out-standing translation in the Chinese section is his human version of Li Po's "Exile's Letter," too long, alas, to quote. It lets one say, however, as do translations by Waley and some of the others, that only in this section, the Chinese, do the great poets of the foreign country seem in English the great poets.

Certainly in the section concerning India, the keynote of whose poetry, says Miss Tietjens, "is its subjectivity," the great poets are hardly worth reading in English. Sir Edwin Arnold comes nearer than any other of the earlier translators to giving life to his material. Fortunately for India's position in the book, there is a modern translator, Arthur W. Ryder, whose work redeems Indian poetry from seeming verbose and vapid. The *Rig-Veda*, the *Artharva-Veda*, even the famous *Mahabharata* and *Ramayana*, seem, in the English they are shown in, tedious performances. Ryder, on the other hand, extracts from the *Panchatantra* (first collected about 200 B.C.) such well-phrased bits of wisdom as the following:

Scholarship is less than sense;
Therefore seek intelligence.

For lost and dead and past
The wise have no laments;
Between the wise and fools
Is just this difference.

> Even a pearl, so smoothly hard and round,
> Is fastened by a thread and safely bound,
> After a way to pierce its heart is found.

Expert as Ryder is in these epigrams, he fails, as completely as translators have failed working at greatness in other Oriental languages, to bring alive the greatness of the poet Kalidasa (about A.D. 400). Nor is any of Kalidasa's translators more successful. Kalidasa, with his *Sakuntala* and other dramas, lies dead in these pages, although "India has long held Kalidasa to be the greatest of her poets." Paul Elmer More vitalizes a lyric called "Warning," from King Bhartrihari of the seventh century:

> O wanderer heart! avoid that haunted grove,
> The body of thy love;
> Nor in her bosom stray, wild mountain fells
> Where Love, the robber, dwells.

A. Berriedale Keith translates from the same King a "Reflection":

> It is easy to satisfy one who is ignorant,
> Even easier to satisfy a connoisseur;
> But not the creator himself can please the man
> Who has just a morsel of knowledge.

Except for fragments like these, Indian poetry in English might as well never have been translated. The translators have left it remote from us. Or is it the essence which is remote? The more subjective the poetry of a country, the more remote from the understanding of other countries? I wonder if we do not come to a conclusion different from that, after having read with Miss Tietjens the classic literature, in English translation, from these five Oriental countries.

First, as to the translations, there is one phenomenon easily to be observed through this review and inevitably, I believe, through the book itself. If my own reactions are any criterion, the successful translations are for the most part epigrams. The translator can apparently make the distance of a short poem with a quick point and turn it into effective English. A long poem seems hard, beyond instance at any rate in this anthology, to carry into another language. The only exceptions are poems from the Chinese. And this brings us to a point which may, I think, clarify the whole problem of translation.

Even in the ancient Chinese poems, dealing with life and customs alien to us through both space and time, there is a universal and enduring humanness. Is Miss Tietjens right in calling Chinese poetry objective and Indian poetry subjective? I doubt it very much. I should even be inclined to reverse her terms. There is a primitive subjectivity in the Arabic poetry, a man's response to his horse, camel, wife, sweetheart, muscle, sword, or whatever. There is a sophisticatedly sentimental subjectivity in both the Persian and the Japanese poetry, sensual and cynical on the one hand, exquisite and wistfully stoic on the other. The Indian subjectivity seems to me to be strikingly objective, a constant projection of the personal spirit to outside persons or things. Chinese poetry, on the other hand, which Miss Tietjens calls objective, is a constant identification of outside persons and things with oneself. May she not have been misled by the fact that the Chinese poet never exaggerates, never lies to himself, almost never boasts or demands, never indulges in unrealities to save himself from truth, never assumes a stature for himself beyond the stature that rightfully relates him to his fellows and to the consoling and consuming earth? This is not objectivity, whatsoever the terms may be in which he considers himself and the world. This is the most accurate subjectivity to which poets have ever been sensitive. And it is this balanced and eternally just subjectivity which makes the reflections, the problems, the considerations and even the surroundings of the Chinese poet more real to us in this generation than all the boasts of the Arabs, all the shrugs of the Persians, all the sighs of the Japanese, and all the reasoned raptures of the Indians. This poised subjectivity, moreover, on the surface of an eternally beautiful earth, is what makes Chinese poetry an easier matter for the translator than the poetry of these other countries.

After all, in spite of my remark that this book is a matter of translators, I suspect that it is fundamentally a matter of poetry.

—Review of *Poetry of the Orient: An Anthology of the Classical Secular Poetry of the Major Eastern Nations*, edited by Eunice Tietjens, New York: Alfred A. Knopf. Published in *The Bookman*, April 1929

Ezra Pound's
Continuing Cantos

· ❧❦❧ ·

Reading Ezra Pound's *Cantos LII–LXXI* and knowing that a review was expected of me, I continued with them to the end. Enough would have been enough a hundred and fifty pages earlier. But a review was expected. And I did find a bit of good rhythm intruding here and there, a well-rounded phrase or sentence and even a bit of the native spirit with which Pound promised in his young lyrics to be a poet. I don't know what he is now. A figure rather than a spirit. But finally not even a figure. I did find in the Chinese section of the book bits I like to remember from histories of China unpretentiously presented in better prose than Ezra's—whose elegant vulgarity, after all, "says nothing not hackneyed six *centuries* before."

> All is lost in the night clubs
> that was gained under good rule.

That's about the best. I did find that.

> And the Emperor TAI TSONG left his son "Notes on Conduct"
> whereof the 3rd treats of selecting men for a cabinet . . .
> The 10th a charter of labour
> and the last on keepin' up kulchur
> Saying "I have spent money on palaces
> too much on 'osses, dogs, falcons
> but I have united the Hempire (and you 'aven't)
> Nothing harder than to conquer a country

and damn'd easy to lose one, in fact there
ain't anything heasier."

I did find that too.

My first impulse was to write a very brief review in regular
prose, as follows:

> One cannot tell, from the *Cantos*, whether the professor
> who gave the lectures was the thickwit, making of life and
> letters one long dreary drone of smatter, or whether the
> smart-aleck student is to blame, whose hodge-podge of
> pidgin-English notes has for some reason been published.

My second impulse was to write a very brief review in
irregular prose, as follows:

<pre>
After such an over-abundance of
        the learned bunk of Babel,
He will all at once learn a new language
        with all the others in it
                a language he will not use at ALL
but he was so rippin' while He lasted
                set such a PACE
                let's go easy
                        nil nisi
    Let him
                        R.I.P.
</pre>

But neither of the "reviews" does so well as for me to add to
my suggestion, that Pound is not a spirit but a figure, the
further suggestion, not too unkind, that he is a figure on a
balcony.

—Unpublished manuscript in the Houghton Library, Harvard University

"Selections from the Three Hundred Poems of the T'ang Dynasty"

· ❧❧❧❧❧ ·

Asked by the editor of *Fantasy* to review *Selections from the Three Hundred Poems of the T'ang Dynasty* by Mr. Soame Jenyns, I found the following in the scholarly, brisk foreword by Mr. Jenyns: "There exists one fairly complete translation in English of the three hundred T'ang poems under the title of *The Jade Mountain* by an American, Mr. Witter Bynner, with whom I should join issue on so many points of translation and interpretation that I will not pursue our differences. The Chinese language is at once so terse and so ambiguous that it provides a thousand and one problems at every turn which offer almost endless opportunities to the unfriendly critic. Only an intimate knowledge of Chinese culture and Chinese ways of thought can hope to elucidate many passages; often the Chinese commentators themselves are at a loss or disagree."

It is natural that this passage should have challenged my attention. It is natural, too, that I should hesitate in the office of reviewer, should feel somewhat embarrassed lest adverse judgment of Mr. Jenyns' work might on my part appear to be a matter of pique. I have chosen therefore to lay before the reader, for his own judgment before I fully state mine, a number of corresponding translations; by Mr. Jenyns in his *Selections* and by myself in *The Jade Mountain*, from the literal texts of my collaborator, the eminent Chinese scholar, Dr. Kiang Kang-hu.

Then the reader will know, by that much comparison at least, how far to respect my conclusions. Incidentally, through this tacit criticism, the sort of detailed comments I might make will become self-evident.

Mr. Jenyns has done, in his volume much briefer than ours, what I was at first tempted to do in *The Jade Mountain*: he has selected only a portion, about a third, of the original anthology and has thus avoided or been spared many of the "puzzling problems" I encountered. Be it remembered that the poems were written between A.D. 618 and 906. With encouragement, however, from my collaborator, I finally undertook the entire task. Not knowing Chinese myself, I could only follow Dr. Kiang's interpretations, except when he would give me several traditional or personal alternatives to choose from according to my preference. Hence Mr. Jenyns' challenges as to interpretation could much better be answered by Dr. Kiang, my two years spent in China not having equipped me to be an interpreter; and my impulse was to submit to the Chinese scholar such divergence as I might discover between him and the English scholar and request the former's comment; but present conference between New Mexico and China would have meant too belated a review.

The first discrepancy indicated by Mr. Jenyns is in his footnote referring to the number of poems comprising the anthology, first published in 1736. Mr. Jenyns says that there are "three hundred and twelve if different parts of the poems are counted separately. Bynner gives the number as three hundred and eleven." Since his foreword states that "some editions omit verses and even whole poems that the others contain" and since in three poems from the edition Mr. Jenyns used there are sections or "parts" not contained in the edition we used, this first "difference" is surely a negligible trifle. A later footnote, to an untitled poem by Li Shang-yin, is more pertinent. It refers to a line translated by Mr. Jenyns, "Beyond the hibiscus pond there is faint thunder." The footnote says, "Of a coming storm and not of wheels." And herein is the only other specific allusion I can find to the "issue" he joins with *The Jade Mountain*, in which the line reads, "And wheels faintly thunder beyond

Hibiscus Pool." Mr. Jenyns is correct inasfar as the text makes no mention of wheels; but Dr. Kiang, explaining his interpretation as warranted by the context, preferred the imaginative to the literal reading, and it is a plausible guess that the Chinese chose a more informed reading than did the Englishman.

Carefully comparing the poems in the Jenyns volume with the same ones in ours, I found few radical contradictions as to ideas presented, and most of those I did find seemed to me a matter of choice on the part of the translator, either variant being permissible. There are three poems and a portion of another in which I instantly point out the superiority of the Jenyns English versions over those in *The Jade Mountain*. He has had signal success with Li Po's famous and much translated "Drinking Alone Under the Moon" (page 35), with the same poet's "The Road That Is Hard to Travel" (page 40), and with Liu Chang-ch'ing's "Farewell to Ling Che" (page 103); but let me quote, as his best reach, without bothering to intrude our version, the apt Jenyns rendering of the last nine lines in Tu Fu's "Song of the War Chariots":

> It has come to this, that to give birth to sons is ruinous,
> And it is actually better to produce girls.
> Girls can always be married to neighbours;
> Sons are only fit to perish like the prairie grass.
> Ah! see you not at the head of the Kokonor
> How the white bones of the long dead lie unburied?
> New ghosts complain bitterly, old ghosts moan,
> The heavens are darkened, the rain falls
> As the ghosts from the past whisper to those that have but
>   lately died.

Mr. Jenyns' version of Liu Chang-ch'ing's poem may be truer to the original than our version:

> Green, green is the monastery in the Bamboo Groves,
> Dim, dim the bell sounds at evening.

The slanting rays of the sun strike the bamboo hat slung on
  your shoulders
As you go back alone to your home among the hills.

—Jenyns

From the temple, deep in its tender bamboos,
Comes the low sound of an evening bell,
While the hat of a pilgrim carries the sunset
Farther and farther down the green mountain.

—Bynner and Kiang

Having destroyed Dr. Kiang's scripts I cannot tell whether or
not in the final line I omitted "alone" and "home" and supplied
"green." I do know, however, that in an English poem I like the
echoing "deep," "evening" and "green" in my first, second and
fourth lines and that in Mr. Jenyns' lines throughout his book
I very much miss an ear for music.

Here are three more poems with versions from both books:
From Wang Wêi:

In the evening of life tranquillity is my only joy.
Ten thousand affairs cease to trouble the heart.
I reflect there is no more excellent scheme than
To give learning a miss and to return to the forests of my
  old home.
Where the wind sighs in the pines I loosen my girdle.
When the hill moon shines I thrum the lute.
If you ask me why I don't care for the proprieties
(I invite you to listen while) over the estuary is wafted to
  me the fisherman's song.

—Jenyns

As the years go by, give me but peace,
Freedom from ten thousand matters.
I ask myself and always answer:
What can be better than coming home?

A wind from the pine-trees blows my sash,
And my lute is bright with the mountain moon.
You ask me about good and evil fortune? . . .
Hark, on the lake there's a fisherman singing!

—Bynner and Kiang

From Tu Ch'iu-niang, a woman poet:

Covet not the gold-threaded coat,
Grasp the years when you are young,
When the flowers open come pluck them;
Do not wait to gather a spent spray from an empty bough.

—Jenyns

Covet not a gold-threaded robe,
Cherish only your young days!
If a bud open, gather it—
Lest you but wait for an empty bough.

—Bynner and Kiang

And Mr. Jenyns adds a footnote: "The moral of this poem is
Herrick's 'Gather ye rose-buds while ye may.'"

From Tu Mu:

Down and out I wander over the waters with a supply of
    wine,
The girls here are like the wasp-waisted beauties of Ch'u,
So light that they could dance on the palm of one's hand.
For ten years I have lived besotted in Yang Chou,
And now all I have to show for it is the reputation for a
    light-of-love in the houses of ill fame.

—Jenyns

With my wine-bottle, watching by river and lake
For a lady so tiny as to dance on my palm,

I awake, after dreaming ten years in Yang-chou,
Known as fickle, even in the Street of Blue Houses.
—Bynner and Kiang

And Mr. Jenyns adds another footnote: "The poem is written in mood of remorse at his wasted life."

I said at the outset that on the whole I found the Jenyns translations and ours fairly parallel as to meaning. There are two instances in which I have found them singularly parallel as to phrase. Note the final verses from Li Po's irregularly lined poem which we call "Endless Yearning" and Mr. Jenyns calls "Unfulfilled Desire":

I think of you far away, beyond the blue sky,
And my eyes that once were sparkling
Are now a well of tears.
. . . Oh, if ever you should doubt this aching of my heart,
Here in my bright mirror come back and look at me!
—Bynner and Kiang

I think of you so far away beyond the blue sky.
Of old times my eyes that sparkled are now full of tears.
Oh! if you doubt this aching of my heart
Here in my bright mirror come back and look at me.
—Jenyns

And there's a prose introduction to a poem by Tu Fu:

(On the 19th of the Tenth-month in the second year of Ta-li, I saw, in the house of the K'uêi-fu official Yüan T'ê, a girl named Li from Lin-ying dancing with a dagger. I admired her skill and asked who was her teacher. She named Lady Kung-sun. I remembered that in the third year of K'ai-yüan at Yen-ch'êng, when I was a little boy, I saw Lady Kung-sun dance. She was the only one in the Imperial Theater who could dance with this weapon. Now she is aged and unknown, and even her pupil has passed the heyday of beauty. I wrote this poem to express my wistfulness. The work of Chang Hsü of the Wu district, that great master of grassy writing, was improved by his having been present when Lady Kung-sun danced in the Yeh district. From this may be judged the art of Kung-sun.)

—Bynner and Kiang

(On the 19th day of the 10th month of the 2nd year of Ta Li I saw in the House Yuan Ch'ih, an official of Kuei Chou, a girl named Li from Lin-ying dance a sword dance. I admired her skill and asked her who had taught her. She said the lady Kung Sun. I remembered that in the third year of K'ai Yuan at Yen-ch'eng, when I was a small boy I had seen lady Kung Sun dance. She was the only one in the Imperial theater who could dance this dance. Now she is aged and unknown and even her pupils have passed the heyday of their beauty. I wrote the poem to express my sorrow. The work of Chang Hsu of the Wu district, the great master of grass writing, was improved by his having been present when the lady Kung Sun danced in the Yeh district. From this may be judged the art of Kung Sun.)

—Jenyns

It seems to me that in these two instances there might have been footnotes of acknowledgment, if not for future students then just for amity.

Mr. Jenyns pays repeated tribute, by the way, to a fellow translator, Mr. W. J. B. Fletcher. For this reason I cannot resist quoting, as characteristic, Mr. Fletcher's version of Wang Wêi's "The Moon":

In bamboo thicket hid, sitting alone am I.
First my guitar I strum, then stop to whistle awhile.
Amid the grove so thick, no mortal can me spy.
But we behold each other, the lucent moon and I.

Could verse be worse? Let me say then, in conclusion, what in my judgment ought to be said about the Jenyns book and other books which purport to be images in English of beautiful, moving and important Chinese originals but are not. Let me say that the usually inept Jenyns translations, though they may convey literal texts, relate very seldom to the spirit of the greater part of the originals, to their life, to their pathos, to their humor, to their wisdom, to their grave beauty, to their deeply wrought simplicity. These pages are dead leaves into which the translators have thought but failed to breathe new sap, new veins. Is it enough that a careful, humorless, unimaginative scholar in the British Museum, because he has studied Chinese history and art, and presumably the art objects which are the written Chinese language, should painstakingly but futilely try to grow poetry for Westerners out of a rich depth of literary soil in an ancient culture? It is not enough. Should one bow and say thank you? No. One should say bluntly—or I should, however reluctant to condemn the results of what has undoubtedly been devoted labor —that most of the English verses offered us by Mr. Jenyns, like those by Mr. W. J. B. Fletcher or Mr. Charles Budd, and unlike those by Mr. Arthur Waley and Mr. Shigeyoshi Obata or—in the case of freer versions—Miss Helen Waddell and Mr. L. Cranmer-Byng—not only bear slight relation to either English or Chinese poetry but make one cringe, somewhat as I cringed years ago in Peking when I received from the American Legation an invitation to "an afternoon of Confusion music."

One of the Jenyns footnotes says: "Chinese wine is spirits. As wine is more poetical than spirits, it is sad Chinese did not use it" (sic, page 100).

—Review of *Selections from the Three Hundred Poems of the T'ang Dynasty*, by Soame Jenyns, New York: E. P. Dutton & Company. Published in *Fantasy*, April 1942.

Patterns of
Eastern Culture

· ❧❦❧ ·

At a time when, allied with one Asian nation, we are warring against another, this compilation of essays on the Orient and what we of the West may derive from its culture is timely and pertinent. At a time when, aided by France, we were warring against Britain, we still respected and cherished the cultures of both countries; and it is well that these considerations of our past, present, and future debt to the Orient deal fairly not only with the cultures of China, India, and the Near East, but with Japan's also.

The editor's opening outline of Oriental influence on Occidental literature from the fifteenth century to the present day, as well as his appended "facts and curiosa" of Indian and Far Eastern trade, present material less familiar to the ordinary reader than that dealt with by the other contributors. Widely informed, erudite but not pedantic, Mr. Christy most interestingly traces the arrival of artistic, intellectual, and spiritual values from East to West in the thought and works of such writers as Voltaire, Goethe, Gautier in Europe, Goldsmith, Johnson, Byron, Southey, Landor, Kipling, Dickinson in England, Franklin, Pound in America. He distinguishes between idealization of the "Noble Savage," the supposed simple and primitive man of the Orient, by poets and romanticists and recognition of the "Noble Sage" from deists and rationalists who were deeply impressed by what they knew of the "practical, social-minded" Confucius and his kind. Mr. Christy seems more aware of influences from "social China" than from "mystic India"; but William York Tindall arrestingly and amusingly complements the case by noting under the title "Transcendentalism in Contemporary Literature" the spirit of Indian mystics in Yeats who came early under the dubious spell of Madame Blavatsky and more or less remained there, in D. H. Lawrence who tried to bring from the *Upanishads* initiation and spiritual exercise for Westerners, and in Aldous Huxley, Gerald Heard, and Christopher Isherwood who brood on the Vedantists near Hollywood. All these cases, he concludes, follow the pattern of "materialism attended with detestation and yearning and followed by theosophy or Hinduism," by "the persisting desire to believe that man's spirit is continuous with a larger spirituality from whose universality are to be derived confidence, courage, and cosmic security."

John Gould Fletcher, spinning the literary tale finer with an account of the effect of Chinese poetry on Imagists, offers more theory than evidence, except in a brief quotation from T. S. Eliot, and much of his essay might better serve as a good chapter in an autobiography than as contribution to the purpose of the present volume. If, as Ananda K. Coomaraswamy points out in his notable contribution, an influence is likely to have been "the more profound the less obviously it can be recognized in outward forms," Mr. Fletcher might more pertinently have considered such poems as Vachel Lindsay's "The Chinese Nightingale" and "The Empire of China is Crumbling Down" than the Japanese rather than Chinese manner of the Imagists.

Lawrence P. Roberts, Director of the Brooklyn Museum, though noting the influence of Japanese print-makers on Manet, Degas, Monet, Gauguin, and Toulouse-Lautrec, as well as on the English Beardsley and our own Whistler and Cassatt, finds Western art hardly touched otherwise by the arts of India, Japan, or China. "Connoisseurs today," he judges, "know more of Chinese art and taste than ever before, but the effect of this knowledge on the artistic life of the West is almost negligible." Mr. Christy had mentioned incidentally, as other American debtors, LaFarge and Saint-Gaudens. Mr. Coomaraswamy's "Understanding and Reunion" deals mainly with the ceremonial arts of dance and drama and their spiritual significance, in contrast to our use of art "for its effect upon our sensations." He observes that "the only drama amongst ourselves that is really what drama means to Hindus, Javanese, or Tibetans is that of the Mass, performed in church, not as a spectacle, but as a sacrifice." I wonder if he ever saw Pueblo Indians at San Felipe, New Mexico, come into the church dressed as deer after the midnight mass on Christmas morning and dance before the Lord. If so, he might well have believed that These States were natively Oriental.

I have long but vainly urged that American institutions invite Chinese scholars, versed in the ancient ways of Han, to study among American Indians our own most immediate Asian legacy. Mr. Coomaraswamy might have said "an Amerindian" when he says: "An Oriental can readily understand and be moved by a Gaelic folksong or by the Gregorian chant, while hardly anything later than Bach will seem to him music at all." To most Western auditors hardly anything later than so-called Confucian music in China will seem music at all; but Curt Sachs concludes his essay on "The Orient and Western Music":

> Faced with Oriental music, the world of 1900 began to realize the limitations of Western music. Maybe for the first time, it dawned upon the European musician and critic that the great achievement in harmony, polyphony, and orchestration had meant sacrifices in other fields; that the unbelievable riches of modes which the Orient still possessed had burnt down to major and minor; that under the straightjacket of harmonic function melody proper had become a poor connecting link between related chords; that rhythm had become an all too simple time-beating.

Incidentally he says: "All the instruments we have used in modern times once came from Asia."

Importations of a quite different kind are noted in an informative paper on "Our Agricultural Debt to Asia," by Walter Swingle, who states that practically all our cereals, food plants, and fruit trees originated in Asia, as well as all our domestic animals except the llama, "an ill-tempered brute," and the turkey.

A cynic might wonder if opium and missionaries were a fair exchange for such benefits; but Oliver J. Caldwell, while admitting faults and weaknesses in some of the missionaries, makes, in "Ties that Bind," an excellent case for most of them as being, through interpretative writing and good works, the "middlemen of friendship between China and America."

William Ernest Hocking in "Living Religions and a World Faith" intimates that our missionaries are taking back to the East what came from the East. When he says, "Whatever forms of religion are alive among us we owe to Asia," he means primarily the Near East; but he summarizes with clear, fine gravity the "prudent pragmatism" of Confucius, the "cure of suffering" through Buddhism, and touches on the tenets of Hinduism and Islam. Granting that "the world views are surely not identical," he does not see them as oppositional. "The ultimate world faith," he believes, "will have to be one in which these differences must be resolved."

Pearl Buck closes the symposium with a balanced "Conclusion," stressing the not dissimilar humanness and common sense of people East and West, the universal basic motive of enlightened self-interest. There's need in the East, she thinks, of more comfort and in the West of more happiness—in both spheres need of interchange. "We are like men digging a tunnel through a mountain," is her apt simile. "We have begun at opposite ends but the goal is the same—human happiness. We ought to meet somewhere one of these days and find that each faces the other's light."

No open-hearted reader could lay down this book and still feel "the white man's burden of superiority" or have any doubt that the white peril and the yellow peril can dissolve in safeguard, golden as the common sun.

—Review of *The Asian Legacy and American Life*, edited by Arthur E. Christy, New York: John Day Company. Published in *The Saturday Review of Literature*, July 21, 1945

Tempest in
a China Teapot

· ❧❦❧ ·

At first glance what is there to say about this book—for a general audience? Mr. MacNair, the editor, with an honest, proper, and due respect for his wife, Florence Ayscough, has very carefully presented and documented her voluminous correspondence with Amy Lowell concerning their collaboration in translating the Chinese poems included in *Fir-Flower Tablets*. At first glance, because of my long preoccupation with translating Chinese poetry into English I felt, as I say, that John Gould Fletcher and I—Eunice Tietjens and Arthur Ficke having died— might be the only two persons in America who would read every paragraph of it with close interest. Except for personal passages and an appended garden essay by Miss Lowell, the book presents only correspondence between two very industrious women concerning the Chinese poems they selected to translate and their method of translating them. On careful rereading of the book, I could but hope that there might be a considerable audience led through these letters to realize the infinite pains that go into such translation. Industry, industry!

In a letter to Harriet Monroe Miss Lowell wrote:

I have made a discovery which I have never before seen mentioned in any Occidental book on Chinese poetry, but which I think must be well-known in Chinese literature; namely, that the roots of the characters are the things which give the poetry its overtones, taking the place of adjectives and imaginary writing with us. . . . Mrs. Ayscough quite agrees with me in this.

The fact of the matter, fully evidenced in the bulk of the book, was that Mrs. Ayscough had made the discovery and that Miss Lowell quite agreed with *her*. The discovery was the fact that Chinese ideographs are compounded of a root idea with other ideas stroked alongside, such as the familiar pictorial word for quarrel: a roof with two women under it. And Mrs. Ayscough had suggested to Miss Lowell that in translating Chinese poems these implicit connotations of individual words should be translated too. Robert Payne in *Forever China* remarks: "The ideographs remain the same; perhaps even the interpretation remains the same; but each ideograph is overlaid with three thousand years of experience and gestation." According to Arthur Waley, "the beauty of the original is bound up with the exact 'auras'—the associative value of the words used."

I agree, as anyone knowing the Chinese response to poetry would agree, that for the native who sees ideographs in print or in the air as he hears them, the underlying strokes vibrate like bracketed notes on a violin; but I still maintain, as I did when the idea was first broached to me of translating these chords or adumbrations, that in wording the enlargement there would be danger of overstress and overweighting. As Dr. Kiang Kang-hu commented when I showed him some early Ayscough-Lowell versions: "This heavy wording tips the poem over." I could not see—and thought my objection fair—that in relation to a poem as a whole the weight of Miss Lowell's phrase, "whirled water of meeting streams," improved upon the direct meaning, whirlpool. In fact I preferred the swift simplicity of the compounded English word. Should a Chinese in translating an English poem give the word breakfast its dictionary meaning, "the meal with which the fast of the night is broken," or expand daybreak into "the day breaking through the night"? For me the stretching out of the Chinese phrase into its ideographic parts definitely distorted its proportionate place in the poem for the sake of an interruptive quaintness. Would it help a Westerner's response to a Chinese poet's thoughts of home to have it translated according to the ideograph, a pig under a roof? (The two women apparently came later.) In the other direction why should what we think of with sufficiently exotic meaning as a phoenix be called a "silver-crested love-pheasant"?

Mrs. Ayscough was afraid of "the naked languages of Europe," too bare for her as compared with the branching jewel-tree words of Cathay. She resisted the fact, moreover, even when Chinese scholars affirmed it, that the words chosen by the T'ang poets were commonplace, colloquial. The Chinese are realists. She was a romantic. She never realized that the exactly fitting connection of commonplace words could make poetry. And Miss Lowell unfortunately acquiesced in the romantic turn. "It sounds pretty," wrote Miss Lowell, "these versions are attractive,"— "our elegant little nosegay." She might have been manufacturing Christmas cards. Both women condescendingly resented, in Arthur Waley's friendly and tempered review of their book, the reminder that "the colloquial of the T'ang dynasty differed very little from the language of poetry." When Li Po wrote about the clouds' resemblance to Yang Kuei-fei's robes, Miss Lowell with Bostonian precision had to uproot and specify the clothing as "upper garments" and "lower garments," apparently approving the fact that the ideograph meant total and not partial clothing. I grant fancy in the idea that varying clouds reflected varying colors or layers of clothing; but fancy is the very weakness from which T'ang poetry for the most part is free.

When I met Mrs. Ayscough in Shanghai in 1920, in spite of her avowed determination to be "discreet" (see below), she informed me of her purpose to search the roots "to their utmost forks" and to use the forks in English. I warned her of the danger of such ramification if put into English wording. She quoted Miss Lowell's agreement with her and I told her that I thought they were being industriously wrong-headed. I had no idea that I was giving grave offense. Mrs. Ayscough in Shanghai, Miss Lowell in New York and Boston, presented an impeccable front, granting me apparently my right to differ with them as to points in the technique of translation and seeming to welcome my zeal in our common wish to accquaint the Western world with

Chinese poetry. But this correspondence reveals pettiness going on behind the screen.

Since many pages of the book discuss me, I feel it only fair to quote a few of the passages for better or worse. Mrs. Ayscough to Miss Lowell: "Witter Bynner is working away in Peking. He is to be down here about a fortnight hence. . . . I shall be very discreet about our work." "Where, I think, he has made a mistake is in choosing an anthology. In the first place, three hundred poems ought to take him about three hundred years to translate. But the principal trouble is this: an anthology always represents the taste of the people who have picked out the poems, and, in the case of a Chinese collection, it represents the taste of scholars who have an entirely different point of view from ours.

"The result is that the poems Mr. Bynner has chosen are fearfully difficult, and complicated." "It makes me so angry to have him come out here and gallop through a T'ang anthology of three hundred poems. He simply can't do such a thing—as I told a little reportress." And Miss Lowell to Mrs. Ayscough, a cable to London: "Bynner has just published 'Hermit on Hill' in *Post*. Wish to answer in correspondence column with original text, your notes, and my version, and sign your name. Do you approve. Cable answer." (According to the book there was never an answer.) "I think it would be a great pity to track Witter Bynner's poems down with the purpose of showing him up. I think we had better ignore him entirely and go ahead with our own work. . . . There's one thing I wish you could find out, and that is something about the man who taught him, Dr. Kiang Kang-hu, because Witter Bynner is going round blowing like anything, saying that he had no idea until he reached China how highly his collaborator was considered there by scholars. . . . Also, can you not give me some sort of an account of Mr. Nung (Mrs. Ayscough's teacher) and make it sound as grand as possible —to show that we have a native Chinaman behind us, for in *Asia*, Bynner said that he did not believe that anyone, even though born in China, could really get the nuances of the poems, which

was, of course, an attempt to cut the ground under your feet. . . .
He throws round a lot of big names of people he met in China,
such as Dr. Hu Shih . . . Princess Der Ling . . . Dr. Ku Hung-
ming. . . . According to Witter, all these people have greatly
praised his work, which I can well believe, for they know nothing
of the English language . . . (*sic!*) What he says of Dr. Kiang . . .
sounds beautifully and may be true, but the position he (Kiang)
held here was in Berkeley, California, and not in one of the older
universities. . . . I think it would be a great mistake to pay any
attention to him (Bynner) whatever. I should merely like to
know these facts in order to punch his pretensions to powder
in case it may be necessary in private conversation."

I remember wondering why Miss Lowell—who used to call
me, I thought jovially, her "official enemy" because we differed
as to points in poetic technique—gloated so heavily when she
said in 1921, the year *Fir-Flower Tablets* was published, "We
have beaten you to it"; but I find running through this book an
undercurrent of the anxiety expressed in her exhortation to Mrs.
Ayscough, "Somebody will get ahead of us if we do not hurry."
Time and again in their letters both ladies seemed to think that I
was in haste. I venture in the light of 1946 to note that eight
years after 1921, years of incessant work, Dr. Kiang and I published *The Jade Mountain* and that twenty-four years after 1921
with the generous help of Arthur Waley and others it was issued
again, the sixth edition revised and improved. The ladies really
need not have hurried.

In 1922 Miss Lowell wrote: "Witter Bynner's book does not
appear, and I do not think it ever will. I think we have given him
a dreadful shock." In 1921 she had written, after an editor's suggestion, that I review *Fir-Flower Tablets*: "I was amused at the
idea of Mr. Bynner as reviewer for the book. I do not think that
he would have helped at all."

She had disliked a review of her book in *The Chinese Students' Monthly* and wrote the editor: "I wonder whether you
think such writing is liable to promote a pleasant feeling between
our two countries." And she wrote Mrs. Ayscough about a dismal

attempt to enjoy an evening with a Chinese professor whom she had bidden to her house: "I gave him a brief outline in my letter of the kind of thing I wanted him to answer without mentioning any specific things. It seems to have given the gentleman's feet chills. . . . I do not find it easy to understand these Chinamen; nor do they find it easy to understand me."

—Review of *Florence Ayscough and Amy Lowell: Correspondence of a Friendship*, edited by Henry Farnsworth MacNair, Chicago: University of Chicago Press. Published in *The Saturday Review of Literature*, March 30, 1946

Indian Drumbeat
in the
Southwest

· ❧❧❦❧ ·

To these skillful drawings and lithographs, John Collier contributes a text that describes the culture of the Southwest Indians as an example for our own materialistic civilization. John Sloan provides an introduction in which he says that the Indians' attitude toward art is traditionally nobler than ours.

Both contributors approach their subject with marked enthusiasm. Mr. Sloan remarks that "the first time I saw the Santo Domingo Corn Dance I felt the same strong emotion from the rhythm of the drums and primitive intensity of that age-old dance ritual that I experienced when I saw Isadora Duncan fill the stage of the Metropolitan Opera House with her great personality."

Miss Duncan may have known better than to say to Mr. Sloan, as she said to me years ago, that "no great art can grow in America, for the reason that no country breeds an art which has not been indigenous to its soil, and America's noise and dance-hops and bright lights are only the natural outcome of the tom-toms, crude hoppings and tinsel adornments of its Indians."

Mr. Collier's reaction toward this heresy would have been scathing, since he states that, "as old as mankind on our earth, . . . classic as Shakespeare almost never is, but as the Greek drama was . . . the sacred drama, at the core of Pueblo life, is a personality-forming, an educative institution, possibly without rival in the world of today."

It is interesting to find Mr. Collier—a former Commissioner of Indian Affairs—making an interpretation of that culture closely akin to D. H. Lawrence's. Mr. Collier sees the spirit of the Indians blending the "twin eternities" of past and future. Lawrence said: "Our immortality is not in the original eternity, neither in the ultimate eternity. God is the utter relation between the two eternities." One wonders in which man the conception arose first. Mr. Collier traces it back to Ceylon. Lawrence had recently come from Ceylon when he began interpreting our Indians to us.

Both men find that, after all, Atlantis is not lost—Collier perceiving, in the present text, that "these mountain heights of the sunken social continent still lift their pinnacles and domes in living air." And both men appear to be convinced that the best service later American civilization could give the world would be to let our ways go by and save the ways of the Indians of the Southwest.

Such rhapsodic faith as Mr. Collier's and Lawrence's is characteristic of converts. A Roman Catholic priest said to me once of Henry Harland, a convert: "He is more Catholic than he needs to be." And a Santo Domingo Indian confided, with an indulgent smile, as to Mary Austin: "She tells us what we believe—and we always say yes."

It is a stimulus, though, to encounter such fervor as Mr. Collier's, accompanying such drawings and lithographs as these by Ira Moskowitz, which are the body of the book. Mr. Moskowitz, living among Indians—Pueblo, Hopi, Navajo, Apache—made many straight-seen drawings of tribal types; and in his impressive lithographs, especially those depicting ceremonies where human figures combine with elemental background of earth, sky or fire, he has caught not static or merely decorative grouping but the very motion of Indian life infused with the flow of the natural world. To paraphrase Lawrence, one feels the drumbeat living in the stone.

Mr. Sloan's introduction concludes that this "work of a real artist, in a technique familiar to our European-trained minds, should do much to awaken our understanding of the Indian people."

—Review of *Patterns and Ceremonials of the Indians of the Southwest*, with drawings by Ira Moskowitz, text by John Collier, introduction by John Sloan, New York: E. P. Dutton & Company. Published in *The New York Times Book Review*, January 1, 1950

A Willa Cather Triptych

· ❧✦❀✦❧ ·

Of these three books dealing with Willa Cather,* E. K. Brown's, completed after his death by Leon Edel, the first in order of publication and of my reading, is, in my judgment, professorially full and orthodox like the chords of a church organist; the second, by Edith Lewis, Miss Cather's longtime friend and housemate, has the meager simplicity of a one-fingered melody heard from a determined child; but the third, by Elizabeth Shepley Sergeant, a writer better endowed and seasoned than the others, is played on the very air of the years through which these two gifted authors knew each other, sharing and comparing their interests, emotions and aspirations.

It is too bad that the three volumes all appear in 1953, since in large degree they have to repeat one another's objective data. The Lewis account, the shortest of them, was in fact prepared originally as material for Mr. Brown's, the longest; and I wish, since much of her text is quoted in his, that all of it might have been used there, that the two books had been made one from the start either through insertion of more passages from Miss Lewis in fitting order or through general collaboration. Even then, though Miss Lewis calls her record *Willa Cather Living*, the result would have remained, as each of the books is now, biography for libraries rather than for persons, for studious reference rather than for quickening warmth. In Miss Sergeant's record, on the other hand, history and environment come alive

---

* *Willa Cather, A Critical Biography*, by E. K. Brown, completed by Leon Edel. New York: Alfred A. Knopf, 1953. 351 pp. $4.00.
Willa Cather Living, A Personal Record, by Edith Lewis. New York: Alfred A. Knopf, 1953. 197 pp. $3.00.
Willa Cather, A Memoir, by Elizabeth Shepley Sergeant. Philadelphia: J. B. Lippincott, 1953. 256 pp. $3.50.

around and through a breathing figure, and Miss Cather's works also come freshly alive as they grew in their creator rather than through outer observation and opinion.

All three books narrate, in varying proportions, how their subject at the age of nine left her comfortable Virginian birthplace and its easy-going neighbors behind for Nebraska and its hard-going pioneers; how with this latter material which might have seemed bleak to someone else, she wrought many of her stories and novels, making lyrical nostalgic memories out of the prairies, and heroic figures out of the Scandinavian and other new neighbors whom she had seen face heavy odds and master them; how she went to school and college in Nebraska, contributed to student journals, sought out the most significant persons in Red Cloud, in Lincoln; how she moved to Pittsburgh, first as magazine contributor, then as schoolteacher, and found there wealthy friends who made life easier for her, with Mr. S. S. McClure soon doing likewise in New York through his eager liking for her work and for herself; then her welcoming of Sarah Orne Jewett in Boston as friend and literary influence; presently her trips to Colorado and New Mexico, from which was to come her memorable revival of the Archbishop; her fifteen years at Bank Street in New York with rental of an apartment kept empty overhead to exclude disturbing footsteps and with a return to the world of people on her Friday afternoons; her retreats to New Hampshire and to Grand Manan, her visits to Europe and especially to her beloved France; her love for Turgeniev, Tolstoi, Flaubert, Henry James and grand opera; her family ties and few close friendships; her growing resentment against the mechanization of modern life; and then, apparently because of deaths among her kin and friends and of a world gone wrong, the decline and withdrawal of her spirit.

As I read the Brown and Lewis books, I became more and more depressed and incredulous. This could not be the Willa Cather I had met and seen often in my early youth. Although she had seemed to me then a more calculating and ruthless person than was now being portrayed, she had also seemed a more intelligent and interesting one, whose life could not possibly have become as dry as these two biographers were making it. Brown had not known her; and among his pages especially the phases of her life lay like pressed flowers, with sap long gone and color dim. There were better specimens pressed in the second book; but from Miss Lewis, who had known her well, how could there come only this transcript of a life appearing for the most part dogged, dull, artificial? Where was the gusto, the joy, the warmth, the great joining with the will of spring, which must come again and again to anyone? Had this life been always literary, never wholly human?

And then I began Miss Sergeant's book—and here was the life I wanted to know about, here was "Willa Cather living," here was the person present behind the young woman I had met at the turn of the century. It is right enough for Miss Lewis to note, "She had a poet's attitude toward weather, to her it was one of the rich, contributive constituents of life," or to remark, "She loved people. She had a gift for immediately creating a personal relationship of some kind with anyone she met. . . . Perhaps it was her instant recognition of their common humanity, of the fact that their claim on life was equal to her own." Such statements unbacked are of as minor use to make a vital portrait as are Mr. Brown's documentations. But when Miss Sergeant speaks, it is not statement, it is occurrence. Miss Cather comes to life at the first meeting: "Her boyish, enthusiastic manner was disarming, and as she led me through the jostle of the outer office, I was affected by the resonance of her Western voice and by the informality of her clothes—it was as if she rebelled at urban conformities." And then: "The door closed behind us with a click bringing me face to face with an—adversary? In the sudden hush and aloneness, like animals in a wood, we stared, making the secret circle around one another. Was it the circle of acceptance? A lively sense of clash and curiosity rose between us like smoke from a new fire." And again: "This Willa Cather filled the whole space between door and window to brimming, as a man might do," which is better than Rebecca West's apt describing of the Cather quality as "mountain-pony sturdiness."

Miss Sergeant sees and easily describes the surface; she also sees through the surface into the nerves and thoughts of people and can express what she finds. Furthermore she not only makes her reader see with her but ponder on what is seen. Her writing echoes her subject and then echoes it again. Her portrait of Mr. S. S. McClure is both flesh and spirit. To anyone who knew Miss Ida Tarbell's "benign, searching look" the three words are as unforgettable as the three about Miss Cather's "blithe made-in-Nebraska look." And then the latter's "eye-in-every-pore quality that took possession of her when she was bent on her own ends." Again, "she slouched her hat farther over her eyes and sat there like a stone," and, concerning the retreats from New York to Nebraska or New Mexico, or from Nebraska or New Mexico to New York or Grand Manan, "she retreated obliquely." You feel the echoing pulses in Miss Sergeant's descriptions, her narrative; you feel them also in her generalizations such as: "Single women making their way to individual destinies—who in the home circle understands them? If they try to share what they have found in their further reach, who wants it?"

The fact that Miss Sergeant is not afraid to criticize her friend adversely now and then, to see weaknesses as well as strength, rather draws the reader to Miss Cather than estranges him from her. Midway in this third book I found myself wondering why I had remembered resentfully for fifty years Miss Cather's cold harshness in refusing to let us withdraw from publication, in *McClure's* magazine, "The Birthmark" which friends of hers assured us at a tense session with her in Mr. McClure's office might ruin the life, even by suicide as in the story, of another friend of hers and theirs upon whose disfigurement and dilemma it was based. I can hear her now, saying briskly: "My art is more important than my friend." The story was published; and friend, as well as art, survived. Miss Sergeant, though she has made no reference to this episode, has so presented and explained Miss Cather that my pity which had long lasted for the friend has shifted to the author.

It was soon after this point where I paused midway through

Miss Sergeant's book, the year in the record being 1920, that its luster began to fail for me, the fault not Miss Sergeant's, but Miss Cather's, for whom, as she herself confessed, the world then broke in two. For her feeling this breakage so deeply, Miss Sergeant suggests reasons other than the world's condition. Perhaps, she says, it was founded on the "poet's response to life, including the typical sense of the lyrical poet that youth and the emotions of youth, because of their great intensity and simplicity, surpass all other emotions. Yet," continues Miss Sergeant, "her ear seems very much less acute in poetry" and might have cited in extreme proof Miss Cather's comparatively youthful but certainly decrepit dedication in "The Song of the Lark."

> On uplands,
> At morning,
> The world was young, the winds were free;
> A garden fair,
> In that blue desert air,
> Its guest invited me to be.

Pursuing her theory that the break in Miss Cather's life came with realization of lost youth, Miss Sergeant quotes from her author a prose dictum on youth's fecundity: "The individual possesses this power for only a little while. He is sent into the world charged with it, but he can't keep it a day beyond his allotted time. He has his hour when he can do, live, become. If he devoted these years to caring for an aged parent—God may punish him but Nature will not forgive him." Not as if God had punished what became in Miss Cather actual filial devotion but as if her "allotted time" of necessary youth had passed, her biographer notes a "spring, now frozen over in talk by fame, or busyness, or just taciturnity," with the former fervors recurring but rarely. And a particularly pertinent and revealing memory follows: "I never heard the sound of a radio or a musical recording in her apartment and only once the sound of a spoken record. That was the romantic voice of Edward the Eighth, abdicating his throne for love." Miss Sergeant might have wondered if her friend were speaking truly when she said, "Life began for me when I ceased to admire and began to remember." Was it life that began then or a lonely kingdom? Elation only in memory is a single stirrup.

Miss Lewis says in her introduction: "I have written about Willa Cather as I knew her; but with the feeling that it is not in any form of biographical writing, but in art alone, that the deepest truth about human beings is to be found." She means, I judge, that Miss Cather's personality and life cannot be better presented than in the art of the author's writings, that art has reasons reason cannot know; which is partially but not wholly true. She forgets that there is an especial art in biography too and that the art of biography can sometimes by-pass the art of story-telling, that for rounded revelation of "the deepest truth" about himself or herself, one artist sometimes needs the presence of another. The fact that Miss Cather's will forbade publication of her letters indicates that she was shy of rounded revelation, that she may have been afraid of the littlenesses which make greatness and that she chose a mirror rather than welcomed the open sky to reflect the features of an artist's being. Her forbidding that her stories be used in films is a different matter, because such treatment would mean an outsider's tampering with something which, however ineffective, inferior or inconsistent, she herself had done.

Art, says Mr. Brown, "was early and late for Willa Cather the chief expression of her mind." After quoting from one of her earliest stories, which appeared in a Nebraska college journal in 1892, "When the moon came up, he sighed restlessly and tore the buffalo pea flower with his bare toes," and commenting with characteristic lameness, "The phrase is not satisfactory; but like many of the unsatisfactory phrases in *Endymion*, and for the same reason, it is full of promise," he quotes from an article printed the following year in the *State Journal* this "explicit statement of her conception of art": "The further the world advances the more it becomes evident that an author's only safe course is to cling to the skirts of his art, forsaking all others, and keep unto her as long as they two shall live. . . . An artist . . . should be among men but not of them, in the world but not of the world." Crudely expressed in her youth, this was a creed to which she adhered through her years. And yet she could write in 1913 about Isadora Duncan a passage which Mr. Brown quotes from *McClure's* magazine: "I agree with the New York reporter who in summing up Miss Duncan's dancing of *The Rubaiyat* said that on the whole he preferred Omar's lines to Miss Duncan's." Though droll from the New York reporter, this was not droll from Miss Cather, whose serious acceptance of grand opera antics makes the more ironic her dismissal of Miss Duncan's triumph over an ungainly body and a reluctant public, through superb art.

To the art in Miss Cather's volumes all three biographers give painstaking and reverent guidance. As to art in detail and in literary style, Miss Sergeant finds that the following passage from *O Pioneers* "evokes" Nebraska's "Divide" "imaginatively and sensuously" and "makes its symbolic image live for us unforgettably, as in a poem":

> . . . The furrows of a single field often lie a mile in length, and the brown earth with such a strong, clean smell, and such a power of growth and fertility in it, yields itself eagerly to the plow; rolls away from the shear, not even dimming the brightness of the metal, with a soft, deep sigh of happiness. . . . The grain is so heavy that it bends toward the blade and cuts like velvet.
>
> There is something frank and joyous and young in the open face of the country. It gives itself ungrudgingly to the moods of the season, holding nothing back. Like the plains of Lombardy, it seems to rise a little to meet the sun. The air and the earth are curiously mated and intermingled, as if the one were the breath of the other. You feel in the atmosphere the same tonic, puissant quality that is in the tilth, the same strength and resoluteness.

Though "as if the one were the breath of the other" is more to my taste than "with a soft, deep sigh of happiness," though I acknowledge Miss Cather's general success in making one feel the atmosphere of her country, and though the people who dwell in it are, I suppose, symbolized by the bodily terms of the writing, this elected passage does not strike me as being indicative of a great artist. It is not Miss Cather's individual style, nor any steady sureness of literary art, which for me makes her work memorable, so much as the cumulative effect of what she is writing about, be it places or persons, and in the long run— despite frequently inept expression—her ability to make that interest count. She seems to me in this respect, though not in what she has called "overfurnishing," to be like Theodore Dreiser. I prefer her naturalness to her "art," though I quickly acclaim both qualities when she gives the sense of a person's whole life in the final four lines of *Lucy Gayheart* or the presence of Nebraska earth and moonlight in a passage like this from the short story, "Two Friends":

> The road, just in front of the sidewalk where I sat and played jacks, would be ankle-deep in dust, and seemed to drink up the moonlight like folds of velvet. It drank up sound too; muffled the wagon-wheels and hoof-beats; lay soft and meek like the last residuum of material things,— the soft bottom resting-place. Nothing in the world, not snow mountains or blue seas, is so beautiful in moonlight as the soft, dry summer roads in a farming country, roads where the white dust falls back from the slow wagon-wheel.

When I first met Miss Cather, I had a quick sense that, though she was only seven or eight years older than I, her child-like smile was set, as by a jeweler, in an elderly, too authoritative face and that the elder would never let it go into a laugh or, on the other hand, feel it graven with tragic vision of magnificent darkness. I had a prescience that she took herself, not life but herself, too seriously to admit and enjoy the health of humor; and I still think that if she had maintained her childlike response to openness of countryside and people, to human mastery of circumstance and of self against raw odds, and yet at the same time been able to laugh down the world's mischief, as Chaucer or Shakespeare or George Meredith or Mark Twain laughed it down (but after all what woman?), she would not have felt in 1920 that the world had broken in two any more than it had always broken. No wonder she repined, the smile dead, the laugh unborn. Her own life, in her forties, was what was breaking in two, through inner rather than outer forces, and not so much with the passing of youth as with the discovery that even the finest art man could create would not be the entirety of his being. The world was not behaving for her as she had planned it. War and death and change had always been. The break in her own world was not due to repetition of chronic human tragedy, nor chiefly due to what Miss Sergeant defines as "conflict between the brave ideals of our pioneer ancestors and mounting materialism." It was due, I am convinced, to her middle-aged suspicion that if there had been less art in her life, there might have been more life in her art. About that art she continued to care deeply, rightly, and sometimes bitterly but seldom if ever with the healing humor which, better than any other gift except love or faith, makes one's proportion to the universe tolerable. Bare of humor, and with love hurt for her by time and death, she turned in her latter years to a given faith; but such faith apparently failed to warm her. And in her facing of disappointments, as Miss Sergeant says about the builder's death in *Alexander's Bridge*, "the great chorus of tragedy failed."

—Review published in *The New Mexico Quarterly*, Autumn 1953

PUBLIC
LETTERS

· ❧❦❧ ·

"Mrs. Warren's Profession"

· ❧❦❧ ·

To the Editor of *The Sun*—*Sir:* In contradistinction to letter writers mentioned by Mr. Daly, who have not seen *Mrs. Warren's Profession*, I hope *The Sun* will give me, who have seen it, space for an exclamation over the uproar brought about by this notorious performance.

What is there so much worse in the play than in *Camille*, for instance, *Zaza* or *Letty*? Why is there this sudden revulsion to righteousness on the part of the press and, in consequence, a deliberately perverted report of it for people who have not seen it, so that to one who has seen it the effect of the notices is of a whimsical, half hysterical conspiracy? The horror-stricken attitude of the press and Police Commissioner must be due not so much to the subject as to Mr. Shaw's methods or to his conclusions or to artificial stimulation of public opinion.

Mr. Shaw's methods are undoubtedly outspoken and unpleasant. In this play, as in none of his others which I have seen, there are sincerity and definite seriousness which make for him a more important position than could any amount of satirical tomfoolery. Without paradox, empty epigram, verbal somersault, except where it is in character, Mr. Shaw treats a grave subject gravely and plainly. His play is not so unpleasant as Ibsen's *Ghosts*; neither is it as deeply and terribly a tract. It is infinitely the hardest, most justifiable slap he has yet given the face of convention. It has little of his usual gay insinuation of moral indifference and none of the effect of an ingeniously arranged drill of iconoclastic tin soldiers. Ordinarily it amuses us to let ourselves be precociously amused by what he does with his tin soldiers. The result is that when he comes to talking sense and moral wisdom we judge him by the tin soldier standard and deny him the rights of free adult speech. We refuse to let him be serious. We insist on being amusingly shocked, and when the shock exceeds the amusement we throw up our hands and cry shame. But maybe it is Mr. Shaw's own fault, maybe in his crowded hour of glorious popularity he has cultivated us to be faithless to him when he shall write sense!

There is humor in *Mrs. Warren's Profession*, but it is grim and sanely based. This freedom of speech is not mere impudent and expert posturing; it is the downright just playing of a man who for once is in earnest.

It does not seem quite possible that the critics and the public could really doubt the terrible meaning of Mr. Shaw's play. The erroneous impression that he defends Mrs. Warren's calling is flatly contradicted by the tragic irony of the effect of her own defense of it. We see all her excuses at their best and then we see much more convincingly that not one of those excuses can prevent the influence of her life from being poisonous and devastating. Every apparent advantage she had gained by what seemed to her a logical sacrifice has turned upon her with venom. She has not only her past and her responsibility to remember, but has made normal human happiness an impossible thing for her daughter and has incapacitated herself for decent living, with no resource, no relief except the activity of continued wrong-doing.

I cannot understand why people who take honest exception to plays of this frank kind have not found in Mr. Pinero's *Letty*, for a recent example, a most pernicious, unwholesome piece of nastiness, as encouraging in its immoral influence as Mr. Shaw's play is blackly discouraging. *Letty* was practically a lesson to the working girl, showing her how far she could go and not have any harm come of it. Not only was there an actual scene of seduction, brightened with the glamour of romance, and containing minute instructions for the impressionable, but there was a damnable moral callousness throughout. Letty's escape from Mrs. Warren's profession was due not to her own principles, nor to the author's deep convincing of the hopelessness of the course she almost followed, but to the need of providing a gullible public with a fourth act wearing the guise of virtue. Implicit in the play was a constant sense of the lure and agreeable features of immorality, which to a really conscientious press and public no amount of fourth act attitudinizing and hypocritical smugness could have offset.

As for Mr. Shaw, not only does he make Mrs. Warren's kind of immorality, when he actually faces it, a deadly and abhorrent thing, blighting all possibilities of happiness; he also reveals, stripped of all its veils of tradition and general acceptance, the equal immorality of such human beings as maintain their respectability on the income which signifies exactly the same sin and suffering as the income with which Mrs. Warren educated her daughter. Not only Mrs. Warren's daughter, and the daughters of men like Sir George Crofts, but the daughters of all hard-brained "employers who pay women less than subsistent wages," are brought up and clothed in the profits of sin. This is an inevitable fact to be faced by the reformer. And this is the fact which Mr. Shaw in *Mrs. Warren's Profession* has preached with a sincerity, vigor, essential cleanness and unpleasantness which have brought the magpie press chattering about his ears, and consequently, as it might not otherwise have done, offended "a hasty, unintelligent and easily duped public conscience."

If there be general public objection to this play, and I'm not so inclined to believe that as is Mr. Daly, the objection is due more than anything else to the "artificial chafing" by the press.

W.B.

—*The New York Sun,* November 5, 1905

Harvard Halls

· ⚡︎〰︎⚡︎ ·

Editor, *Harvard Alumni Bulletin:*

As a Harvard graduate, I ask leave to protest in the columns of the *Bulletin* against the refusal by the acting authorities at Harvard to grant the request of an earnest body of Harvard undergraduates to be allowed, in accordance with precedent, the use of one of the Harvard halls, to hear a distinguished speaker.

Only a few years ago Sanders Theater was judiciously opened to students and the public for a lecture by an eminent American actress. Today it is closed, partly on the grounds of sex, to a noted English reformer.

Whatever may be thought of the methods of the English Suffragettes, the result of their agitation has been an impetus to the cause of Equal Suffrage not only in Washington and California but all over the world; and wherever their leader, Mrs. Pankhurst, has been heard to present her case, disgust has given way not perhaps to sympathy but to understanding and respect.

Mrs. Pankhurst, on a brief visit to the United States, had shown the Harvard Men's League for Woman Suffrage a great courtesy and rearranged her plans to comply with their request that under their auspices she give an address to Harvard students. The action of the authorities in refusing a hall to the Harvard Men's League seems to me not only to be discourteous, ill-advised and unfair, but to justify, in this particular, Harvard's name as a closed shop.

At Cornell last winter Dr. Anna Shaw, President of the National American Woman Suffrage Association, having been given the use of one of the University halls for a lecture, had to march across the campus with her overflowing audience to the largest hall in Cornell. I was myself in that audience; and it was easy to see hundreds of fellows who had gone to the lecture with one idea of the subject come away with either the opposite idea or with a realization of its being a serious, two-sided question.

I cannot do better than to quote the memorable words of Wendell Phillips in his address delivered in Sanders Theater, "The Scholar in a Republic," probably of all addresses ever delivered there the brightest and best.

"Timid scholarship," said he, "either shrinks from sharing in these agitations or denounces them as vulgar and dangerous interference by incompetent hands with matters above them— it shrinks from that free speech which is God's normal school for educating men, throwing upon them the grave responsibility of deciding great questions and so lifting them to a higher level of intellectual and moral life. Trust the people—the wise and the ignorant, the good and the bad—with the gravest questions and in the end you educate the race. Men are educated and the State is uplifted by allowing all—everyone—to broach all their mistakes and advocate all their errors. I urge on college-bred men that as a class they fail in republican duty when they allow others to lead in the agitation of the great social questions which stir and educate the age."

Very truly yours,

Witter Bynner, '02

—*The Harvard Alumni Bulletin*, November 29, 1911

"Tiger"

· ❧✠❧ ·

To the Editor of *The Forum*

Dear Sir,—Last May you had the courage to print "Tiger" in *The Forum*. Its theme since then has been variously used in longer plays, it has appeared in book form, been barred from sale by the Comstocks of Boston, been played by students before members of the Dartmouth College Faculty and by a professional cast at the Little Theater in Philadelphia. Though most of the critics have treated it with understanding and sympathy, it has received, as was to be expected, a certain amount of censure. And I ask leave, in the magazine which first published the play, to make briefly an accumulated reply to its official and unofficial censors.

"Tiger" has been referred to as a "white slave play" at a time when platitudinous people are obscuring the question with that easy quibble, "There is no such thing as white slavery." Whatever may be the fact as to an organized ring of kidnappers or system of procuring girls against their will, it is an indisputable fact that there are enough girls in the business of prostitution who have been betrayed into it by individuals and forced to remain in it by society to justify the use of the term "white slavery." And it is this wider kind of white slavery which "Tiger" symbolizes. I am careful to symbolize it fairly by including Annabel, corrupt and more or less contented. The trouble with the sentimentalist who declares prostitution to be a picturesque affair and no particular hardship to most of the girls concerned is that he finds in the type, Annabel, an excuse for him to believe as he comfortably prefers to believe. He prefers to say, "A white slave is a girl living in seduced circumstances," and to treat the whole situation as a joke and a convenience. The theorist abets him by insisting that virtue—even at five a week—is not only its own reward but its own protection. And the vacuist tries his best to draw into his vacuum not only vice, the dust, but knowledge, the floor. What I venture to suggest to this group, to the anti-suffragist, to the feudalist generally, is that, in my reading of Christ, we are all "members one of another," responsible to one another and eventually identified with one another. Objection to the coincidence in the play, that of a father meeting his own entrapped daughter in a disorderly house, is of no validity against the meaning of the coincidence in this essential tragedy of prostitution: Lust demanding and Greed supplying us with members of our own human family.

By some critics, by poets especially, I have been taken to task for telling the story of "Tiger" in blank verse. I started to write it in prose, but I soon found that the narrative in prose would require a more detailed account than I should need to set down in verse. I found that the verse carried in its rhythm an edge of artistic suggestion which gave a truer effect than I could accomplish by the accuracy of prose. It was the same picture; but the verse heightened and yet softened it, like a carbon enlargement. I suspect that had I given the characters in the play the distinction of title or removed them to Persia, there would have been little or no objection to my use of blank verse; its heroic associations would not have been soiled. Certainly I have not written heroic blank verse in "Tiger." It is rough, disjointed, sometimes almost syncopated. But running through it, here and there audible, I hope, is something of the rhythm of beauty, just as something of the grace of life runs through the Tenderloin.

Witter Bynner

New York

—*The Forum*, April 1914

The Imagists

· ❧❁❧ ·

I wish I could honor the Imagists as you do. Hueffer wrote "On Heaven" (not imagistic); and Pound wrote well before he affected a school . . . Pound has a rhythm he can't kill. But none of them, except Hueffer, says anything worth mentioning. They build poems around phrases, usually around adjectives. George Meredith has thousands of imagist poems incidental to each of his novels. But he knows their use and their beauty. These people wring tiny beauties dry. I can imagine a good poet using their methods on occasion, but he wouldn't be so damn conscious about it. On the whole, the Imagists strike me as being purveyors of more or less potent cosmetics, their whole interest being in the cosmetic itself, not even in its application. Poetry gave signs of becoming poetry again and of touching life—when these fellows showed up, to make us all ridiculous.

Witter Bynner

Windsor, Vermont

—*The Little Review*, August 1915

Pacifism

· ❧❧❧❧❧ ·

To the Editor of *The Tribune*

Sir: Answering Mr. Berton Braley, as well as those of my critics who would rather reason through the spleen, let me resume point by point:

1. I am not protesting that at this stage of civilization the war was avoidable. But now that we are in it I am urging that, contrary to the Prussians, we should add to the use of arms the use of brains. The advance of Prussianism is only half with their swords; it invades us daily through our own minds. Just so the defeat of Prussianism can be only half with our swords and half through German minds. No, I have not forgotten the *Lusitania*, the *Arabic*—nor the *Maine*; but I should rather be thinking forward than backward, thinking as decently and constructively forward as I can. A German Mayor of Chicago is preferable to a Prussian Governor of Illinois.

2. I am not proposing peace with "a man-eating tiger." I am urging peace with the German people—precisely what the President urged in his note to the Pope.

3. I am not asking for the exposure of military secrets. I am urging the open statement of general war aims and rejoicing that the United States has defined its purposes.

4. I am not counseling "obscenity," "grossness," sedition or treason. I am urging fair play for people whose views seem to me to be merely more like those of one set of respected citizens than like those of another set of respected citizens, more like those of H. G. Wells, Charles W. Eliot, Hiram Johnson and Woodrow Wilson than like those of Cleveland Moffett, Elihu Root, William Hohenzollern and Theodore Roosevelt.

5. I wish Mr. Braley had not made it seem, by the use of quotation marks, that I spoke of our government as an "irresponsible government." I did not. I clearly applied the phrase to the German government. And I am not opposing majority rule. I am only urging people against such Prussian folly as military or police suppression of law-abiding minorities.

In conclusion: I am not with the People's Council in their present fight against conscription. I am not with them in their effort, if such it be, to stop the war without restoration or internationalization of invaded territories (including, if possible, Bosnia, Herzegovina, Alsace and Lorraine, as well as the German colonies), without reasonable reparation of damage, and without a responsible pledge of future peace, made through the military and naval disarmament of nations and through the establishment of an international police force. But I am with them to the extent of believing that a clean peace and the safety of democracy should be kept in our minds, not only after the war but during it, with as much friendliness toward the peoples we are fighting as is compatible with or conducive to the attaining of those purposes. And I cannot feel that our official persecution of reputable citizens presenting reputable views is likely to advance those purposes, whether here or in Russia or in Germany. I judge of the views of the People's Council, not from the flippancies of a reporter, but from their Chicago resolution and the planks of their platform as printed in *The Tribune*. And I cannot see that they have done anything toward embarrassing our government in the prosecution of the war comparable to certain efforts by officers of the Navy League.

I make the following final points, because a reasonable human being is liable these days to misrepresentation: I am not a spy. I am not in the pay or employ of the German government. I am not pro-Prussian. I am not and never have been a member of the Socialist party. I am not Irish. I am not a bigoted pacifist.

In fact, my nearest approach to political bigotry is my admiration for President Wilson, whose leadership has been from the beginning a leadership of the minds rather than of the sensations of the American people.

Thanking you, sir, for your willingness to print both sides.

Witter Bynner

New York

—*The New York Tribune*, September 11, 1917

Out of the Bag

· ✄✄✄✄✄ ·

Editors of *Poetry*:

In your June issue A.C.H. contends that "*Spectra*, then, proves nothing against the method of free verse as such, though it may hit off very cleverly some of the practitioners thereof." May I call the attention of A.C.H. to the fact that all but one or two of Emanuel Morgan's contributions to *Spectra* are what might be called "rhymed jingles," and to this paragraph from the book's preface:

> Emanuel Morgan . . . has found the best expression of his genius in regular metrical forms and rhyme. Anne Knish, on the other hand, has used only free verse. We wish to make it clear that the spectric manner does not necessitate the employment of either of these metrical systems to the exclusion of the other.

Our intent in publishing the book was not to question the use of free verse and not to "bait the public," but to satirize fussy pretense; and if we have in any degree focused laughter on pomp and circumstance among poets we shall have had enough satisfaction in our fun. I frankly admit that my approach to the game may have been with an excess of impatience, but I ask you if it is not true that I who came to scoff remained to play. Having given vent to Witter Bynner's irritation at smug and pedantic pretenses, Emanuel Morgan soon found himself a liberated identity glad to be agog with a sort of laughing or crying abandon, of which, in other poets, the New England soul of Witter Bynner had been too conscientiously suspicious. And so I am eager for a chance in the pages of *Poetry* to make amends

for whatever may have been unworthy in Witter Bynner's intention and manners, and to thank the editors of *Poetry, Others,
The Little Review* and *Reedy's Mirror* for their encouragement.

After various inaccurate and unjust statements in the press,
let me say here accurately and justly that I think now of my
later work even better than you do, that I count on having the
readers of *Poetry* place my hand in yours when they read the
group of my verses you have accepted, and then place your hand
in mine when they read, if they will, my new volume, *Songs of
the Beloved Stranger,** which I am going to publish not preten-
tiously but seriously, and well aware of the likelihood that some
of the critics may mock it according to their cue.

Yours more than ever,

Emanuel Morgan

Note by the Editor: Thanks for your thanks, Emanuel! But has
Poetry ever printed you? or so much as mentioned *Spectra*? It
was a pleasure to "accept" the poems of so clever a joker, but
why all this hand-clasping?

But don't be proud—don't quite obliterate Mr. Bynner!
Have you read Mr. Arthur J. Eddy's tribute to you and Miss
Knish in *Reedy's Mirror*? "Believe me," he says, "they are not
half bad! . . . No one can read them without being instantly
impressed with the importance of the so-called burlesques as
revelations of the *real* Bynner and the *real* Ficke—and if all the
'poems' are as good as the few printed in the *Times*, delightful
revelations they are of two personalities who are betrayed to be
more human, more natural, more hail-fellow-well-met than their
serious verse indicates them to be. And by conventional standards their serious verse is good—good but *conscious*, while their
burlesques are the gleeful outpourings of their unrestrained—
say boyish—selves. Their burlesques are their own while their
serious verse is largely *literature*—traditional. How true this is of
Ficke's sonnets—many of them fine—attempts to cast the

---

* Published as *The Beloved Stranger* (1919).

thoughts and feelings of an Iowa lawyer (a good one) in Roman mold! Admirable, as attempts, but why try to fit the youth, the surge, the radicalism of America into the most rigid of antique armors?

"I should say both Bynner and Ficke simply 'broke loose' in their burlesques and, for the *first* time in their lives, abandoned their literary pose under the cover of pseudonyms, just as many another man has been able best to express himself anonymously."

—*Poetry*, August 1918

Confessions

· ❧✣✣✣✣✦ ·

Dear Fanny Butcher: In asking me what book I would rather
have written than any other, you probably expect me to name
a book of poems. You might shrewdly have guessed *Leaves of
Grass*. For a long time I have enjoyed the sense, which Whitman
cannily imparts, of being a personal element in his book. In
his large way he draws me, with unnumbered readers into his
consciousness, into his power, almost into his identity. If you
make me name verse, I shall say, then, *Leaves of Grass* is my
book, because of the whacking great pulse of it, the magnificently
delivered ego, the vibrant circumferences. It is especially comfortable in this moment when literature is petty and querulous,
to be with a spirit who knew how to accept the universe and
how to phrase his acceptance. When Margaret Fuller said "I
accept the universe," Carlyle remarked, "By gad, she'd better."
Whitman accepts the universe not because he had better, but
because he just does. In spite of his occasional pettiness, that
rocking chair of his in Camden covers more leagues than an
airplane. In a way, the old boy is, himself, the universe.

But you have not obliged me to name a book of verse; and
I am almost surprised to find myself answering your question by
naming, instead of poems and plays, or any of the formal kinds
of literary art, a book of letters.

Over the figure of George Meredith rests a temporary
shadow. Nervousness is more in vogue than emotion, cleverness
than beauty, irritation than content. But when the clouds clear,
the mountain will be there. Besides having enlarged English
literature with the ripest and richest style since Shakespeare,
Meredith has offered, it seems to me, the noblest and soundest
creative counsel in English for thoughtful spirits. Full as his
novels are of wisdom and of wit, glittering with a million

imagist poems, concentrating into luminously human men and women, yet in none of them has he let shine so clear as in his letters that "celestial sunlight of the mind."

In a poem of mine written the year his letters were published, I called them "high hearted." That adjective, better than any other I might summon, expresses the quality of the man which makes me wish I might have been able so to set myself down, for my friends and for later readers, as a man who had learned "to see life steadily, and to see it whole."

Even in the dull and stilted early letters of Meredith, when considered with the masterly messages that came later, there is a solace. The stature of Whitman was fixed, immutable, magnificent.

To have written a part of the Bible? To have been mistaken for God?

I should rather have written *The Letters of George Meredith.*

Sincerely yours,

Witter Bynner

—*The Chicago Tribune,* August 11, 1923

A Few Pointed Questions—
A Snappy Comeback

· ✄✗✗ ·

A FEW POINTED QUESTIONS FOR MR. WITTER BYNNER

In view of the stand taken by Mr. Witter Bynner, one of the Democratic candidates for the legislative house from the county of Santa Fe, in favor of the Hannett program, policies and methods, and in view of the high importance and responsibility of the position of member of the law-making body of the state of New Mexico, it seems timely to address some questions to Mr. Bynner on the issues of the campaign.

These include, of course, the tariff question; the matter of the administration of the bonded indebtedness of the state; the matter of collection of delinquent taxes; the police power of the state; the election code; the Rio Grande compact with Colorado; and other vital issues.

The *New Mexican* will take up these outstanding matters in the order given, with a view to getting Mr. Bynner clearly on record so that the taxpayers of Santa Fe county may know exactly how he stands, and if elected what may be expected from him in the way of support of legislation of this or that type, which will affect the interests of his constituents, along with the interests of the remainder of the 350,000 people of New Mexico who will be affected by his vote in the state house of representatives. It is only fair to the people that Mr. Bynner should answer specifically the questions asked, without evasion or indirection. . . .

—*The Santa Fe New Mexican*, October 22, 1926

SNAPPY COMEBACK BY BYNNER ON 6 QUESTIONS

To the Editor

Dear Sir:

The *New Mexican*'s six questions, addressed to me as a candidate for the Legislature, seem to me to have almost as little to do with real issues of the campaign as the bulk of the *New Mexican*'s political comments during the past month or two. Nonetheless I shall answer to the best of my ability.

1. "For the protection of home industries, where does Mr. Bynner stand on the question of Oriental labor; more specifically what tax does he regard as proper to be imposed in Santa Fe on Chinese laundries?"

Velly Good!

Orientals are universally known as hard workers, as giving always a full measure of labor. From that point of view, perhaps the *New Mexican* in using the term "Oriental labor," refers to the devoted and unsparing labor of the present Democratic administration for the public good. My answer is that I would protect it at any cost from the danger of being interrupted by accidental labor on the part of Republicans.

As to "Chinese laundries," I am not quite sure of the queue, but I approve of any business that makes for cleanness.

2. "Is it public policy to bond the taxpayers of the state for support of barber-shops?"

Check!

Not believing in a poll tax, how can I believe in a barber-pole tax? I do believe in cutting hair, in cutting taxes and in almost any kind of cutting, except dates and Bronson.

3. "Does Mr. Bynner favor the placing in the hands of the district attorney or special attorneys employed by the state the matter of collecting of delinquent poets' licenses?"

Bull's-eye!

I believe that the license of delinquent poets is a negligible issue in Santa Fe county, as compared with the license of delinquent editors. License taken with fancy is a light matter compared to license taken with fact.

4. "Will he vote in favor of a law regulating and restricting, and calling upon the governor to enforce such regulation, restriction and limitation on the Santa Fe style in clothes?"

I believe in individual freedom as to dress—but not as to overdress, at least in public. I would impose no limitation on clothing, nor any restriction on personal adornment, whether Pueblo or Kiwanis.

5. "Should the Rio Grande compact be inlaid with mother-of-pearl, or passementerie, and is it in the public interest that white or flesh colored powder be used?"

Gunpowder?

As a politician I am not interested in trimming. If you imply that the Rio Grande compact is a skin-game, then gunpowder might be appropriate; but I believe that the latter should be used as seldom as possible.

Biff!

6. "Where will Mr. Bynner stand on the proposed election of David Lawrence as poet laureate of Santa Fe?"

Please name me the disloyal citizen who proposes that one of the highest offices in America should be given to a foreigner.

Noting once more that the *New Mexican*'s six queries seem to me as wide of the mark as most of its political observations, I turn to some of the incidental and preliminary challenges, which come somewhat nearer:

Fair Enough, Hal

As to the election code, I shall have plenty of time, if elected to the legislature, to study this joint nonpartisan recommendation of Republicans and Democrats and to vote for or against any amendment to it which any Republican or Democrat may offer, in the place where it will properly come up for discussion and action. I am sure that the Republicans who helped frame the proposed code know as well as the Democrats that the Constitution of New Mexico prevents any "disfranchisement," and I feel proud that most of the attacks against the Hannett administration have been on this unreal and ridiculous issue, proving the complete hollowness of the Republican opposition.

As to the collection of taxes, my common sense as a layman would advocate definite notice mailed to each taxpayer, telling him how much this tax is and when it is due. I say this, because I am in a fog as to what I myself may now owe, in spite of having made both written and personal inquiry.

As to the tariff (on which the New Mexican legislature votes so often!—and yet I am grateful for the chance of a word concerning it), I am against a tariff drawn for the further fattening of interests already too fat; I am against the kind of tariff the Republicans always enact, a tariff calculated to increase dividends to the rich and costs to the poor.

With thanks to you for asking my opinion on these latter questions, and with confidence that you will give my answers as conspicuous a place as you gave your inquiries, I am,

Very truly yours,

Witter Bynner

—*The Santa Fe New Mexican*, October 26, 1926

Bynner Urges President-Elect to Put Al in Cabinet

· ❧❦❧ ·

Dear Mr. Hoover:

In greeting you as our new president selected by a majority of the American people, I venture to urge upon you a step which may already have occurred to you as characteristic of yourself in the role of an American rather than in the role of a Republican. Not only did you receive a record Republican vote; Gov. Smith received a record Democratic vote. In spite of press verdicts as to "landslides," the result was more an electoral than a popular phenomenon; and Gov. Smith stands beside you today as a second figure unprecedentedly beloved, honored and trusted by the American people.

Would Create Precedent

One of the outstanding attributes in your own career is your indifference to party as compared with principle. And I adjure you, in many more names than my own, to consider whether or not you who whole-heartedly and usefully served Woodrow Wilson might as whole-heartedly and usefully be served by Alfred Smith. You yourself have notably refrained from be-littling in any way Governor Smith's superb record as a public servant. You are not only with Woodrow Wilson in recognizing Smith's statesmanlike qualities but with Charles Evans Hughes and other Republicans. Why not, then, create a vigorous, human, honest and influential precedent in our politics by appointing Governor Smith to a cabinet post, possibly secretary of the interior, and win, not only by so generous a gesture in politics but by so deserved a rebuke to bigotry, unending respect?

Please present my regards to Mrs. Hoover and believe with her that this letter is written in a conviction that its rightness will appeal to you beyond any partisan superstition. I trust that you will not mind my feeling the suggestion pertinent enough and patriotic enough to be made an open letter.

Sincerely yours,

Witter Bynner

—*The Santa Fe New Mexican*, November 17, 1928

"Not a Drop to Drink"

· 〰〰〰 ·

"Religious groups have unjustly and bitterly fought against the right of the people to express its voice in this matter," says Witter Bynner of Santa Fe, replying to a letter from Miss Adela Holmquist of Albuquerque attacking his position in the state prohibition controversy. Miss Holmquist's letter was published in the *New Mexican* and Bynner's reply follows:

March 4, 1931

My dear Miss Holmquist:

I have read your personal letter to me in the matter of the referendum and reread it as published in *The Santa Fe New Mexican*. With all deference to the sincerity of your motives, I am not in the least convinced by your arguments.

In the first place, you argue entirely away from the point, which—since I concerned myself not with the dispensary bill but only with the referendum—was the question whether or not the people of New Mexico have a right to speak for themselves on as important a question as prohibition. The contention that it had once been decided argues that people do not develop in 14 years. It argues also that a voting population of 40,000 at that time should govern the present voting population of 120,000. These arguments seem to me undemocratic and untenable. And it is in this connection only that I attack ministers as reflecting discredit on the church. Not only in states but nationally, religious groups have unjustly and bitterly fought against the right of the people to express its voice in this matter. There is every indication that the majority of Americans are convinced of the failure of prohibition. Ministerial groups, as a whole, seem determined to prevent that majority from expressing itself.

Such an expression, to be sure, would have no immediate

effect. It would, however, strengthen the growing number of legislators, both at Washington and in the states, who are shifting from myth to common sense.

I am not in the least opposed to ministers exercising their rights as citizens or as heads of institutions to influence and persuade the people on the actual case of prohibition. I noticed last night in a magazine that the Rev. Randolph Ray, rector of the Church of the Transfiguration in New York, has said: "Prohibition or censorship in the hands of the state immediately becomes a political matter, is very badly administered, and my observation has been that it is always a failure." Dr. Ray has as much right to his judgment as any of the ministers who arrived here the other day from Albuquerque, and I know that there are a great many of the clergy who agree with Dr. Ray. I do not think, however, that Dr. Ray would oppose the right of the people to pass judgment in the matter.

Selfish Arguments

Since you devote your arguments entirely to prohibition per se and not to the point in question, I beg also to suggest that your arguments are on the whole the selfish ones of your own case under present conditions. Because you do not encounter drunkards on the streets of Albuquerque, or over-gay parties at tables near yours in restaurants, you go counter, it seems to me, to the best advised judgment from all over the country as to the results of prohibition. Although the Wickersham commission advocated attempts at enforcement—this presumably because of the administration pressure, I beg you to note the following passages from its report:

"Organized distribution has out-stripped organized enforcement"; "enforcement is not reaching the sources of production and distribution so as to materially affect the supply." The commission points out the absolute necessity of obtaining "full, voluntary cooperation between state and nation but it recognizes that this involves the expenditure of large funds by the states and that this cooperation can only be obtained by a complete change in public opinion." "From the beginning ours has been a government of public opinion. We expect legislation to conform to public opinion, not public opinion to yield to legislation." "It is axiomatic that under any system of reasonably free government a law will be observed and may be enforced only when and to the extent that it reflects or is an expression of the general opinion of the normally law-abiding elements of the community." "From its inception to the present time, the law has been to a constantly increasing degree deprived of that support in public opinion which is essential for its general observance or effective enforcement."

Thanking you for letting us hear your private opinion,

Very truly yours,

Witter Bynner

—*The Santa Fe New Mexican*, March 6, 1931

"Young Harvard"

· ❧❈❧ ·

My dear Miss Matzen:

"Early Struggle for Recognition as a Poet?" I do not remember that I thought much about that, feeling too much absorbed in what I was writing. Of course, when the first book appeared, called now *Young Harvard*, but called then *An Ode to Harvard*, I was anxious to have it right. The publishers sent it about to eminent persons in this country and England; and praiseful responses from such poets as William Butler Yeats, Edmund Clarence Stedman, Alfred Noyes, A. E. Housman and Louise Imogene Guiney, put enough heart into me at the age of twenty-five so that I have not cared very much since then what might be said about my later work. In fact, the only person for a poet to please, is himself. As soon as he does that, the rest is so much velvet. How I might have felt about it if I had not received prompt recognition from the only persons whose judgment I valued, I do not know, nor how that circumstance might have affected the advice you ask me to give to young poets. As it is, the only advice that seems to me of much importance is that the young poet write things he believes in and in his own terms. I should say to him also, to be very wary of academic influences, to look out against becoming imitative of the established poets, especially of poets who wrote in language belonging to other periods than his own.

Now that more attention is being given than heretofore, in preparatory schools and colleges to the work of contemporary writers, it is not so bad for a young poet to follow models; but the essential business of a young poet is to face the theme which he wishes to express, with no literary influence intervening between it and himself—to express it and himself just as straightly and natively as he can. I might add that it is important for a young poet either to have an income at the outset or to assure himself of livelihood through some other occupation than writing. There is a reward in poetry, but it is not financial.

Sincerely yours,

Witter Bynner

—*The Plotweaver*, May 1931

Red Hearing
Is Postponed

· ❦❧❦❧ ·

Pair Arrested Holding Meeting in Plaza
Will Go on Trial This Afternoon

Three self-professed Communists, who spoke in the Plaza Saturday afternoon, will be given a hearing at 5 p. m. today in the
justice of the peace court of Judge Berardinelli at the jail. The
charge is vagrancy, which covers a wide range of offenses as
described in Section 35—3813 of the Code of 1929.

The defendants are Carl Howe, Juan Ochoa and Harry
Managenis. Howe was at Gallup during the coal strike and later
came to Santa Fe, addressing a meeting held some months ago at
Gonzales Hall, on the Camino. Ochoa is from Old Mexico, and
Managenis is a native of Greece.

The arrests were made Saturday by order of Chief E. J.
House of the state motor patrol.

The case was set for yesterday afternoon but the failure of
two witnesses for the prosecution to be present at the jail when
the hearing opened, caused Judge Berardinelli to order a post-
ponement.

As the hearing began, Howe stated that he and his companions expected to ask for a jury trial. He added that he thought
they were entitled to a jury trial "if our liberty is at stake." He
asked for a copy of the complaint and Judge Berardinelli replied: "The charge is vagrancy."

The defendants were released in the custody of Witter
Bynner, poet and writer, and resident of Santa Fe.

Several writers and artists were at the jail, seeking an opportunity to attend the hearing.

They Had a Permit

The Communists contend that they spoke Saturday in the Plaza only after a permit had been obtained from Mayor Barker, that the meeting was orderly, and that after it was over, they offered for sale literature entered as second or fourth class matter by the U. S. post office.

Mayor Barker says that he issued a permit, but the permit distinctly stated that the speakers would have to abide "by the law."

Group Protests Holding Three on Vagrancy Charges

A protest has been filed with the attorney general against the detention of three Communists who were arrested here Saturday on a charge of vagrancy.

The protest is as follows:

We, the undersigned citizens of Santa Fe, vigorously protest the unwarranted detainment in the Santa Fe county jail of Carl Howe, Harry Managenis, and Juan Ochoa, on July 21, 1934; and we ask in the future a guarantee and reaffirmation of the constitutional rights of all citizens, as written in the Bill of Rights of the Constitution of the United States, of free speech, free assembly, and immunity from unwarranted search and seizure—which we feel have been inexcusably withheld on this occasion.

Signed by: Joe Fresquez, Vivian Dunton, Helen N. Mc-Crossen, Rose A. Mora, Frances N. Gutierrez, Cuca Dominguez, Nabor Archuleta, Mrs. Gonzales, Ann Webster, Marjorie Thirer, Paul Lantz, John Flanner, Andrea Asbjornsen, Joe L. Servin, Willard Nash, Witter Bynner, Robert Pfanner, Philip Stevenson, George McCrossen, Anne Pfanner, Gladys Stevenson, Alberto Ortiz, Lloyd A. Lauer, Robert Hunt, Jesus Pallaris, John Gould Fletcher, Henry Schmeltzer, Ernest Knee, Edith Nash, Helen

Cramp McCrossen, Preston McCrossen, Hellen Cunningham, Lura Oak, Catherine Gay, Forrester A. Blake, Ivan Dunton.

—*The Santa Fe New Mexican*, July 24, 1934

To the Editor
The Santa Fe New Mexican
Santa Fe, N.M.
Dear Sir:

Inasmuch as in *The Santa Fe New Mexican* we were mentioned together with Philip Stevenson as unavailingly interested in releasing the three Communist speakers from jail on Saturday night, and inasmuch as one of us gladly took them into his custody the next day until they should have their hearing on Monday, and inasmuch as both of us appeared with sympathy at the hearing on Monday and at the postponed hearing on Tuesday, noting each time that the witnesses for the prosecution were curiously absent, we would like to make a brief joint statement to the effect that unlike our much admired friend, Philip Stevenson, we are neither of us in the slightest degree Communists. We happen, on the other hand, to be human beings and as such to resent the fact that these three speakers were arrested through the instigation of someone apparently afraid to back his charges. According to the admirable statement of Judge Berardinelli when the case was dismissed for lack of evidence, the defendants, representatives of an accredited political party with as much right to present their case as representatives of any other party and with a definite permit from the mayor to speak on this occasion, had made, as far as the judge could learn, no illegal appeal, been guilty of no disorderly conduct, or done anything that any self-respecting citizens might not do to advance their political opinions. In common decency we stood by them; and we feel it to be a pity that they are not financially in a position to bring charges against the mysterious person or persons who unjustly caused their detention for a night in jail.

Yours very truly,

Witter Bynner
Willard Nash

—*The Santa Fe New Mexican*, July 26, 1934

SFAA

· ❊❊❊❊❊ ·

Editor:
The Santa Fe New Mexican
Santa Fe, New Mexico
Dear Sir:
While I was away in Mexico, I was asked to join The Santa
Fe Arts Association and did so with hopeful purpose. I believed,
and still believe, that active organization by artists may mean to
them material benefits offsetting to a certain degree disservice
done them through diversion of their energy from devotedly individual practice of their arts. I believed, and still believe, that
a guild combination of artists or craftsmen on an honest and
nonpolitical basis has come to be in this modern world, for a
while at least, a proper and necessary procedure to safeguard
their interests for general economic advancement; but I am convinced, by what I have noted of the activities of this particular
organization to which I might conceivably adhere, that my
adherence would be disloyalty to what I consider the interests of
either art or intelligence.

Uninformed of the exact qualifications for service by writers
or artists under the WPA, and closely aware only of what is
happening here in Santa Fe, I cannot feel: (1) That, for the
WPA, work done or offered should be work unsatisfactory to
the responsible administrators; (2) That the personnel doing the
work should be dictated by a self-appointed group of persons
almost completely misrepresentative, not only of art in Santa Fe
but of residence here; or (3) That there should much longer be
any such work done at all.

In view of the fact that I am a writer with an income independent of my writing, I speak with a natural discomfort
about the status of writers or artists less fortunate than I. None-

theless I affirm that an artist should prefer receiving relief from the government, if he needs it, on an economic rather than on an artistic basis; I register my protest, both as an artist and as a political liberal of long-standing (regardless of what that term may mean to persons not seasoned into liberalism) against governmental discrimination which provides bounty in favor of artists above or below any other group of citizens, and I assert my opinion that financial favor to this special interest is doing even less good morally to the individual artist than it is aesthetically to the public. An instance in point, as regards the moral effect, is the claim of newcomers in Santa Fe to benefits which, if they should accrue at all, should accrue to established residents. In the present agitation by The Santa Fe Arts Association I see only new evidence that the whole policy of special privilege to artists, any more than to plumbers, is mistaken, undemocratic and dangerous.

I urge that the government should bounteously employ good artists, and I grant that most artists consider themselves good; but I maintain that the measure of such employment should, for the general benefit, be the best possible gauge of merit and not a gauge of economic need. Artists and writers in need should, apart from the normal laws of preference which apply as well to art as to industry, take their respectful place in line with other respected people and be treated on an equal basis with those others.

I happen to know that one of the protestants in outcry against the present local administration of largesse to artists, though represented as dependent upon strangers for payment of his grocers' bills, has neglected for some days even to acknowledge offer of employment which would take care of him adequately. I happen also to feel that the kind of employment offered him—and let me add that he is a very recent arrival in this region—would be of more benefit to him, and therefore to all of us, than any post to which he might be appointed under the WPA.

In view of what seems to me a disingenuous and unworthy attitude on the part of an apparent majority of my fellow-members, the remedy for which should be abolition of special privilege to artists, I hereby make public my resignation from The Santa Fe Arts Association if I am a member with dues paid —or, if I am a member with dues unpaid, my resignation with responsible acknowledgment of my dues to date.

Very truly yours,

Witter Bynner

—*The Santa Fe New Mexican*, March 16, 1937

Rich vs. Poor

· ❦❧❦❧ ·

As a North American who has lived in Mexico from time to time for twenty years, I have submitted to officials in Washington, and should like to submit to your readers also, a suggestion concerning the serious economic state here and our relation to it.

It has been reported recently that the cost of living in the United States has risen 24 per cent since Jan. 1, 1941, and food prices 46 per cent. In Mexico food prices have doubled and even tripled within a year and are causing among the poor acute hardship. While the rich flourish because of new industry and widening activity for export, the poor—despite slightly higher wages—keep asking the eternal poser for economists: "What does more money amount to when it buys less food?" A very grave aspect of the stringency is a widespread and resentful impression, with due blame for profiteers in Mexico, that the United States is callously absorbing Mexican necessities—its import of cattle and hogs, for instance, speeding up the cost here of meat, milk, lard, and leather. And it is wondered why we should be taking basic necessities out of a country where the increase in cost of living is almost ten times greater than it is north of the border and far greater than that in proportion to wages.

Is my lay mind too simple when I ask if our government might not declare its willingness to put the good-neighbor principle into needed practice; its willingness to arrange with the Mexican Government that further importation of foodstuffs and other basic necessities be suspended at least until such time as the rise in cost of living is approximately level in the two countries?

Witter Bynner

Chapala, Jalisco, Mexico

—*Newsweek*, August 16, 1943

E. P.'s Shadow

· ❦❦❦ ·

Chapala, Jalisco, Mexico

To the Editors: Your October 20 and November 10 issues arrived here together, bringing at the same time the Ezra Pound article by Oliver Evans and the letter of protest against it from J. J. Cohane.

Having known Pound and watched his career from the earliest days, I cannot see why the Evans estimate is not a square statement of opinion, besides being intelligently and ably written. Credits and debits are both there and, to my mind, are presented without wartime prejudice. If Pound is out on a limb in limbo, he asked for it, it is to his taste and, if I know him at all, he can take it. Surely not "tragedy" to him, Mr. Cohane, just experience—and perhaps fame.

Witter Bynner

—*Commonweal*, December 22, 1944

The New Atom

· ❧❧❧ ·

Dear Sir:

Although the Chamber of Commerce has sent its members the following communication from a group which is initiating the Santa Fe Citizens' Committee on Atomic Information, I wonder if you will not circulate it in your columns to help notify Santa Feans of an important occasion and opportunity: the open meeting at Seth Hall, Saturday evening, December 8th, at 8:30, when several of the distinguished scientists from Los Alamos will speak and answer questions. Those of us who attended the preliminary meeting at the Laboratory, where facts were presented in terms laymen could understand and where counsel was given with impressive earnestness, came away clarified and moved.

The members of the Chamber of Commerce, the churches and the various organized civic, professional and social groups in Santa Fe are invited to join a townwide Citizens' Committee on Atomic Information to cooperate with scientists at Los Alamos in spreading here and elsewhere knowledge of the potentialities of nuclear energy and quick search for the best and most constructive method of controlling it. It is said that most of the scientists at Los Alamos, as well as throughout the country, are convinced that the solution and safeguard for ourselves and all civilization is international control, while many laymen and scientists feel that the present form of control is for the best. These men, with their common sense, are aware that lack of international cooperation may mean international suicide, but their hopeful human spirit, racially composite and decent, and their belief that this world deserves to continue living and to become harmonious inspires them in their belief.

It might be if our government had not heeded Albert Einstein's letter in 1939, warning us that Germany was already blocking exports of uranium from Czechoslovakia and was intending control of uranium deposits in the Belgian Congo, and if scientists had not persuaded the government to set up in June 1940 its Office of Scientific Research Development, that very few American citizens would be existent today and be privileged, as we are, to receive similar warnings even more urgent and portentous. We Santa Feans who have long been mystified neighbors of these men should now be their usefully respectful associates, should be promptly and proudly active in impelling for them as immediate and wide a hearing as their knowledge, their eminence, their record and their grave warning demand.

Witter Bynner

—*The Santa Fe New Mexican*, December 5, 1945

String Too Short
to Be Saved

· ❧❦❧ ·

SIR: Noting among "Letters to the Editor" objections to Lin
Yutang's statement that "the material must be the basis for the
spiritual well-being" [*SRL* Aug. 26], I am reminded of a remark
I heard more than once years ago from Dr. Anna Howard Shaw,
who was not only a suffrage leader but a Methodist minister and
a Christian wit, to the effect that in the Lord's prayer ". . . give
us this day our daily bread" precedes ". . . forgive us our trespasses. . . ."

It seems to me that Mr. Lin is making a point which not
only Americans but perhaps others in the world might need to
hear. A great part of the basis of modern life is material waste.

I remember well the satisfaction we children used to feel in
New England when we carefully untied all string which came on
packages and wound it carefully on little wooden shafts for
future use. We even spread out the flaps of envelopes and twisted
the resultant paper into neat squills, which stood in a little vase
on the mantel over the fireplace, later to be lit from the embers
and used instead of the old fumacious sulphur matches. The
whole accent of life and activity was on preservation and use,
and the good business of our fingers helped considerably not
only in keeping children happy but in ridding our elders of
wasteful or harmful thoughts. When people waste substance, as
they so largely do in the world now, the step is short toward a
psychology where the waste of life seems a natural part of the
world's order.

Westerners would do well to give a more attentive ear to
the soundness of Eastern thought as it comes to us through Mr.

Lin's balanced mind. I grant that wasting of life has occurred on a stupendous scale in the Orient, the reasons being obvious; but I maintain that happiness or serenity of spirit has widely survived in the Orient because of its being partly based on such material measures as Lin Yutang recommends.

Witter Bynner

—*The Saturday Review of Literature*, April 30, 1950

ESSAYS
AND
OCCASIONAL
PIECES

The Spectra Hoax

The Spectric School
of Poetry

· ❧❦❧ ·

ANNE KNISH AND
EMANUEL MORGAN*

The Vorticist School of poetry died an ignominious death in
London, snuffed out by the explosion of the war. This was no
great loss, because the experiments of this school, though interesting, were actuated by a wrong theory of poetic expression.
These writers underestimated the amount of clarity which even
the most daring poetic sketches must have; as a result, their
works hardly resembled human speech.

The Spectric School has tried to avoid this pitfall which
menaces all really original poets. Even in its most novel efforts
at advancing the frontier of the known world of poetry, it has
retained a measurable degree of communication with the world
of everyday speech. It has done this in spite of the fact that it
was engaged in working out a theory that might easily have
led to excesses of abstraction.

The theory of the Spectric School is not difficult to grasp
if one comes to it with an open mind. Its formula divides itself
naturally into two propositions, alike in essence but different
in application.

The first of these propositions affects the mental attitude of
the poet in so far as he is a perceiver of objects and a recipient
of impressions; the second affects him in so far as he is the

---

* These are the pseudonyms used by Arthur Ficke and Witter Bynner in
their hoax, Spectra.

portrayer of objects and the creator of expressions. We may take them up separately.

Every object, scene, person, and episode of the human world is to be regarded by the Spectric poet as a concrete focus of infinities. The subject of every Spectric poem has the function of a prism, upon which falls the white light of universal and immeasurable possible experience; and this flood of colorless and infinite light, passing through the particular limitations of the concrete episode before us, is broken up, refracted and diffused into a variety of many-colored rays. Some one of these rays will impress the poet more than others; and he will necessarily color his whole poem with its hue. But in so doing—and no amount of care can enable him to do otherwise—he must, if he is to create a fine work, have regard for the fragmentary nature of his perception, and allow his creative imagination to indicate some relation between his limited and single-colored vision and the great stream of pure light from which the vision originally was separated. As is said in the preface to the forthcoming book *Spectra*, by Emanuel Morgan, the discoverer of the theory, and Anne Knish, "the theme of a poem is to be regarded as a prism, upon which the colorless white light of experience falls and is broken up into glowing, beautiful, and intelligible hues." This preface omits to point out the fact that the poet must by means of his reconstructive vision bring to the reader some hint of the original light in all its completeness. Spectrists, however, are putting this extension of the theory into effect.

The second proposition of the Spectric School relates to the method of expression; and involves some consideration of the psychological processes by which the mind forms images of the outside world. The senses, and the mind behind them, act to a certain extent as a prism in relation to the emanations of the physical world. Vibrations of sound, color, or heat impact upon the sensory nerves, are conveyed in the form of a totally different kind of vibration to the brain, and there become once more transformed into some variety of emotion or motor impulse. Thus a flower, when it reaches the conscious intelligence via this devious channel, is no longer the flower of the outer world; it is the plexus of a number of different impressions. Just as a beam of white light breaks up in passing through a prism, and becomes a spectrum, so the entity of the flower is dismembered when it enters the consciousness. We perceive the color, the qualities of its form in space, the scent of the pollen and the stem, its coolness and smoothness and softness to the touch, its faint rustle as the wind stirs it. Out of these elements the mind, behind the prism of the senses, must recombine by another act of the intelligence the parted rays, in order that it may grasp the unity, the white light, the Platonic Idea of the original flower.

In art, particularly in poetry, it is a great gain to be clearly aware of these facts, and to take conscious advantage of them. This is the aim of the Spectrist. He tries, not to give the flower in its original unity, which is impossible, but to make perceptible the various rays, the various elements, out of which the perceiving mind would have, in the case of an actual first-hand perception, to create its idea of the flower. Or, to choose a more complex example, if he wishes to describe a landscape, he will not attempt a map, but will put down those winged emotions, those fantastic analogies, which the real scene awakens in his own mind. In practice this will be found to be the vividest of all modes of communication, as the touch of hands quickens a mere exchange of names.

The Imagists, suicidally advertised by a concerted reciprocal chorus of poet-reviewers, might once have been capable of employing this very theory in a tentative way. The time is past, however, when Spectrists can hope for cooperation in this quarter; and the latest of the modern movements in poetry must be content to go its own way after the fashion of "the spear that knows no brother."

Opus 181
Anne Knish

Skeptical cat,
Calm your eyes, and come to me.
For long ago, in some palméd forest,
I too felt claws crawling
Within my fingers. . . .
Moons wax and wane;
My eyes, too, once narrowed and widened.
Why do you shrink back?
Come to me: let me pat you—
Come, vast-eyed one . . .
Or I will spring upon you
And with steel-hook fingers
Tear you limb from limb. . . .
      There were twins in my cradle. . . .

Opus 45
Emanuel Morgan

An angel, bringing incense, prays
Forever in that tree;
I go blind still when the locust sways
Those honey-domes for me.

      All the fragrances of dew, O angel, are there;—
The myrrhic rapture of young hair,
The lips of lust;
And all the stenches of dust;—
Even the palm and the fingers of a hand burnt bare
With a curling sweet-smelling crust,
And the bitter staleness of old hair,
Powder on a withering bust.

The moon came through the window to our bed.
And the shadows of the locust-tree
On your sweet white body made of me,
Of my lips, a drunken bee.

O tree-like Spring, O blossoming days,
I, who some day shall be dead,
Shall have ever a lover to sway with me.
For when my face decays
And the earth molds in my nostrils, shall there not be
The breath therein of a locust-tree,
The seed, the shoot of a locust-tree,
The honey-domes of a locust-tree?—
Until lovers go blind and sway with me—

O tree-like Spring, O blossomy days,
To sway as long as the locust sways!

—*The Forum*, June 1916

The Spectric Poets*

· ❧❧❧ ·

There is a new school of poets, a new term to reckon with, a
new theory to comprehend, a new manner to notice, a new
humor to enjoy. It is the Spectric School; composed, as far as the
present publication goes, of a man, the cornerstone, and a
woman, the keystone—Emanuel Morgan and Anne Knish. In
the preface to the volume just issued under the title *Spectra*,
Anne Knish refers to "our group"; so that I suppose we shall
soon be hearing the names of other members of the spectric
edifice. Meantime we must be content with the rhymes of a
"founder" and the free verse of an "interpreter."

The term "Spectra" obviously means poems written according to the spectric theory and manner, poems which these
two authors, after the fashion of composers, see fit to number
confusingly, "Opus" this and "Opus" that. Their theory is as
heavily presented by Anne Knish as if she were a graduate of
some German university. Perhaps her birth in Hungary accounts
for the effect. Here is a summary of the preface. The theme of
a poem is a spectrum through which all the light there is
separates into rays, then recombines or focuses into a certain
concentrated point of something or other in the reader's brain.
It's a case of seeing the point. The complementary vision in the
eyelid, "after the exposure of the eye to intense light," is called
spectric, "the after-colors of the poet's initial vision"; and still
further use is made of the term in the sense of spectral, "the
spectres which for the poet haunt all objects." In other words,
the apparently unrelated impressions reflecting through a theme

---

* In an essay also published in this volume, "The Story of the Spectric
School of Poetry," Bynner describes how he came to review his own hoax
for *The New Republic*.

or idea may be artfully enough selected or directly enough recorded, without the conventional mental or verbal bridges, to reproduce, in the reader's mind, their effect in the mind of the poet.

It may be that the Spectrists are offering us a means toward the creation or understanding of the essential magic of poetry. Their attempt, at any rate, goes deeper than the attempts of any of the other latter-day schools in that it cuts under mere technique. Not that we fail to welcome dusters of technique or to realize that the Imagists' insistence on natural cadence and clear-driven expression is a salutary insistence. But we are always looking for something inside technique, something to hold and keep. And, though the Imagists seem to be surviving the Chorists and the Vorticists, yet I feel sure that they will not count so much in themselves as in their jacking-up of the technique of poets through whom vibrate richer matters than the tickling of a leaf on a windowpane or the flickering of water in a bathtub. The Imagists note with admirable accuracy all sorts of small adventures of the nerves, but very seldom for me relate those adventures to heart, head, and—or even stomach. They don't connect. They give the heightened, localized nervous sensations of a sick-bed, as though all the faculties were paralyzed except a finger-tip or one eye or one ear. Perhaps, without them, we should not have had the group of poets represented in *Others* who, to me, show more interesting vigor, even though most of their experiments are in gayer vein than those of the Imagists. The Spectrists, true to their expressed plea for humor, often share this gayer mood with the Kreymborg poets; as, for instance, in Morgan's "Opus 104" or Knish's "Opus 118."

Opus 104
Emanuel Morgan

How terrible it is to entertain a lunatic!
To keep his earnestness from coming close!

A Madagascar land-crab once
Lifted blue claws at me
And rattled long black eyes
That would have got me
Had I not been gay.

Opus 118
Anne Knish

If bathing were a virtue, not a lust,
I would be dirtiest.

To some, housecleaning is a holy rite.
For myself, houses would be empty
But for the golden motes dancing in sunbeams.

Tax assessors frequently overlook valuables.
Today they noted my jade.
But my memory of you, escaped them.

But on the whole these later comers bring to the "new poetry"
a quality it had rather lacked. They have more than fancifulness
to add to discernment: they penetrate the surface with a curious
vibrancy of imagination. Many of their poems, such as the
Morgan poem on war ("Opus 29") and the Knish poem on the
Greek vase ("Opus 135") are strangely, richly and memorably
done. "Madagascar," as it happens, is one of only two done in
free verse by Morgan.

What little we are told of the poets personally, is that they
are now Pittsburghers, that Anne Knish had lived till lately on
the Continent and has written a volume in Russian, and that
Morgan, an American, had been for years painting in Paris before
his hand was turned to poetry through Remy de Gourmont, to
whom *Spectra* is dedicated:

To Remy de Gourmont

> Poet, a wreath!
> No matter how we had combined our flowers,
> You would have worn them—being ours. . . .
> On you, on them, the showers—
>   O roots beneath!

Perhaps a wider experience of life and of media has made the Spectrists' ability in English verse more flexible and more potent than that of the other poets we may compare with them. Certainly their theory demands an art not stopping short with direct notation by the senses, but reaching connotation of all kinds. And they are ambitious, without being too solemn!

If I have overestimated the importance of *Spectra*, it is because of my constant hope that out of these various succeeding "schools" something better may develop than an aesthetic dalliance of eyeglass and bluestocking. But, whether or not there be meaning or magic in the book, I can promise that there is amusement in it and that it takes a challenging place among current literary impressionistic phenomena.

—*The New Republic*, November 18, 1916

The Story of the Spectric School of Poetry

· ❧✖❧✖❧ ·

In answer to many inquiries, I set down this brief story.

In 1914 when the poetic world was being stirred and amazed by the vagaries of various "schools" such as the "Imagist," "Vorticist," etc., I found myself feeling not only skeptical but resentful. There had been a widespread revival of interest in poetry, in response to a remarkably fine output of verse by the soldier poets. The public was recovering from the distaste it had felt toward poetry on account of fantastic and dubious excesses in the nineties. Everything was set, it seemed to me, for the coming of a period when a very large audience would be soundly and properly interested in poetry. Then came the interrupting antics of the more bizarre aesthetes.

Partly because of irritation, and partly out of amusement, I had the idea at the back of my head that anyone with a comparative knowledge of poetic diction and technique could play any sort of prank he liked with verse, talk about it sententiously and get away with it. This thought grew into a resolution. I decided to found, under cover, a school of verse and to have fun with the extremists and with those of the critics who were over-anxious to be in the van. I needed a name for the school; and it happened that on the way to visit Arthur Davison Ficke in Davenport, Iowa, I stopped at Chicago and saw the Russians give a ballet called "Le Spectre de la Rose." The suggestiveness and fitness of the word Spectral or Spectric flashed over me. Between Chicago and Davenport, I wrote the first few Spectric poems; and within ten days after I had reached Davenport, and Ficke had kindled to the idea, we had written nearly all of the poems which were later collected in the volume *Spectra*, and many others which were a bit too wild for inclusion.

The method of composition was simple. Sometimes we would start with an idea, sometimes with only a phrase, but the procedure was to let all reins go, to give the idea or the phrase complete head, to take whatever road or field or fence it chose. In other words it was a sort of runaway poetry, the poet seated in the wagon but the reins flung aside. Some of the results seemed so good to us that Ficke and I signed, sealed, and filed a solemn document swearing that the whole performance had been done as a joke. I see now that in some respects this method of letting the subconscious do the writing was not an altogether bad method. In fact, leaving the jocose intention aside, I employed the method later in writing the poems in *The Beloved Stranger*.

With only three persons in the secret, the manuscript of *Spectra* was submitted to Mitchell Kennerley who promptly accepted it. Not long after, proofs of the book were lying on my desk at Cornish, New Hampshire, when the editor of one of our leading weeklies chanced upon them and became enthusiastic about the poems. To cover my confusion I told him that Mr. Kennerley had sent me, with an idea of my reviewing it, an advance copy of this work by the founders of a new school, Anne Knish and Emanuel Morgan, which were the names Ficke and I had chosen for disguise. The editor at once asked me to let his journal have the review. I accepted and at about the time the book was issued, *The New Republic* printed my article giving the new poets an astonished, amused, but respectful send-off. With few exceptions, critics and reviewers took the book seriously, many more of them praising than damning it. Poetry followers all over the country responded to it with zeal. Magazine editors accepted Spectric poems. Ardent enthusiasts bought many copies for voluntary distribution, and the Spectric School had become an established institution alongside the schools it secretly parodied. Its vogue indeed was so great that Ficke and I were put to it to conceal our friends Miss Knish and Mr. Morgan from the pursuit of newspapermen. The two new poets moved about from place to place, always eluding on some pretext or other the inquisitive interviewers. We had of course to let one or two others into our game: friends who in cities remote from our own dwelling places conducted a considerable correspondence. We would write the letters and our friends would sign and post them. Among the hundreds of congratulations we received there was one from an American poet, as well known as any, which told us "whereas the Imagists merely prick at the surface, you probe to the core." Ficke and I threw dice all afternoon to see which of us should be the owner of that letter. I won the throws and highly value the document.

Demands for Spectric verse became so insistent that we decided to enlarge our school. Oddly enough, the particular trick of writing Spectric verse proved not so easy. Somewhere I have a sheaf of poems from the late George Sterling who was let in as a disciple, poems which, after all, by common consent had to be excluded from the Spectric output. The only one of several poets who caught the trick, and that after weeks of arduous and determined labor, was Marjorie Allen Seiffert who joined the ranks under the pseudonym Elijah Hay, and was soon involved as we were in considerable and sometimes embarrassing correspondence as a Spectrist.

Alfred Kreymborg told me one day at lunch in New York that he had persuaded the Spectrists to compile an issue of his magazine *Others*. Illuminating my vague knowledge of the group, he told me of friends of his who knew both of the founders, and assured me with a real gleam in his eye that Anne Knish was a great beauty. The poems which the three of us contributed to *Others* were even more extreme than those in the volume, were in fact somewhat calculated to give the secret away to the knowing, but the Spectric vogue had taken too firm a hold. It seems incredible now, when one looks at that issue of *Others*, that readers could have taken the verse seriously. On the other hand, it was no worse nor wilder than pieces solemnly offered by many an Imagist.

One of the strangest episodes connected with the hoax happened in Paris in 1917, when Ficke was a Lieutenant-Colonel. An officer who had been ordered to the front came to Ficke and confided to him that on the eve of possible death he thought he ought to leave behind him announcement of the authorship of *Spectra*. By word of mouth to Ficke and also in a sealed envelope he claimed the authorship as his own.

Although there had been a number of leaks, the hoax was still holding water two years after the appearance of the book, but maintaining it was growing more and more difficult. It broke finally and publicly in Detroit. In the course of a lecture I was giving there on modern American poetry, I touched as usual on the Spectric School. A man in the audience rose and interrupted me with a direct challenge as to whether or not Ficke and I had written the poems. A direct and large lie was too much for me. To the huge amusement of the audience, I thereupon told for the first time the complete story.

Many a discerning critic of poetry is convinced to this day that, liberated by our pseudonyms and by complete freedom of manner, Ficke and I wrote better as Knish and Morgan than we have written in our own persons. Once in a while we think so ourselves.

—*Palms*, March 1928

Poet to Poet

· ❧❀❧ ·

I have been asked what living poet has most influenced me in my work. I can answer, without hesitation: Witter Bynner. This may seem strange to some of my more impatient fellows. It does seem strange to Mrs. Knish, the most interested adherent of the Spectric idea, who contends that Mr. Bynner's forms are old-fashioned, that he seldom shows a glimmer of the principles we are advancing in our book, *Spectra*, that he has in fact publicly questioned and even belittled our writings. I answer that my admiration for his work does not depend on his for mine and that it is not for him but for us to apply our principles and prove their validity. And I answer finally and in a word that if *The New World* is old-fashioned, so is any classic. I remember in his early volume, unprepossessingly called *An Ode to Harvard* and published nine or ten years ago, a poem, "The Fruits of the Earth," written in excellent free verse. I point to "Tiger," in which Mr. Bynner broke ground for the unhindered use of colloquialism in verse and was much criticized therefor. I instance his *Iphigenia in Tauris*, marking a line of cleavage in English between the old-fashioned literary translation and the new-fashioned human translation. And even in such of his lyrics as the magazines print—he owes the public a volume of short poems—I find a simplicity, a reality and, above all, an artful modernity, definitely characterizing him among his contemporaries. But it is for something more than form that I owe acknowledgment to Bynner. It is for poetry.

By all odds his major poem is *The New World*. It may well have taken him the five years to write, which the publisher's note indicates. For there is something rare if not unique in American literature: a long subjective poem, sharply human, presenting—oftener through autobiographical narrative than by pronouncement—a deeply evolved philosophy of life. Whitman's *Leaves of Grass* gathered the manifold experiences of life into a book of poetry, a number of poems related to one another not so much by order or art as by spirit. Greatly he commingled and enumerated and luxuriated. He was not only a great lover, he was a great artist: especially in his painstaking adjustment of words, a far greater artist than most of his readers will allow or guess. Let them compare passages in the various editions he revised and watch through form after form the fluctuant true evolution. Witter Bynner, a patent and avowed follower of Whitman, proves himself in *The New World* not only an artist in the arrangement of words into rhythmic and magical sentences: he has mastered in this sixty-page book the arrangement into a single poem of most of the experiences and meanings of a life. Through his love of "Celia" he quickens his own perception and mine of the love of God. In fact he shows in Celia, or in the woman you or I love, the everlasting mother and maker of God. He overturns theology. Through beauty to the heart of man he reveals the divine creative impulse as the one fact which beyond all peradventure we know to be God. And into that creative impulse he receives all the power and glory and tenderness of the dead, illuminating through their intimate presence and vitality the miracle blindly apprehended by the old theological phrase: "dying in the Lord." All life, as Bynner sees it, is part of a process which is creating God. The poet forsakes the ancient lazy absurdity that out of Perfection, out of an absolute Godhead, can come imperfect life. He ignores that other absurdity, that an apparent imperfection is disguised perfection; he does not need even to intimate that the creation of beings so imperfect that they cannot understand the perfection of God is nothing at all but God's own vicarious imperfection. He glorifies with paeans of beauty the new consciousness of God, which embraces and explains all the woe and all the wonder of the human adventure. If this is not poetry, I do not know what is.

Most of us come and go, idling and repining. But the poet who comes and stays brings with his gift of beauty almost always a healing touch and a quickening vision. Who in America since Walt Whitman has made life sing to its very core as it does in *The New World*? This is no "idle singer of an empty day," but a seer of visions, a prophet of joy!

And though I cannot always keep high courage burning in my heart—as perhaps he cannot always in his—let me at least bring to the altar of his ministry my tribute and my laughter, my praises and my poems!

—Unpublished manuscript, signed "Emanuel Morgan," in the Houghton Library, Harvard University

Pueblo

"From Him That Hath Not"

· ❧❦❧❦❧ ·

Tomasito Benavides, a young Indian from the pueblo of Santo Domingo, New Mexico, stood recently before a Chinese painting of a hunt which hung in the Santa Fe Museum. After a quiet survey of the various figures, some of them horsemen, Tomasito turned and said: "There is much grass in China." And when I asked why he thought so, he explained: "Fat horses."

Over eight thousand Pueblo Indians live in New Mexico, scattered among their twenty adobe villages—their pueblos. While New Mexico was still old Mexico, each of these villages was the center of approximately a seventeen-thousand-acre patented land grant from the Spanish crown, a grant subsequently confirmed by the Mexican Republic. After this northern part of old Mexico became the Territory of New Mexico the American Government, in 1848, guaranteed to the Pueblo Indians the validity of all their land grants except the grant centering around the pueblo of Zuñi, which for some reason was not recognized. The Zuñis, a branch of the Pueblo tribe, are therefore living on a Government Reservation, like Indians in other States; but all the rest of the Pueblos, unlike Indians anywhere else in America, are living on land which belongs to them in their own legal right.

I have seen in Santo Domingo one of the canes which were presented by Abraham Lincoln to the various Pueblo governors when the Spanish and Mexican grants were made supposedly firm under American law. It seems, though, that a cane may be a solider thing than a scrap of paper. It seems that the American Government, in dealing with the Pueblo Indians, has cared very little about its word.

For three-quarters of a century the Pueblos have been asking that Washington keep its word and prevent the steady illegal encroachments upon their territory. So little has it mattered to Washington that there are today several whole towns of Americans on Indian land in New Mexico. Much of this old mischief cannot now be undone without grievous consequences, but new mischief can be obstructed and recent mischief remedied. A few Americans, acquainted with this dishonorable history, undertook a while ago in and near Santa Fe a public defense of the Pueblos, a defense which ought to have originated in Washington.

An Indian from San Juan, learning of the efforts of these citizens to bring about even a lame and belated justice, exclaimed, sincerely: "I did not know we had a single friend in New Mexico!"

The New Mexico Association on Indian Affairs consists, not only of New Mexicans, but of many now from outside the State who, like myself, have come into touch with the Pueblo Indians and by the threatened passage of the Bursum Indian Bill have been made to realize with a shock the ignominious cruelty of the American people toward its wards. Other societies have arisen East and West. The press has responded vigorously, and the public is waking up.

To the eye of a casual observer Indian territory looks large on the map—large enough, it would seem, for a vanishing race.

Let it be said at once that the Indians are not numerically a vanishing race. On the contrary, their number has increased during the last decade. Culturally they are being hard pressed. They dare to differ; they dare to ignore our mechanical standards; they dare to maintain customs and privacies we do not understand; they dare to be simple, to be natural, to be sincere, to be religious; they dare, in New Mexico, to find happiness under a communal system of landownership. And by all these offenses they have earned hitherto a passing glance from American tourists, a compassing glance from American capitalists, hostility from American hypocrites, contempt from American puppets, and, worse than all, deliberate betrayal or careless neglect from the expensive officials appointed to guide and to guard them.

Even culturally speaking the Pueblos might not be a vanishing race were it not for their vanishing land. Statistics are as dull as sermons, but briefer. Here, then, are a few, with chapter and verse.

First, a hint of what had already happened to Pueblo lands in New Mexico before the Senate passed the Bursum Indian Bill:

San Juan's 4,000 irrigable acres had been reduced by encroachments to 568, so that the total average cash income and value of product there per capita per annum for its 431 inhabitants is about $32. Contrary to general opinion, the only governmental addition to this meager livelihood is the tutelage, board, lodging, and clothing of schoolchildren. It may be added that San Juan is better situated as regards land and water than any of the Northern Pueblos save Taos, and one of only two or three which have had enough, or nearly enough, water for their lands this season.

Tesuque struggles along on an average income of $16.68 for the year, with practically all its irrigation appropriated by non-Indians.

The average annual income per capita in San Ildefonso is $13.11! Of the 12,000 acres granted to the San Ildefonso Indians in 1680 there are about 1,250 productive acres. The Indians have been left of these only 248 acres. In all, outsiders hold 3,500 acres of the best cultivated and pasture lands belonging to the San Ildefonso Pueblo. Only a day or two ago I was welcomed into some of the new houses which these gentle and gifted people are being obliged to build outside their own town, relinquishing their beloved plaza and its great cottonwood tree to the invaders.

At Nambe only 280 acres of the 3,000 irrigable acres of Indian land are now held by Indians.

These various lands were lost to the Pueblos in various ways. Sometimes there were conflicting grants from Spanish or Mexican authorities or squatter claims antedating 1848; but oftenest trespass and theft came about more simply.

Let John Dixon, an Indian Judge at Cochiti, tell in his own

way what happened to the people of his pueblo. "When the Navajos came here to fight and steal because they were hungry, my people took in Mexicans to help protect them. The Mexicans say, 'Let me have one little room for my wife and family.' Then, 'Compadre, could you not let me have a little lot for a little house?' 'All right, compadre, you build a little house.' All the Mexicans, they just came in that way—did not buy. Then he would move, and sell his land to some other Mexican. When the Republican party issued pamphlets in the State campaign, old Mexican women would come to have me read for them. I say to one old woman—and there was another old woman together with her—'What is it Republican party says? It says: Vote Republican, vote for Bursum Bill. Then all Mexican neighbors in a village like this, if they had a house, would get a title. Now, old women, you got a room here. You can vote for a title.'" This, in simple talk, indicates the process by which many of the claims have grown up, claims which even without color of title would have been confirmed by the Bursum Indian Bill.

It happens that the Pueblo Indian tracts are all owned by the community; different portions being devised by the pueblo authorities to different families for use, but not for individual ownership. It may at once be seen that no title transferred by an individual Indian has any legal validity except what might accrue to it through the harmless-appearing provisions of this bill.

As though there had not been enough depredation and deprivation already, consider what the Bursum Indian Bill proposed and might have accomplished but for the vigilance of a handful of private citizens. . . .

—*The Outlook*, January 17, 1923

Pueblo Dances

· ❦❧❦❧ ·

Once upon a time, I jotted down the following remarks from the lips of the Governor of the Indian pueblo, San Juan de los Caballeros, who was introducing a dance to a group of white watchers.

"This is a very old dance—maybe five hundred years back. The elders of the pueblo have taught us this dance, which we danced before the Spaniards, Mexicans and Americans came to this country; when there were only Indians who have had no records except in their heads and in their hearts. The elders have bidden us, as long as the world exists, never to forget this dance. It is an important dance. When we dance it, we have an abundance of everything. Now you are to see this dance. The man who will dance it is of a high position in the pueblo, one of the caciques, and an elderly man, a very religious man in the Pueblo religion."

Not long ago, a New Yorker who had heard much about Indian dances came to New Mexico, eager to see them. He saw one, and his interest waned. Because the dances are not dances.

After experience of the black maze of dances in Harlem, with this or that individual's personality shining through it as sharply as his teeth, our friend found Pueblo dances unexciting. After watching Isadora Duncan's infinite and subtle variety, he found the Pueblo motions monotonous. After watching through many seasons many fine bodies on the New York and European stage, each exhibiting its own particular and highly conscious beauty through sensual human graces and intricacies, he was chilled to find Indian dances as aloof as blown treetops that tip toward the moon. He wanted what he had seen before. He wanted the personal, the immediate, the physical; something to excite his nerves with outward sensation. He encountered the impersonal, the remote, the spiritual; something that constricts the heart of both dancer and onlooker within its own innermost beat.

Preparing for a dance, a Pueblo may be as careful as the vainest of us that he shall look well, that his costume shall accurately and properly befit an occasion. Once he has entered the dance, his vanity seems to leave him. He seems unaware not only of the foreign friend looking on from a housetop but even of the dancer nearest to him in the shifting lines and figures of the devotional mass-movement. One wonders, feeling the withdrawnness of each man and woman in the dance, how they manage their turns and changes without occasional conflict of body against body. They hardly seem to be hearing the equally rapt chorus of men who are singing and treading and weaving the song, they seem to have forgotten the perfect tempo of the drum. Their footbeats are like heartbeats, pulsing as inevitably through varied and interrupted rhythms as the inlet and outlet of breath in a living body. And yet, with as many as four or five score other persons between them, the two end persons in a line of dance will be touching the earth in a rapid entrancement of unison. While the dance interval lasts, the whole group moves as lightly and surely as a single swallow. If Patricio or Alfonso or Rafael steps out of the dance to have betweentimes a smoke and a laugh with you, your wonder is all the greater when he steps back into the dance again and becomes someone who existed a thousand years ago, is now and ever shall be. They are of the earth and the earth is of heaven. They are blown by a wind from the sky, like the many drops of the rain they dance for. And like the rain itself, the falling of their feet is an everlasting motion against death.

Granted that there are dances which the Pueblos borrow from other tribes, dances given in a lighter and more playful spirit; granted that some of their own dances are deliberately comical or whimsical or surprisingly primitive and candid; granted that youngsters at Indian schools away from their homes develop competitive steps in a mood rather athletic than religious, and that such institutions as the Santa Fe Fiesta and the Gallup Ceremonial, where Indians present their dances before large commercial audiences, tend to break down the original meaning and inner intent of the ceremonies; granted all this, there remains in the Pueblo dance-rituals as conserved at stricter villages like Santo Domingo, a devout beauty which explains to us moderns what the ancients meant when they danced before the Lord. Only by watching them in their own spirit, may any one of us deserve to see them.

Specialists there are who can explain the symbolism, the details of movement and costume, the definite religious import of the Moqui Snake Dance, the Zuñi Shalako, an Eagle Dance at Santa Clara, a Buffalo Dance at Santo Domingo. And often the specialists are right. When we learn that the snake dancers, for instance, their tribe being descended from a Snake Princess, carry rattlers and other reptiles in their mouths in order that these earth creatures may have a happily rhythmical reminder of human friendliness and then be sent back underground bearing to the Snake Princess good report of her people above ground, we cease from our inquisitive abhorrence and we respect this Indian sacrifice to a better god than those many gods, including Jehovah, who have demanded even to this day blood-sacrifice and death.

Several years ago at Zuñi, the morning after the tall gods had come down from their mountain to bless each new hearth with stately ceremonies, to confer on all dwellers in new homes the dignity of ancient homes, I saw a grave accident. At the muddy edge of the river, during a final rite before departure for the year, one of the tall gods slipped and fell. Instantly his attendants hid him from sight with a circle of upheld blankets; and just as instantly the people of Zuñi were swept as by an unseen wind into their houses, and the clusters of visiting Navajo on their horses were struck away into the distance as on a thunderbolt.

Zuñi was deserted—except for a lone figure here and there, including a single Navajo who had dismounted after the ill omen and stood waiting like the others, motionless. Thereupon the Fire God strode across the river with a switch in his hand and lashed the scapegoats one by one on their bowed shoulders. When those few had taken upon themselves the punishment due all their fellows, because they had all profaned the god by viewing his mishap, the town began to breathe again, resumed its life. The symbol had been clear. It was the vicarious atonement.

However pertinent these explanations and parallels may be, no detail or episode can deeply illumine the onlooker, unless he be in his own nature attuned at the outset, unless he feel, almost from the very first drumbeat of the first dance he sees, an intimate and solemn sense of participation in the forces of heaven and earth, unless his private perverse individuality subside into the common rhythm of life, unless he hear the beat of timelessness countering the beat of time, and unless the drouth in his heart be ended by the coolness of an inner rain. Let the outer rain come, too, if it will. First the faith, and then the adding of all things.

It sometimes seems as if these people, in their heightened moments, had cherished alive through the centuries the Taoist wisdom of Laotzu and as if their dances were an outward and still visible sign of his inward invisible grace.

There are certain dances—a part of this wisdom—celebrating with honest, gay and proper acceptance, out in the open, before men, women and children, the necessary processes of nature which belong to this creative earth and which are by no means, to the Pueblos, a sly continuance of the original sin. I have watched one or two of these dances and find nothing to criticize.

This is no brief for the moral or intellectual character of Pueblos. It is a simple acknowledgment of the religious beauty in their ceremonies, a beauty that grows from their quiet faith in the earth.

They are of the earth and the earth is of heaven. They are

blown by a wind from the sky, like the many drops of the rain they dance for. And like the rain itself, the falling of their feet is an everlasting motion against death.

—*They Know New Mexico: Intimate Sketches by Western Writers,*
Passenger Department: The Atchison, Topeka and Santa Fe
Railroad, 1928

Paintings by
Pueblo Children

· ❧❧❧ ·

The Pueblo Indians of the Southwest have had for centuries, like their mysterious predecessors in this region, an extraordinary sense of conventionalized design, as unearthed prehistoric pottery markedly proves. In these old pots and utensils, combined with the symbolic shapes and lines, there are often to be found realistically painted birds, animals, and even fish. From these figures to the minutely realistic figures of persons as well as of animals, which have been drawn and painted by the present generation of Pueblos, there is, it seems clear to me, a direct descent. The delicate precision in the painting of a deer or bear or skunk by Awa Tsireh of San Ildefonso or by Ma Pe Wi of Zia, in spite of the fact that these have come more or less under the influence of this or that archaeologist in Santa Fe, who has encouraged and tried to guide them, relates, after all, more closely to the art of their forbears, as seen in details painted on pottery, than to the art of the white race.

It would appear that eminent Indian painters, like the two named, whose work has been exhibited in various American cities and is to be shown this winter all over the United States by the Exposition of Indian Tribal Arts, need by no means be exceptional individuals. Almost every Indian child begins with a native aptitude for expressing in line and color objects that he sees about him. White children very commonly make drawings at an early age, but these drawings are crude and unobservant when compared with the work of Indian children.

There has been, unfortunately, a widespread attempt on the part of teachers in our Indian schools to divert the youngsters from their natural choice of subject and their natural bent in technique. At exhibitions from the various schools shown in connection with the Gallup Inter-Tribal Ceremonial or the Santa Fe Fiesta, there are far too many copies by Indian children of current magazine covers or of birds and flowers found in white men's books. There are even landscapes painted with an attempt at the white man's use of perspective, instead of suggested by the symbolic lines representing mesas, wind, rain, rainbows or desert in the manner indigenous to the Southwest before the whites ever came here. On one occasion, at Gallup, in looking over work by pupils at one of the Indian schools, I selected with relish from among many specimens of imitative work, several dance figures recorded by pupils in their own characteristic clear-cut manner. The teachers in charge of the exhibit were not pleased with my choice, indicating clearly that they disprized these particular pieces and trying their best to turn my favor to some of the more pretentious imitations of white man's art. One could almost feel, in the paintings I chose, the presence of the little Indians insisting upon their own way against official neglect and even displeasure. If only the native work of these Indians, the gift common to most of them at the start, might be appreciated in its purity and importance by a large enough section of the American public, it is likely that the attitude and apparent policy of many teachers in the Indian Service might be altered for the general good. The instinctive and distinctive native ability of our Indians is a precious inheritance of these states which ought not to be distorted and lost. It is true that against all manner of oppression, against force of environment, against economic need, against the general might of pale-skin civilization, the Indians of the Southwest have, with impressive tenacity, continued their traditions, their identification of themselves with the natural world about them, their devotional ceremonies toward the elements, and their various detailed manners and customs. A young Indian, returning from our schools to this or that pueblo, does not take long to forget most of the pressure exerted upon him to outgrow the ways of his people and he returns, with apparent satisfaction, to the beliefs, traditions, and manners of his kin. Nevertheless, it is a pity that during the formative years these children cannot be taught to value, cherish, and enrich the best qualities and gifts of their inheritance and to relate properly and helpfully to our white civilization traits of character and aesthetic gifts which are distinctly their own.

Here and there in the Indian Service we encounter teachers who have a deep and dedicated sense of this need—a realization that for both races it is wiser that the Indians become their own best selves rather than half-bewildered mimics of their white neighbors. Among these more discerning teachers I may mention Miss Clara Brignac, who teaches at Zuñi. The effect of her enlightened intention was easily visible at the Gallup show in the paintings and drawings done by her pupils. In her zeal she reminded me of some of the teachers I met in Old Mexico where the native artistic ability of Indian children all over the country was recognized and fostered under the leadership of Señor José Vasconcelos when he was Minister of Education. Not only was he largely responsible for the phenomenal showing of Mexican art by older painters, as it appears through frescoes in public buildings at Mexico City and elsewhere, but he instilled among teachers in the smallest villages an intelligent and patriotic sense of the marked ability of numberless small Mexicans in drawing and painting. The Mexican Government issued in 1926 the *Monografia de Las Escuelas de Pintura al Aire Libre*, a beautifully printed volume of work done by these children in their outdoor schools. Many of the paintings are reproduced in color, a signal evidence of enlightened governmental activity. Although Señor Vasconcelos is no longer in favor among the forces that govern his country, I understand that his policy in respect to the teaching of art is being continued.

In sad contrast to this attitude, I have encountered cases of definite suppression, by our government and its agents, of the art instincts of Indian children. Here in Santa Fe I have had a number of Indians arrive and beg for the use of my room and my drum, in order that they might sing their own songs. It seems that they were forbidden to sing these songs at the school. It also seems that the local superintendent was only carrying out orders from Washington. Indian songs, as anyone knows who has lived in the Southwest and been magnetized by the unison and beautiful cadences of Indian voices, are again a distinctive and valuable art expression which our people should respect and cherish. Under the present administration, it appears that there is a friendly change of attitude toward the aesthetic life of the Indian. . . .

—*The School Arts Magazine*, April 1932

Designs for Beauty

· ❧❧❧ ·

For many years Indian blankets and basketry from this or that tribe have been not only familiar to collectors but useful and ornamental in houses throughout the United States. Much more lately has come a knowledge and use of Navajo silver jewelry with its setting of turquoise.

Beadwork and chains made of wampum or of bone or of porcupine quills have always been associated in the mind of the American newcomer with his idea of the original American; but this jewelry made of silver and turquoise, designs which might as well be thought to have come from China or Rumania as from among our own American plains and mountains, is a comparatively recent discovery on Main Street. So also was its making a later activity among Indians than the crafts of weaving and braiding.

It is an odd fact that most Indian blankets and most Indian jewelry are made now by the nomadic Navajo and are called by his name, whereas he learned the craft of blanket-weaving from the Pueblo and Hopi Indians, and according to good authority, the craft of metal-work from the itinerant Spanish silversmiths who plied their trade throughout New Mexico.

Fifteen years ago when I first came to Santa Fe I was shown a collection of Zuñi bracelets and earrings which the painter Andrew Dasburg had brought back from his trips in New Mexico and Arizona, a collection which I have not since seen matched anywhere. Dasburg unfortunately sold his collection piece by piece, so that certain examples of earlier Zuñi work, which ought to have been held together for their rarity and as examples of artistic invention antedating the influence of Indian traders and American buyers, have been dispersed. Following Dasburg's lead and enthusiasm, I soon found myself collecting

Indian jewelry: delving indefatigably into every far corner of the Pueblo, Navajo and Hopi regions and, like a pearl-diver, coming out of them sometimes with treasure.

All I had to do was to see an Indian woman hiding her wrists with a shawl or blanket, to be sure that the finest bracelet, the rarest ring, was hidden thereunder. First I would indicate a ring or bracelet of my own with gestures meaning that I would like more of the same; then, exasperated by her staid stolidity or pretended ignorance, I would tug at the edges of her blanket, even to the point once in a while of alarming her virtue. Eventually I would succeed in uncovering silver and turquoise. And this or that piece of it came home with me.

It was the same with the men. I would fondle the hand of a motionless horseman, studying ring or bracelet. Then the bargaining. Then the prize trophy. Now that I have assembled thousands of such trophies, I doubt if there exists a design, either old or new, which could arouse in me that fever of the collector, that hunger for the variants which will make a collection; but I still admire.

It is a fact that a collector within the scope of his collection acquires a knowledge without knowledge. To this day I know nothing of the history of silver-work among Indians, nothing of the origin or significance of the designs they use. For me that is not the point. I can only wheeze with other amateurs that I know what I like. But at the same time I can instinctively and instantly reject the false design, the design which means nothing to its maker except foreign instruction or intended sale. The quality which makes any object beautiful is the love which goes into its making. Left alone, the Indian could not conceivably create anything without love, without delight. The blanket, the basket, the pot or the necklace may eventually be an object for commerce. In fact our Indians are distinctive among men for lack of the possessive instinct. To make a thing beautiful is important, but to keep it is not important. They make you feel at times, as the Chinese do, that remembering is better than keeping, or let's say that remembering is the real keeping. But aesthetic integrity in the making of things is as natural to Indians as a race as it is among other races to specialists in beauty.

Let's go back. Let's remember that there was a Navajo living sixteen miles from Fort Defiance, Arizona, whose Indian name was Hosteen Ah-tsi'di and who as a young man was called Iron-maker because he made bits for bridles and then with variations copied fancy bridles from Spanish horses, singing songs perhaps at his work about their dead riders. Let us remember, since Mary Roberts and Dane Coolidge have reminded us of it in their book *The Navajo Indians*, that when members of this tribe were herded into Bosque Redondo in 1864 to become farmers there were issued to them coils of brass and copper wire and that they made bracelets of the wire and that after the Navajos were sent back to their old country their smiths made similar bracelets from silver coins and evolved new shapes and decorations; that they learned about 1900 the better silver content in Mexican coinage than in ours, that they gradually developed a racial craft with which to ornament themselves, both men and women, that they became gifted and important silversmiths, that they combined with silver their anciently loved turquoise and that when turquoise is worn, rattlesnake will not bite nor lightning strike.

Let me myself remember in the wide Navajo country a family of Indians guiding their sheep to new grazing-places, a canopy of branches set up against sun and rain, an outdoor loom for the women to weave on and a little satchel with tools in it and silver and turquoise so that one of the men out there under the sky could hammer and weld and inlay small bits of beauty to his heart's content.

What matter if the pendant which he makes means different things to different men. He himself could tell me that the horse-shoe shape with its inner prong is the Navajo war-god's dagger. A Pueblo Indian, having dug turquoise from the old mine at Los Cerrillos over which the Pueblos had assumed semi-mystic ownership from time long since until Tiffany of New York bought and closed and guarded it to make such beauty more expensive, would bring back his pendant from the Navajo country and translate its meaning into phallic symbolism or the peace-signal of a rainbow. Let archaeologists and scholars worry concerning such matters. Let poets and people take beautiful craftsmanship into their hands and find their own meanings.

But let poets and people, and most people are poets without knowing it, be cautious against factories. For factories can take art away from Indians and poetry out of people. And the fact is that many Americans, with their creative minds destroyed by the effect of factory products, can come even into this mountain country whose clear air should clean their taste, and prefer Indian jewelry made wholesale in factories at Denver or Albuquerque or in the petty factories set up by white traders where Indians sit in small rows and fabricate jewelry under white direction, with arrows and swastikas and thunderbirds provided in stamps by the factory-keeper. An unimaginative and tinny jewelry is being imposed upon credulous and tasteless buyers in the name of Indians who, left alone, let me repeat and repeat, can create for themselves and through themselves for us, decorative belongings as distinguished and personal and aesthetically important as the decorative belongings which for centuries have graced the Orient and reflected there in man's response and in all the uses of life the importance of each separate cherry blossom.

—*New Mexico*, August 1936

At War

·❧❦❧·

The Writer and the War

· ❦❧❦ ·

Those who heard last year's forum on "Regional Literature" will remember that, after the heat of discussion, after apparent differences had swayed this way and that, the four or five of us roughening like human waves, we all subsided at the end into a calm sea or bay or backwater or pond or pool or pellucidly bubbling spring, whatever it was—and the region which, for all of us, turned out to be important to literature, as to life, was the region of the heart. The heart has a region *separate* regions cannot know.

I doubt if, on this topic, "The Writer and the War," there will be as much incidental, superficial disunity to divide us and divert you. The topic connects with too much gravity for us to be playful with it or to do aught but focus on it our clearest intelligence as exactly and earnestly as we may.

When the topic came to me in the leaflet, it came to me first objectively: the effect of the war on the output of writers as one sees it in print. I admit that my mind stumbled, at the outset, over the morass of advertisement one sees and hears in journals and on radio. Something has been done, I believe, to curb aerial use of flag and country for rhetoric and appeal which come from regions less of the heart than of the pocket; but printed advertisement of every sort continues to vex us with circus-barker cheapening of whatever plot may lie behind this dark curtain we face, mysterious, solemn and sobering to all of us.

Perhaps, in the sense of the word "Writer," as we are considering it tonight, advertising men are not writers. But I notice that through such agencies as the Writers' War Board, the League of American Writers, the Council for Democracy (with its excellent "Write Now" department), and through other organized groups, some of them connected with the government, the individual writer is being urged to contribute his thought and skill to a campaign of what is, after all, advertising: advertising the issues of the war and the needs involved in its prosecution as well by the lives of men as by their money.

In this campaign, which to most of us seems not only necessary but right, the writer, the serious, honest writer, has a worthy and commanding task. He can do much to keep our war propaganda within the bounds of truth, to keep clean our motives, our procedure and our thinking. I, for one, am convinced that the people do not need lies and would be immune even to the big ones that Hitler advocates. There is evidence on all sides that the people want this time no nonsense, no fanfare, no mere flag-waving, no ballyhoo, but choose to face facts, to take the war as straightly and justly as they may be allowed to do. Blind hatred is not deeply in us this time, nor must it be put there by misinformation or pig-headed patriotism. The writers taking part either officially or personally have a grave job and responsibility to keep their standard at least as high as that of the people they assume or are enrolled to advise or direct. The spirit abroad in These States is not so much apathy, not so much cynicism, as it is a rooted desire for fact-facing and a stoic desire for fact-making: desires which, by writers in books, articles, editorials, radio scripts, and in press columns as far as possible, should be deepened, strengthened and actuated toward significant victory.

Still considering our theme objectively, we see everywhere an increase of writing, or at least of publishing, in departments economic, industrial, military, diplomatic, reportorial, and a lessening of printed matter in belles lettres, in the sphere of imaginative writing. That is natural. A proportion of "escapist" writing arrives and is salutary as well for the writer as the reader. The mind and heart crave relief these days, God knows, and must have it, lest they snap with fever or fall into coma from concentration on the temporary aspects of this conflict or on the endless futility of war, all war, and man's refusal to learn or grow. Let us pray that the people's present temper means that the refusal is weakening, that man *is* learning and growing.

Let me turn for a moment to a moot case which seems to me to have bearing for all of us in connection with the war, with any war, for writer and for reader too. I may tread on toes when I affirm my conviction that among American writers working soundly and vigorously for the proper understanding of this war, for the human principles which ought to be animating the United Nations and which, by the grace of God and man, can be made to animate them, for an open-eyed facing of faults in our national or personal judgment and conduct, for a firm, sincere campaign, widely followed, toward binding of diverse racial and social elements into fundamental unity and decency and toward a victory deserved and worth winning—I may be treading on toes when I affirm my conviction that among such publicity men in America, Ralph Ingersoll stands first. He has enemies at home as well as in the Axis. He seems to some of my acquaintances too radical, to be more kind than kin. But by and large I adjudge him, so far, our best literary soldier. His accounts of life, in Britain, in Russia, in our own country, have been reportorial or factual writing; but in the big sense they have been imaginative writing too, in the sense of the imagination which can live inside ideas, emotions, lives seemingly unlike our own, understand them and effect through words the spread of that understanding. You are doubtless familiar with the evidence in his case: that he was inducted in his forties for the army and that his employer, Marshall Field, owner of *P.M.* which Ingersoll publishes and edits, appealed for deferment on the ground of indispensability to the newspaper. The underlying basis, whatever the wording of the appeal, was the man's greater value to his country as a writer than as a soldier. To this issue it is an irrelevant fact that Ingersoll was a soldier in the First World War. The issue lies apart from that sort of consideration, the only sort given him by his enemies and critics who cry slacker and would enforce his induction into the ranks. It is my belief that their concern is not for impartial induction, any more than it is for the drafting of one additional soldier. They don't like his ideas and they want him quenched and with him, if possible, the paper in which he is the lifeblood. I do like his ideas, as I think most writers must: and I like his actual achievements through editorial campaigns in ridding our forces of men rightly suspect, in blasting brass-hattery in places however high, in forcing as often as he can our fine democratic words into deeds and in keeping high before a large following the banner of a positive, creative cause we can respect. Sensational journalism now and then, yes, and errors of taste—but a spirit firm and true—and a writer. My contention then is that Ingersoll and carefully chosen men like him should be deferred, honorably and emphatically, for the national service they can render in fields quite as important as factory or office—where deferment for important service is taken for granted. No man is indispensable; but some men are nearly indispensable and should be so accounted—even if they be only writers—when our government disposes its forces. Therefore this special pleading for a journalist.

And now as to the poet. We see poets working in the war, with words: Archibald MacLeish with radio plays and other activities, Stephen Vincent Benét similarly—a new series of radio plays under way now called "Dear Adolph" and representing the American attitudes of farmer, businessman, worker, housewife, soldier and immigrant. My old friends, Roark Bradford and Franklin Adams, are at work in some such way. So is my new friend, Carl Carmer. So is Eric Knight who won your hearts here last year. And there is the Boadicean leadership of Pearl Buck in her fine, wise, stalwart campaign against racial discrimination. And Edna Millay early in the game issued a book of war poems, a book—because of heat and haste—not so well-written as it might have been but moving nonetheless as the irrepressible battle-cry of a doughty democrat, small *d*.

In this connection, and because I was writing war poems too, I received a letter in January from a friend, a poet: "If *you* are going back on us, I am going to cry. I have given up all hope of Edna; but I cannot bear the thought of your being a casualty too; and when I see signs that you are planning to put your intelligence on ice for the duration, I protest. I think this is a time

when we should remain strictly silent about all the little superficial aspects of events and not write at all unless we can dig
very deeply into our emotions and speak of those things that
are true and eternal. I have made a resolution for myself that
I will not during this war write one line that would not seem
true to a sensitive and honest spirit in Germany or anywhere else.
Though I am as well aware as anyone that we are obliged to fight
now in a life and death struggle with an enemy, I regard the
deep, moral issues as so obscure, tangled and rooted in the
deep abysses of human nature and human society, that I do not
believe any fine or honest poetry can be written about the
partisan aspects of the struggle, but only about those tragic
elements in the human heart which have made the struggle
possible. I believe that we are indeed obliged to fight with our
whole strength, yet that deep inexpressible loathing should be
reserved for that element in our own selves which has made
such a situation possible—our own greed, lack of humanity,
failure to devote all our energies to the cure of national and
international conditions which could not possibly result in anything but revolution and war. If you and I believe one single
word of this hooey about freedom and democracy and our own
wonderful purity, then we shall have learned nothing from this
tragedy, and the peace when it at last comes will be only another
armistice."

I agree with my friend that the poet is primarily a writer in
the imaginative sphere. War poems that we remember, to go
no further back than World War I, have depended, at least in
part, on the fact that the poets who wrote them were slain by
the war. Nor do we remember the poems as bugle-calls to a particular conflict of arms. No. That wasn't it. The poems were, for
the most part, personal reactions to an experience that happened
to be war. And their implications, for the most part, related to
that ever older, ever newer war than any that shall ever be fought
with arms: the conflict in the inner man.

Among the manuscripts I have so far read submitted at this
conference I have found a finely thought and wrought sonnet

sequence concerning this inner conflict—or, rather, the next thing to it, the devoted conflict between man and wife, but written in terms of outer war and definitely bearing on it, since issues in macrocosm can best be studied, understood and solved if first seen clearly in microcosm—if clarity begins at home.

This is the attitude of the friend who wrote me and is only mistaken when it goes too far, bends over backward and refuses to relate the temporary to the eternal.

The sudden, current popularity of Tolstoi's *War and Peace* does not stem mainly from an interest in the military strategy and maneuvers of an elder war nor from the analogy between that war and the present invasion of Russia, and our hope that history will repeat itself, but from an interest in the phenomena of war as exhibited by imaginative genius and the revelation of its causes and effects, the ignoble results of the carelessness of mankind. Here are universally curative properties in the work of a man of imagination. And there is constant need of the work of such men, relating not only to this or to any other particular war but to the war which lies behind all others, the war within the human spirit, its causes, its campaigns, its defeats, its victories.

So—*marchons!*

—Lecture at the Writers' Conference, University of Colorado, July 22, 1942

Some Roots

Tuckerman

· ❧❧❧❧ ·

Frederick Goddard Tuckerman, an American poet, published one book. It was issued by Ticknor and Fields at Boston and went through three editions. The first was printed privately in 1860; the others, in response to a decade of approval, in 1864 and 1869. There was also an English edition in 1863, which may have been the result of Tennyson's interest. Like Tennyson in England, Emerson and Longfellow in the United States seem to have been impressed with a more than casual and passing quality in Tuckerman's poetry. The established poets happened to notice and prefer the lesser side of Tuckerman, a side which allied him as a craftsman somewhat with themselves. His great work escaped them and has escaped, since then, every anthologist and professional critic of American poetry. This mishap may be due to the fact that the initial and longer section of the volume was devoted to poems akin to the current verse of Tuckerman's time, the playful pastorals and correct lyrics of a New England gentleman, interspersed with Wordsworthian and Tennysonian narratives, which gave little or no inkling of matter hidden behind manner or of a master hidden behind his generation. And yet how could they have missed the beauty of this?

> Under the mountain, as when first I knew
> Its low black roof and chimney creeper-twined,
> The red house stands; and yet my footsteps find,
> Vague in the walks, waste balm and feverfew.
> But they are gone; no soft-eyed sisters trip
> Across the porch or lintels; where, behind,
> The mother sat,—sat knitting with pursed lip.
> The house stands vacant in its green recess,

Absent of beauty as a broken heart.
The wild rain enters; and the sunset wind
Sighs in the chambers of their loveliness,
Or shakes the pane; and in the silent noons
The glass falls from the window, part by part,
And ringeth faintly in the grassy stones.

A quarter of a century ago, Mr. Louis How was preparing a less conventional anthology of American poetry than he could find in print. In this anthology, unpublished then, unpublished still, Mr. Walter Prichard Eaton discovered two sonnets by Tuckerman and through these poems was led to unearth the volume called *Poems*. In *The Forum* of January 1909, Mr. Eaton announced his amazement that "this introspective, withdrawing, contemplative man, for all the metrical faults and the slender bulk of his verse, was so absolutely unknown in the history of American letters. . . . It did not seem just or right. . . . His was a rare if imperfect poetic faculty; and certain portions of his verse are worthy of perpetuation."

Mr. Eaton quoted six of the sonnets which comprise this present edition and spoke, advisedly, of their "passionate dignity." He quoted also from several of the poems in the earlier section of the original volume. Here are five stanzas from a long poem, the rest of which, in my judgment, he well dismissed.

I took from its glass a flower,
To lay on her grave with dull, accusing tears;
But the heart of the flower fell out as I handled the rose,
And my heart is shattered and soon will wither away.

I watched the changing shadows
And the patch of windy sunshine upon the hill
And the long blue woods; and a grief no tongue can tell
Breaks at my eyes in drops of bitter rain.

> I hear her baby wagon,
> And the little wheels go over my heart:
> Oh, when will the light of the darkened house return?
> Oh, when will she come who made the hills so fair?
>
> I sit by the parlor window,
> When twilight deepens and winds grow cold without;
> But the blessed feet no more come up the walk,
> And my little girl and I cry softly together.

Such phrasing as "the windy sunshine," "and the long blue woods," are interestingly akin to the phrasing of the great Chinese poets concerning nature: concentrated, simple and accurate. Tuckerman, moreover, often deals as directly as they do with emotion between persons. Compare, for instance, the last line in the passage just quoted with the ending of Wêi Ying-wu's poem, "To My Daughter on Her Marriage into the Yang Family."

> I always try to hide my feelings—
> They are suddenly too much for me,
> When I turn and see my younger daughter
> With the tears running down her cheek.

There is a Chinese note in Tuckerman's quick combination of the homely and the grand. . . .

Respectfully and not without reluctance, I have chosen for the present edition only seventy-seven from the two hundred and forty-four pages printed during the poet's life. Partly from the published volume and partly from the manuscript notebooks which led to it, I am impelled, however, to quote a few unrelated lines, for their own sake. The first of them connects obviously with the mood of "Margites":

> Nor born to fame beneath some rare conspiracy of stars.

The others are at random.

> Pines and scrubbed oaks half dead and tailed with moss.

> Brooding in dim solicitude
> On earlier other times
> And yon dark-purple wing of wood
> That o'er the mountain climbs.

> An awkward youth in the dark angle there,
> Dangling and flapping like a maple-key
> Caught in a cobweb.

> America, the country of the world,
> The half-the-world that should have changed the whole,
> The model flowering of all modern time,
> Dropping to pieces like a three days' rose.

> Loving the white truth as a boy his bride.

There is enough pure poetry in these instances and excerpts to have drawn a reader, though he had never seen the sonnets, toward as clearly poised a poet as any of Tuckerman's contemporaries. The sonnets constitute poetry apart not only from his contemporaries but in a way from Tuckerman himself as a literary figure of his time. In the 1854 manuscript version of his book, after all the other poems, he set down the first twelve sonnets of the first sequence under the heading, *Personal Sonnets*, almost as though he had not intended to include them in a printed book, as though they were too tender, too close. And, unless I am wrong, after my twenty-one years' conviction, it is here that Tuckerman begins to count among the poets. Not only are the sonnets the fine thoughts of a devout stoic, they are the subtly fine craft of a devout poet. Mr. Eaton, if he referred to the sonnets, was misled when he spoke of "metrical faults" and questioned Tuckerman's "sense of form and style" and was certainly unjust when he said, "there is not a perfectly formed sonnet in the volume," though he was reverently just in noting "the passionate dignity," "the magical simplicity," "the flashes of pure gold in imagination," "something piercing and beautiful," "the simple, stinging grief." While surmising as cause for public neglect of Tuckerman, "his lack of a sustained and well-wrought style," Mr. Eaton left himself room when he said that Tuckerman "either scorned or did not know the rules of the sonnet form." In the light of Tuckerman's obvious familiarity with the classics, in the light of recent experiment with variation in verse, in the light of present knowledge that Walt Whitman and Emily Dickinson had ears more sensitive than their contemporaries had, we may be sure that Tuckerman knew what he was doing when he ended a sonnet with an Alexandrine or shortened the last line by a foot, or when he shuffled the rhyme-scheme to suit the roll and rise and fall of his meaning. He was as aware of his irregularity, as was George Meredith in "Modern Love" adding to the sonnet the two extra lines. He was as tenderly conscious of his form as was ever any maker of the sonnet. Instead of bungling or staling the sonnet-form, he renewed it and, molding it to his emotion, made it inevitable. Along with the tide of his words flowed the tide of his thought, cresting in breathless images.

Related to this personal and differentiated use of rhyme-form in the sonnet, to an anachronistic fondness for the juxta-position of fine and homely phrases and images, was Tuckerman's delight in the invention or resyllabling of words: tamerac, for instance, instead of the obsolete word tameric for tamarisk. Some of his seemingly classical references, while bearing the earmarks of validity, are to persons and events that seem to have existed only in his own imagination. And in the eighth sonnet of the final sequence, his homesick line written in the city and mindful of trees near a beloved country dwelling is compact, through in-wrought words, of poignant connotations. The passage runs,

> The low-built cottage buried in the vale,
> Wooded and over-wooded, bushed about
> With holm tree, ople tree, and sycamine.

Involved in the rich sound of the concluding line is a combination elm and home, apple and opal, sycamore and mine: an apparently whimsical but really emotional use of words that Edgar Allan Poe might has envied.

II

Tuckerman's daughter-in-law, Mrs. Frederick Tuckerman, and his granddaughter, Mrs. Orton Clark, have graciously given me access to the poet's manuscripts, correspondence and other papers. In a tiny manuscript book which might easily have been destroyed or lost or overlooked, we discovered three sequences of unpublished sonnets, the final three sequences in this volume. My first impression on reading these later poems, composed apparently in 1872, eighteen years after the earliest record of the first sequence, was that the poet's mastery had lessened. I know now that I was wrong. I am convinced that every line of these later, rougher-seeming poems was carefully intended to stand exactly as it stands. I have touched only two or three words in all of them, at places where the poet had apparently been in doubt and had left his doubts unsolved. The manuscripts are otherwise identical with this printed version, both in the single copy of these last poems and in the several copies of the first two sequences. Just once was there evidence of a continued problem in phrase. A notebook apparently antedating 1854 showed, in the twelfth sonnet of the first sequence, these lines:

> There where his shield shed arrows, and his helm
> Rang like a bell beaten with axe and brand,
> He pushed the battle backward, realm on realm.

Already he had interwritten an alternative:

There where his shield shed arrows, and the clank
Played on his helm of battle-axe, rank on rank,
He pushed the battle backward, realm on realm.

In the manuscript book of 1854, written in Litchfield, England,
the first two lines were set down the second way, then stricken
out and restored to the first version. It was probably in proof
that the sure form arrived in 1860:

Tall stately plants with spikes and forks of gold
Crowd every slope: my heart repeats its cry—
A cry for strength, for strength and victory:
The will to strive, the courage overbold
That would have moved me once to turn indeed
And level with the dust each lordly weed.
But now I weep upon my wayside walks
And sigh for those fair days, when glorying
I stood a boy amid the mullein-stalks
And dreamed myself like him the Lion-King.
There, where his shield shed arrows and the clank
Clashed on his helm of battle-axe and brand,
He pushed the battle backward, rank on rank
Fallen in the sword-swing of his stormy hand.

In Tuckerman's early notebooks were jotted such rhythms as
"traffic," "Sapphic," "welfare," "elf-hair," "clumsy," "Tecum-
seh," and other indications of the mood in which he wrote
as a young man, taking verse to be the ingenious, suitable and
amiable pastime of a well-born and well-bred country-gentleman.
In his published book, he collected evidences of this mood under
such titles as "A Sample of Coffee Beans," "A Latter-Day Saint"
and "Anybody's Critic." It would appear that he had enjoyed
Thomas Hood and *The Ingoldsby Legends* as well as Tennyson,
Poe and Longfellow. Wordsworth seems to have been the poet
who guided him most deeply under the surface; but in the end,

all outer literary influences gave way to his own emotion and to a voice of his own. The death of his wife and his consequent withdrawal from the world left him an intimate sense of life and an intimate need to express it; and grief-stricken isolation swept him into poetry.

Tuckerman, in his sonnets, seems to me not only the peer of his great contemporaries but the equal of his most important successors. To this day, despite a few dated phrases and for all his soberness, he is as modern as any twentieth century sonneteer. Though Robinson and Millay and Masefield have undoubtedly never read him, they would seem to have tapped his philosophy as well as his diction. His quality, as theirs may prove to be, is more than modernness. And it is not only in time that he penetrates. He is as Chinese as he is American. He is a poet permanently important in any literature. He happened to belong in New England, nevertheless, at its great literary period. It was an apex of civilization in an American region that had reached a full pitch of fine living. Our civilization is scattered now and ready to become ripely civilized in other sections than New England. A phenomenon of that earlier regional civilization, a phenomenon which may repeat itself, was a withdrawal from society on the part of at least four of its great figures, Emerson, Thoreau, Emily Dickinson, and Tuckerman, and their austere, ennobling, gracious sobriety. . . .

From first to last, the substance of Tuckerman's sonnets was a deep and baffled concern in his personal relation to life and its meaning, a concern so sincerely felt and wrought that the reader too is stricken by grief, is comforted by the uncomforting earth and in the end is soberly willing to accept the beautiful and bitter miracle of life. Tuckerman himself, for all his long sadness, justifies, as in the final sonnet of the first sequence, "the round, natural world," "the deep mind" and the far-away unknown purpose, by reflecting both their changes and their permanence and by meeting their eternal challenge. Never did a man write poetry more straightly to himself—with nothing fictitious. He is isolated in an intense integrity toward nature, toward his own mind, and toward the unknown God.

The austere melancholy which dominates the sonnets is tempered throughout, let me stress, with his sense of natural beauty, which heals even while it wounds:

> Yet Nature, where the thunder leaves its trace
> On the high hemlock pine or sandstone bank,
> Hating all shock of hue or contrast rank,
> With some consenting colour heals the place.

Tuckerman continually feels and expresses the endless contradictions of existence, of life and death, of joy and grief, of yes and no, the endless interbinding of positive and negative. . . .

All in all, if my judgment is in any way sound, Tuckerman's sonnets rank with the noblest in the language and dignify America with poems not bettered in their kind by anyone of his time or since.

—From the introduction to *The Sonnets of Frederick Goddard Tuckerman*, New York: Alfred A. Knopf, 1931

Credo*

· ❧❧❧ ·

Most formalized religions have been engendered in the assumption of a more or less personal God, the creator and control of life. But the latest theism is as baffled as was the earliest by the question: "What and why was the beginning of God?" By assuming a God, we only place the mystery a remove away. Humanity, moreover, has equipped Godhead with perfection and omnipotence; and then it has accepted the basic impossibility that out of perfection and omnipotence can come the creation, in humanity at least, of imperfection, frailty, ignorance, and evil. We attempt to explain the paradox by attributing to the Godhead perfect motives beyond our comprehension; but the fact that we remain uncomprehending victims and witnesses of injustice and barbarity supposedly concocted in heaven for our good, the fact that we suffer by not understanding, is an imperfection or an impotence which no such explaining explains. So the religions impose still other paradoxes on our conception of the Godhead. They direct us, for instance, to pray to Him for defense and benefit, although such prayer infringes upon God's all-wisdom and contradicts the orthodox doctrine of our ignorance as to what is good for us. Truly faithful or logical acceptance of a perfect God would exact of human beings complete acquiescence and inaction. If perfection stood all-powerful, what judgment or action by us would be necessary?

The Western world has dramatized the difficulty by having us try to cast out imperfection as with the help of a father. Even Christ kept, in his own personality, something of the old Hebrew authority of a father. But Christianity has acknowledged

---

* This Credo, phrased mostly as here, was set down in my twenties. In my seventies I find little reason to change it.—W.B.

more than it realizes of a deeper Christ when it calls its God the son of man, approaching therein a concept of the evolution of God through all life. When Jesus says that the Kingdom of God is within us, he would seem to mean that we are members not only of one another but of inherent perfection. His most considerable group of modern interpreters have met the basic issue another way. Sensing the weakness of the ancient idea that evil can be coexistent with a perfect God, they have denied the existence of evil except as a human illusion. They try to bolster the perfection of God by foisting the mistake of imperfection upon us, although we are parts of God: a perfect whole with imperfect parts. They attribute "error" to the handiwork of a perfect Creator: their God, without need of making mistakes, yet errs through us. Theirs is still the error of trying to believe in an already perfect God.

This historical conception of a personal God, of a force outside us, wholly powerful, was sure, moreover, to become for the human individual a conception of his own image given power over his fellows. It is this persistent conception which has caused and sanctioned wars and blind obedience, jealousies, and woes. And of a part with the conception of fixed divine identity has been the conception of fixed human identities. No life can be individual and separate in the sense that it can exclude other lives or can be life at all if it ceases to grow and change. Only as it becomes consciously inclusive of other lives and included in them can it become conscious of the spirit of life. An individual's vanity, his wish to proceed in some later existence with the same separate personality he has had here, seems to be an obstacle of pain and untruth against the way of life. Are we what we mean when we call ourselves individuals? Are we not many people inside ourselves? Do we not begin, compact of many ancestors? Do we not add still other lives from lovers, friends, and books? If identity survives, does death conclude its bounds? Must one's separate soul continue at the age of ten, twenty, or sixty, according to the date of the body's death? Is the spirit to be molded by the happening of death into an endless fixity? Surely if we are to continue in consciousness, it can only be as we realize all life to be our final and very self. Experimenting, suffering, learning with God in His growth toward that perfection which is in His blood and ours, a man becomes mankind and mankind God. The meaning dawns in life, in hope, in thought, in deed. If evil comes, or error, it is not as something which might be prevented by an existent omnipotence, it is not some discipline which omnipotence visits upon us in a cryptic tyranny; it is as something in the growing experience of God. And by use of evil, as by use of good, it is God as well as ourselves who can lose or gain. You, no less than any man and no more, except by degree of realization, may be coexistent and coeternal with God. Happiness consists in the consciousness and use of that existence. A hint of the sweetness of such faith, such possible consummation, is given your body through its dissolving union with the body of one whom you love. Even though the fruit of such union seems to be a furtherance of separateness, the desire of lover for lover is a desire to enclose and to be enclosed, an urge and ache for oneness. And with the separation of bodies by death may come still more strongly the realization of oneness, the penetration of peace through chance and change, the gradual integration. For

> . . . who shall be my enemy
> When he is I and I am he?

Such rumination may of course be only one more happy guess: but, without the morbidity of most religions, it is a stimulus to responsible and helpful living, a human or divine hope like that of Mark Twain's child, found written in her diary after her death, that there may be "a God in heaven or something better."

—*Unity*, September–October 1958

On Writing

Ten Commandments
for Poets

· ❧❧❧ ·

   I. Don't be a poet, or marry, or use adjectives, as long as you can help it.

  II. Don't secrete words from both thought and emotion, for the sake of a verbal intrigue.

 III. Don't let lines fix themselves in your head before they run their course, lest they be on their mark and get set—but never go.

 IV. Don't, by connecting the words in the line, disconnect the line from the stanza nor, by connecting the words in the stanza, disconnect the stanza from the poem.

  V. Don't use two images when one will do better, nor any at all that are graven.

 VI. Don't let poets who prefer to be monkeys deter you from being a person.

VII. Don't be daunted by don'ts.

VIII. Don't be cornered, or pigeonholed, by form, fashion, label, fear, habit, critic or editor.

 IX. Don't write a book but a life.

  X. Don't think a book is finished until you are.

—*Palms*, Autumn 1923

On Teaching the Young Laurel to Shoot

· ❧❦❧ ·

Can the writing of poetry be taught? To poets, yes; to others, no. There, in two sentences, is the question I asked myself at the University of California in January 1919, and the answer I brought away in June.

When Dean Gayley offered me a class for poetic experiment and assured me complete freedom of procedure, I admitted members according to specimens of their work, letting the first-chosen students combine their judgments with mine as to doubtful cases. In this way we reduced the class from seventy-nine applicants to twenty-three members and three irregulars. In a university where a class is often a whole township, I especially realized the advantage of working with a small group. And so there were twenty-seven of us, thirteen girls and fourteen boys, and plenty of blank paper.

Every Friday afternoon, for three hours, I gathered my group around a long table. Smoking was not permitted in the university buildings, but I construed that ledges of open windows were not strictly inside; and sometimes we met under eucalyptus trees where we needed no window ledges, and always after hours sections of the class would adjourn to my rooms where there were no rules against smoking. In other words, I wanted the students to be at ease and natural with one another and with me. Soon we were more like a club than like a class, a chapter of widely divergent personalities, enjoying one another.

As to enjoying one another's verse, I followed the excellent plan of the Poetry Society of America. Everything was submitted to me and to the class, including verse of my own, anonymously. This lent a latitude and relish to our criticism, both attack and defense, and an interest, both amusing and surprising, to the guesses and confessions at the end of our periods. Little by little, the lessons developed. The whole class taught and the whole class learned.

In America, we believe too often that he snarls best who snarls first. Our humor is largely a humor of fear. It is an ill humor. It is like the spirit-wall a Chinese builds across his gateway. We believe that if we but make a devious entrance to our hearts mirth will not injure us. William James surmised fear of poverty to be the demon that haunted us worst. Surely the next demon in the unholy hierarchy is fear of ridicule. Afraid to be gaily exposing our hearts, we laugh at our own good qualities in others and in ourselves. Here is an immediate case in point. A girl who is honorably mentioned by the judges of the P. S. A. Undergraduate Verse Contest for 1923, writes me from Vassar: "I seem to run to superficial subjects, and I'm afraid that flippancy is a habit with me. I think that I poke fun at my own verses in order to beat the other fellow to it!" The Berkeley class on the whole agreed with me that this is no mood in which to write poetry. Ingenuous verse stood its ground with us against clever criticism. I have noticed, since, that those of our members who were the smartest critics have become the dumbest poets. Their glitter was not gold. It was a glitter of apprehensive malice, a glitter which youth likes to exhibit, mistaking it for a flash of maturity. For the most part, however, we developed a glow rather than a glitter, a warmth of laughter rather than a chill. Like all wise mortals, we knew the need of laughter from the heart.

So they smoked and laughed and made friends, you say. What else? Well, let's see.

We discussed our favorite poets. We had poets read to us and talk with us: Vachel Lindsay, Ruth Comfort Mitchell, Stella Benson, and others. We heard about Chinese poetry from Kiang Kang-hu and about Serbian poetry from Milutin Krunich. We had many other visitors, who sometimes took part in our conversations. We had one of our irregular members—Eugenia Buyko, now of Yvette Guilbert's Company in Paris—sing Russian songs to us, tell us the English meanings and patiently give us the musical beat, that we might try our hands at lyrical translation. We celebrated in a grove the centenary of Walt Whitman's birth. We remember the many townspeople who assembled with us, all sitting on the ground except one old lady so deaf that we fetched her a chair and let her perch craning in the very shadow of the speakers. We wondered where they had come from, those Whitmanites whom we had never seen before, most of them elderly people with wise and gentle faces. Von Neumayer told us about visiting the poet at Camden. Sam Hume read from *Leaves of Grass*. The students had written of Whitman, praising, appraising, dispraising. Their poems were read, of all three kinds. John Cowper Powys, contributing his eloquence, doubted if there had ever been a gathering in Whitman's name that the poet himself would rather have attended. Powys ended with a quotation from one of the passages prophetic of a just and generous brotherliness on earth; and a professor from the University of Chicago hissed because he thought the passage had a Bolshevik sound.

You can see what fun it was, all of it. And yet I would never do it again. Not with a new group. The old group met with me further in 1921, unofficially but regularly. That was different. We were continuing. A new group would have necessitated repetition. No. Only once that "first fine careless rapture." Similar classes have met successfully at Berkeley with W. W. Lyman and Leonard Bacon. None of us three is any longer connected with the university. The powers, I understand, attribute our absence to the fact that none of us held a doctor's degree. Doubtless each of us regards the young lives we have touched with our own lives as a composite thesis more valuable to himself and to the world than any paper in which we might have been solemnly guilty of wrapping old bones for the university. My brief experience as instructor has put me in pitying awe of teachers who have to give out of their creative selves, not progressively, not directly, but the same thing over and over again, through others, others, others, term after automatic term. It has made me wish there might be a form of conscription under which men and women eminent in this or that field of life might ardently and profitably share a year of their development with the young at our universities. There would be a freshness then and a gain for both teacher and student. But perhaps this passage has a Bolshevik sound!

Calculable results from the class? Already several of the students who had made themselves known to me have made themselves known to others. Three of them have published volumes: Stanton A. Coblentz, Hildegarde Flanner and Genevieve Taggard. Coblentz, four years ago, pleased us best as a grave young Aesop, rhyming his satire, a member more sober than lyrical; and I notice him today coming to the fore rather as critic than poet. Hildegarde Flanner was a poet from the first and has so proved herself, with a delicately firm touch. Genevieve Taggard, who had written in 1918 verse that compares well with what she has done since, began as a visiting member of the class but was soon a regular attendant and participant. Her work is now impressing outsiders with the emotional turns and subtle rhythms that impressed her smaller audience. David Greenhood, still working off his obscurities, is producing from time to time poems of importance, especially in the Hebrew rhythms which have always charmed him. Eda Lou Walton's highly distinctive short lines have become familiar to magazine readers. With her quiet humanness and individual style, she has always seemed to me sure of a place in the poetry of her time,—thus far, if my other students will forgive me, the most likely of them all. Her translations of songs from the Navajos and Blackfeet are, in my judgment, by all odds the finest Indian poems that have been produced in English, the nearest to the spirit of their source. This may be because Miss Walton grew up among the people she is interpreting: an Indian nurse sang the songs into the little poet's heart. There are able figures to name in my class, including Vernon Patterson, a later member than the rest. But the last I shall mention now is Idella Purnell, who has not only published her own worthy verse in other people's magazines, but other people's verse (and not hers) in her own *Palms*, which she publishes at Guadalajara, Mexico. Critics in England, as well as here, have noticed *Palms* as already rivaling the longer-established verse magazines for excellence and freshness of content. This is the more remarkable in view of the fact that the young editor supports her venture from earnings in a consular office. She is her own hard-working angel.

It is natural for me to feel pride in my poets. On the other hand, as I announced at the start, they were poets when I met them. I take no credit for their gifts but only for my discernment; and I have wished to express myself here not as their teacher but as their friend and fellow worker.

If there are others who would like to teach poets and would be interested in more specific advice resultant from my experiences, here it is. I might invest it in Freudian formulas, fashionable prescriptions for genius; but I prefer it in honest American.

Catch your poets young. Not too many of them. Knock the nonsense out of them—the affectations, the self-deceptions, the guesses toward what will seem poetry to others, the catches at vogue. Release them from the dead hand of English literature. Disabuse them of fear, disabuse them of "modestovanitas," as Lamb called false modesty. Lead them to distinguish between self-importance and self-confidence, between push and poise, between patter and poetry, between pretense and truth. Send them outdoors. Encourage them to write in the open: to give terms of themselves to the sky and, as far as possible, those same terms to their neighbor, whether or no the neighbor like it. Show them that there is neither shame nor distinction but just humanness in their being as ridiculously natural as they are prompted to be. Let them laugh. Let them smoke. Let them say or write anything which genuinely impels them, discovering among one another that honesty is the best poetry. And, above all, after you have made sure that they understand your general and particular judgments, let them, without pride or prejudice, believe their own differing judgments to be as good as yours—or better.

I asked at the outset of these remarks, "Can the writing of poetry be taught?" I answered, "To poets, yes; to others, no." And I might add in conclusion, for the unobservant, that there are more poets born than insurance agents.

—*The New Republic*, December 5, 1923

On Judging Poetry

· ❧❧❧❧❧ ·

There are three approaches to judgment of any art. First, there is the simple untutored approach, which has been over-ridiculed by the satirical echo: "I don't know anything about art, but I know what I like." Second, there is the approach of the cultured individual who tries to combine his own judgment with the majority judgment among those whom he considers his peers. Third, there is the conventionalized approach of the complete academician who subdues personal judgment to the cumulated judgments of other academicians deader than he is. The first approach is human, respectable and, in the end, conclusive. The second is one of those compromises by which we live. The third, fortunately the rarest of the three, has nevertheless an influence out of all proportion to its value: a great influence, for instance, on schoolbooks. The first approach is of the heart, without which the others are only shadows. The first might be called a love-letter, the second an invitation to tea, the third an obituary.

Granting various amalgamations of these attitudes, let me consider them as concerns poetry, and let me do away with the usual disguises of ego. On the whole, when any of us says "one thinks" or "we think" or "it is thought," he means "I think."

Not long ago I was driven to a New York station by a happy taxi-man. The question whether or not his state had anything to do with prohibition may have nothing to do with poetry or may have a great deal to do with it. At any rate, he was singing. While I listened, I noticed that he was one of the children of Israel for whom the countless Red Seas of Manhattan divide at regular intervals of time and space. And yet the tune he was improvising carried a hundred repetitions of the American colonial lines,

Listen, my children, and you shall hear
Of the midnight ride of Paul Revere.

I wondered if he had been a school-parrot learning, as I had done, a routine Longfellow poem, and if he was unconsciously recalling it at a moment when his heart felt like a song. Samuel Johnson's dictionary gave oatmeal as a food for men in Scotland and for horses in England. Similarly it might be said that Longfellow is a poet for men in England and for children in America. Critical England still venerates Longfellow as a poet, while critical America shrugs a shoulder at him. How are we to tell which judgment is right? By any or all of the three approaches, Longfellow might be regarded as an important or unimportant poet. For myself, with due deference to men in England and with still more deference to children in America, I have only to pick up a volume of Longfellow and to shake my head. He is not for me. If he is for you, I make no argument. In fact, I confess with humility a judgment out of gear with superior taste in both countries, inasmuch as I have finally set aside the reverential college courses in which I studied English poetry and have decided and hereby avow that Milton has never meant much of anything to my heart nor Shelley to my ear. For thirty years now I have read these two poets from time to time and have doubted my own judgment; but at last, against overwhelming opinion to the contrary, I ease my soul by declaring that Milton, in spite of his blind eyes, is little more to me than a swollen old bore, and that Shelley, in spite of his open life, is little more than a stretcher of thin and unmusical platitude. One man's platitude may be another man's pleasure. To Bernard Shaw, for instance, even Shakespeare is a dresser of platitude. To many a modern, Wordsworth is a dreary old sheep, Whitman a blatant old rooster. To me, Shakespeare, Wordsworth, Keats, and Whitman are, at their best, the four dominant glories of English poetry.

Where are we, then? I can only tell you where I am. Let me look back a minute. At the turn of the century, I was expostulating with my Harvard professor in American literature against the inclusion of Walt Whitman as a subject worthy of study; a few years later, I was reading Whitman again and feeling as if the sun had risen after a long darkness. Still later, I was drawing ridicule from Harriet Monroe by preferring Moira O'Neill's Irish poems to those of W. B. Yeats, was being pitied by the Poetry Society of America for liking some of the war ballads of Robert W. Service, and was finding critics in general apathetic toward my favorite latter-day American poet, Edna St. Vincent Millay. These may have been good judgments or bad. They were mine. I was not demanding that others should agree with them. I was not considering my judgments superior to those of others, nor inferior either. I was not sure that my judgments might not change, in any direction. Once upon a time, Edgar Poe and Sidney Lanier seemed to me much more important poets than they seem today. They not only seemed more important; they were more important, because they were more important to me. By the same token, Milton and Shelley remain unimportant. If they be not poets to me, what care I whose poets they be! On the other hand, how do I know that I may not wake some morning and find myself in a single stroke the thrall of Milton, Shelley, Ella Wheeler Wilcox, and Edgar Guest.

Am I suggesting irresponsible egotism? No, but egotism honestly responsible to itself. Candid egotism is a wholesome quality. Arrogant egotism, however, is as bad as arrogant hypocrisy. Arrogance is the stupid and offensive quality, not egotism. Let me then, to the best of my ability, know what I feel and think and, to the best of my manners, say what I feel and think. And let me bear in mind always that, unless I seal my mind with dry arrogance or my heart with dry rot, I shall find life to be change and change to be growth. As long as there's life, there's change; and as long as there's intelligence, the change may be the change that comes with growth, instead of the change that comes with decay. Therefore, in judging anything or anybody, a poem or a neighbor, let me be honest as far as I have gone already, and open-minded as far as I may be able to go in the future. If there be a God, let him hold absolute judgments as to poetry and everything else and let him, in the relief of Nirvana, forget the ennui of those judgments. No living man can trespass upon such prerogatives and such repose. Until we take a possible eventual share in absolute knowledge, we have the more imaginable joy of watering our faculties to blossom and resting them under temporary snows.

Desiring, then, to judge poetry: first be sure that you read it, that you are not judging by hearsay; then be square with yourself as to feeling it, liking it, respecting it, or the opposite; then keep your heart and mind open by listening.

Although a liking for poetry is not to be reasoned into the system, it has many avenues. Our vibrations may be changed in many ways, ways of which we may be aware or unaware. Love of poetry is akin to personal love: subject to the sway of currents deeper than even Freud can probe.

Poetry, sprung from the seed of man, has many flowers. If you choose poppy, shall you forbid your neighbor columbine? Though you marvel over priest-nurtured peonies in a Chinese temple, may you not turn to a stray bamboo outside the gate, or from an American Beauty to a wild rose?

I have said nothing about a knowledge of the art of poetry, of the technique, the subtleties, the finer patterns and melodies. Obviously, with an increase of such knowledge, the appreciator's taste becomes more acute, more sensitized. "Heard melodies are sweet, but those unheard are sweeter." But oh, the ears of the experts! Those tutored ears, how differently they hear! The poets themselves, or those most fitly equipped in the appreciation of poetry, become a jury of hopeless confusion when they are brought away from all signposts and set to choosing new paths by the poetic stars. Watching the choices of my fellow judges in a score of poetic contests, mostly from among anonymous offerings, I have been amazed by our flatly contradictory tastes. If any man insist upon knowing beyond fault which may be the vital poems in a contest or in a generation, let him first be dead a thousand years. Meantime he has his immediate right to judge, not only against his fellows but against posterity; and the poem that dies, with only him for partisan, may conceivably be the better poem.

With poems, then, as with persons, choose for yourself, enjoy for yourself, reject for yourself; and the devil take the hindmost. If he be a better judge than you, so be it.

—*The Scholastic*, May 29, 1926

Statement of Belief

· ✹✹✹✹ ·

Brought up in New England with Puritan surroundings, I managed, nonetheless, a happy boyhood. Perhaps my sentimental beginnings as a poet were due to the fact that Puritanism is a constipated form of sentimentality. At Harvard and at New York I found a more laxative environment, and a gradual cure from the earlier affliction. And yet, as late as 1903 I remember O. Henry protesting against my use of such words as "train" and "sidewalk" in a poem. I disagreed with him, persisted; and when my verse appeared with commonplace words in it, I was regarded as a liberal. Years later, in *Spectra*, my revolt had turned against other poetical liberals who by that time seemed to me as sentimental and long-headed as ever were the Puritans. Today I am quietly concerned in opposing the traditional Western attitude that poetry is an escape from life—concerned in my faith that true poetry ought to be, on the contrary, and can be, as with the great Chinese poets, the sheerest and most crystalline focus on life and the natural world. And in spite of certain modern novelists, I maintain that this focus reveals pain, to be sure, but the birth-pain of something worth bearing.

—*The Bookman*, October 1928

The Persistence of Poetry

· ❧❦❧ ·

Definitions, rather than realities, have for centuries cost blood and brains. Therefore the tender heart sinks a little when it essays definition. Especially is it uncomfortable, trying to define poetry. For poetry is not so much a matter of hemming about, as of releasing. Can you bridle Pegasus with definition? Can Wordsworth by defining poetry as "passion remembered in tranquillity" prevent its being, on occasion, tranquillity remembered in passion? Do the "infinite capacity for taking pains" and "the first fine careless rapture" deny each other? Where angels might fear to tread, I have rushed in and have tried to devise a phrase which, though not necessarily implying the "sensuous" and the "noble" as exacted by Milton, would epitomize for my own satisfaction the nature and practice of poetry. I have made the phrase as brief as I could. Perhaps its very brevity will leave it vague enough to cover or suggest the reaches of poetry, better than if I had expanded the idea into words more specific and debatable. Here is it then. Two words. *Passionate patience.*

Of all the arts, music and poetry are those nearest to the heart, and most immediately echo the heart. Any definition of the elements of poetry must define also the elements of life nearest to the heart. No one would question passion as the prime element in live things; nor would anyone, I think, considering the cosmic silence which meets man's passionate and thwarted demands, question the element of patience as necessarily inhering in the life we have to live and try to understand.

Primarily, poetry like music—as a matter of fact with music —came out of the heart and lips of simple mankind. One who lives in New Mexico and wanders sometimes among Indians has an opportunity, rare in this modern world, of feeling and hearing poetry at its primitive source. Although the Indians have not themselves recorded their songs, they have followed the custom of all primitive folk and handed down words and music from father to son for many generations; so that we are undoubtedly hearing, in the choruses that accompany tribal ceremonies, a poetry which antedates our own coming to this continent. Besides those traditional racial songs, there are countless personal poems springing up yesterday and today from this or that individual in the Pueblo villages or the Navajo hogans. These poems come with their own music and are extremely simple. They are haunting, as such primitive rhythms always are, whether one hear them from a Navajo shepherd setting his heartbeat to coyote music on some invisible hill at night, or from a Hopi herdsboy singing his cattle back to the mesa, or from a Swiss mountaineer yodeling, or from a boat-boy on the Yangtsze River translating into ancient loves and hopes his own young emotions.

The modern European or American inherits a very different kind of poetry. Through a vast cumulation of books, there have come to him not only these original wellings from man's rhythmic heart, but also the subsequent literary adaptings of primal impulses to the complicated needs and tastes of a gradually cultured civilization. In medieval literature we have on the one hand folk-poetry and on the other hand poetry of the court. Now that republics succeed kingdoms we have forgotten the enforced flatteries due from minstrels to their patrons; and the folk-songs are no longer our own. The middle class is now the patron. The patron has become diffused and impersonal, but it still holds the purse and pays the poet. Its vanity is as great as that of the feudal lords, and its taste not necessarily better. The upper class, on our modern financial basis, has pretty well outgrown the uses of poetry; it has been twisted, for the most part, too far away from natural life, and the middle class now expects primal elements of poetry to be infused and tempered with those qualities of intelligence which are the due of sophisticated and cultured beings.

Culture brings with it a satiety and a fatigue. We know too much, or think we do. At least we have studied too much. We have killed the songsters and dissected their throats. There is nothing new under the sun. We compete with one another in meticulous shades of artificial taste. We are intellectually estranged from the simple sources of poetry. It would seem that in the noisy midst of a mechanistic civilization, poetry must perforce atrophy. Clearly, however, this is not what happens behind our busy and, on the whole, unpoetic lives. Any newspaperman, in touch with the more sensational events happening amongst our millions, knows how the passionate lover, the murderer, the suicide, or even the bandit, inclines to set down his crude emotions in crude verse. Any magazine editor knows from what thousands and thousands of the inarticulate in every American town and village come manuscripts of verse. Even a quarter of a century ago, when the public attitude toward poetry was far less serious, far less friendly, than it is today, the multitude dared secretly to express in verse its emotions and aspirations. Often in the emotional output there would be, and there continues to be, a thought, an impulse, a line, a phrase, of genuine worth or beauty. Unfortunately, busy editors cannot also be tutors. And though it would seem that these utterances from primitive individuals might contain the qualities which inform and beautify utterances from people racially primitive, the fact is otherwise. The environment of a comparative culture and of mechanistic progress intrudes on the simple person. In these days, a certain amount of instruction is necessary, except in the rarest of instances, for a poet to be a poet.

And here, between the impulse and the craft, we realize the extraordinarily delicate edge on which a modern poet must tread. Shakespeare, writing for both the aristocracy and the pit, trod this edge with a genius almost inexplicable. Although his language derived from sources that might have seemed above the ears of the herd, they could listen and understand, even while the Euphuists applauded. To this day, despite the most earnest efforts of pedagogues to annihilate in the mind of a college student an intuitive acceptance of the right and rhythmic beauty of Shakespeare, the profoundly human and poetic quality of the dramatist reaches modern listeners or readers as vividly as it did theater audiences in his own time. And this reach depends not at all upon Shakespeare's knowledge of Latin or Greek, nor upon his acquaintance with the earlier plays which he metamorphosed, nor upon the Elizabethan meaning of his terminology, nor upon anything except his passionate understanding of the emotional values of living and of the vibrations universal in man, and upon his ability so to phrase those emotions and vibrations as to make them, even in a language partly archaic to us, the living speech of human hearts. This passionate gift is genius. And in whatever time it happen, whether it be the time of Li Po or of Homer, of Chaucer or of Shakespeare, it is the rhythm by which men feel their own impulses, their own emotions, their own thoughts. A poet's office is to catch this rhythm and give it to the multitude which has tried to express itself in heart-felt words but has missed the soul-felt rhythm. When a master lives who can so use language that a whole vast sky of words seems as simple as a petal, then the genius arrives who in poetry expresses men to themselves. In our own day two lyric poets, one in England and one in America, have caught this semi-mystical accent. A. E. Housman, in forms and in an austerity of phrase which he might not have used but for his intimate acquaintance with Greek literature, has set down in imperishably distinguished verse, world-old and many times retold emotions. Edna St. Vincent Millay in a different language, more Shakespearean perhaps and yet with an occasional aside that might have been spoken in a village on the coast of Maine, has performed the same magic.

There are countless artificers, over-cultured and jaded, who with extensive knowledge of the world's poets and with the most highly self-conscious uses of prosody, fabricate words into strained and intellectualized meanings which pass for a season among the literary fashionables as poetry, but which are about as important to the singing heart of man as the latest sartorial trick from Paris. Amy Lowell was the high priestess of this cult. Indefatigable as she was in her hours of writing, self-convinced as she was in her theories of art, defiant as she was in her version of herself as a poet, diverting and intriguing as she was in witty polemics, she has already ceased to hold the imagination, except as an arresting and picturesque personality. There is a whole tribe of her nature who might, if they would, do better than she did, and yet who may be equipped, after all, to serve only as haberdashers for contemporary culture.

The Navajo Indians are supposed to be able, with concerted incantation, to make corn or cactus grow a month a minute. Around the seedling they hold a screen of blankets, while they sing their spell. When they move away, the seedling is a few inches high. And so it goes, spell by spell, until the plant or flower is complete. This kind of magic is for children, young or old, so credulous of miracle in the outside world that they will always lend themselves to the sorcerer. Poetry is another kind of magic. A true poet makes a flower of life grow in the heart. It may be a flower of good, it may be a flower of evil. It may be the morning-glory, it may be the deadly nightshade. The true poets are the priests of the inner miracle. There is all the difference in the world between these flowers in the heart and the outer flowers which are fabricated by craftsmen.

Like most of us who are schooled in this Western world, I was afforded in my youth a study of culture flowing mainly from two sources, the Greek and the Hebrew. I had come to feel that poetic literature must contain streams from one or the other of those two sources: on the one hand the clean, objective, symmetrical, athletic beauty of the Greek, on the other hand the turgid, subjective, distorted, elaborated beauty of the Hebrew. Like my fellow students, I had been offered nothing of the literature of the Far East. I am still doubtful that I could ever feel any real adherence to the ornate and entranced literature of India; but I have come by accident into as close touch with Chinese poetry as a Westerner is able to come without a knowledge of the Chinese tongue. And I feel with conviction, that in the matter of poetry, I have begun to receive a new, finer and deeper education than had come to me from the Hebrew or the Greek.

Centuries ago, cultured Chinese had reached the point of intellectual saturation which has tired the mind of the modern European. The Chinese gentleman knew the ancient folk-songs, compiled by Confucius. He knew also, all around him, a profoundly rich civilization, a more poised and particularized sophistication than we Westerners have yet attained. Through the Asian centuries, everyone has written verse. In fact, from early imperial days down to these even worse disordered days of the republic, the sense of poetry as a natural and solacing part of life has lasted among the Chinese people. Whether or not the individual may form or enjoy his poetry in metrical shape, he is constantly aware of the kinship between the beauty of the world and the beauty of imaginative phrase. On any Chinese mountain-climb toward a temple, rock after rock with its terse and suggestive inscription will bear witness to this temper. So will the street-cries of the peddlers, or the names of the teahouses and on many hilltops and lakesides the casual but reverent jottings of this or that anonymous appreciator of natural beauty. When Whitman said, "To have great poets there must be great audiences too," he must have had in the back of his mind enriched generations like the Elizabethan in England or like almost any generation in China. In those great audiences each man, to the limit of his capacity and with natural ease, was a poet.

There is a simple secret in the Oriental ease. It is told in a pamphlet by an old Chinese scholar who till a few years ago was still living in Peking, and still with infinite passion adhering to the precepts of his ancestors and with infinite patience, acceptably expressed by the way among foreigners, adhering to his conviction that foreigners impair the health of China. His name is Ku Hung-ming. His pamphlet, written in English, one of the five languages of which he was master, is called *The Spirit of the Chinese People.* In it he advances, as reason for the eternal youth of the Chinese people, the fact that the average Chinese has managed to maintain within himself the head of a man and the heart of a child. On this brief he is absorbingly interesting, explaining the continuance of Chinese culture, the only ancient culture still racially existent. My immediate concern with his brief is more special. I detect in it something that he does not specify; a reason for the continuance of poetry as a live factor among his people and, more than that, the best reason I know of for the persistence of poetry anywhere among cultured races.

Music may be the most intimate of the arts; I am not sure. Except for simple melodies, music is beyond the reach of any individual who is not a technician. Painting and sculpture are obviously arts expressing themselves in single given objects, which although they may be duplicated and so circulated are for the most part accessible only to the privileged or to those who make pilgrimages. Poetry more than any other of the arts may be carried about by a man either in his own remembering heart or else in compact and easily available printed form. It belongs to anyone. It is of all the arts the closest to a man; and it will so continue to be, in spite of the apparent shocks given it by the noises of modern commerce and science and jazz.

It has been an age-old custom in China that poets, even the best of them, have devoted their earlier years to some form of public service. Century after century, Chinese poems reflect this deep devotion of their authors to the good of the state,— their unwavering allegiance to righteousness, even when it meant demotion or exile or death. In modern Western times there have been periods when poetry has seemed to be a candle-lit and thin-blooded occupation. I venture to surmise that poetry written in that sort of atmosphere grows with time less and less valid, less and less noticed. As a matter of fact, the outstanding English poets have been acutely concerned with the happiness of their fellow men and have given themselves warmly to public causes in which they believed. Similarly, present-day poets in America, with amazingly few exceptions, have clustered to the defense of noble souls at bay like Eugene Debs, or have been quick to protest against doubtful justice as in the case of Sacco and Vanzetti. This sort of zeal may not result in poetry of a high order immediately connected with the specific cause; but there is no question that but for this bravery, this heat on behalf of man's better nature, there would not be in the hearts of the poets so fine a crucible for their more personal alchemies.

These various remarks bind together, I think. I have been trying to focus my thoughts on the place of the poet and poetry, in a time of cumulated and over-materialistic culture. I have remarked that the art of a poet is by no means only craft, but inheres in his life; that there is a special gift by which a particular poet now and then expresses the poetic impulse in the hearts of other men; but that the element is common to us all, and is an element inextricably mingled with the element of life itself.

I have said very little about the craft, the skill, the technique of verse. At the risk of setting my general observations out of gear, I must before I finish say a word as to the method of Chinese poetry. I am not referring to the superficial tricks by which a Chinese poet makes his words balanced and melodious. The discovery which has largely undone my early convictions as to the way of writing poetry has really to do with use of substance rather than with turns of expression. Mencius said long ago, in reference to the Odes collected by Confucius: "Those who explain the Odes must not insist on one term so as to do violence to a sentence, nor on a sentence so as to do violence to the general scope. They must try with their thoughts to meet that scope, and then they will apprehend it." In the poetry of the West we are accustomed to let our appreciative minds accept with joy this or that passage in a poem,—to prefer the occasional glitter of a jewel to the straight light of the sun. The Chinese poet seldom lets any portion of what he is saying unbalance the entirety. Moreover, with the exception of a particular class of writing—adulatory verse written for the court—Chinese poetry rarely trespasses beyond the bounds of actuality. Whereas Western poets will take actualities as points of departure for exaggeration or fantasy or else as shadows of contrast against dreams of unreality, the great Chinese poets accept the world exactly as they find it in all its terms, and with profound simplicity find therein sufficient solace. Even in phraseology they seldom talk about one thing in terms of another, but are able enough and sure enough as artists to make the ultimately exact terms become the beautiful terms. If a metaphor is used, it is a metaphor directly relating to the theme, not something borrowed from the ends of the earth. The metaphor must be concurrent with the action or flow of the poem; not merely superinduced, but an integral part of both the scene and the emotion.

Wordsworth, of our poets, comes closest to the Chinese; but their poetry cleaves even nearer than his to nature. They perform the miracle of identifying the wonder of beauty with common sense. Rather, they prove that the simplest common sense, the most salutary, and the most nearly universal, is the sense of the beauty of nature, quickened and yet sobered by the wistful warmth of human friendship.

For our taste, used as we are to the operatic in poetry, the substance of Chinese poems seems often mild or even trivial; but if we will be honest with ourselves and with our appreciation of what is lastingly important, we shall find these very same poems to be momentous details in the immense patience of beauty. They are the heart of an intimate letter. They bring the true, the beautiful, the everlasting, into simple easy touch with the human, the homely and the immediate. And I predict that future Western poets will go to school with the masters of the T'ang Dynasty, as well as with the masters of the golden age of Greece, or with the Hebrew prophets, or with the English dramatists or romanticists—to learn how best may be expressed, for themselves and others, that passionate patience which is the core of life.

It is not necessary that culture bring about the death of poetry, as it did in the Rome of Virgil. The cynics are wrong who see in our future no place for an art which belongs, they say, to the childhood of the race. The head of a man and the heart of a child working together as in the Chinese have made possible with one race and may make possible with any race, even in the thick of the most intricate culture, the persistence of the purest poetry.

—Part of this essay appeared as Witter Bynner's introduction to *The Jade Mountain*, an anthology of 300 poems of the T'ang Dynasty, translated from the Chinese by Witter Bynner and Kiang Kang-hu. A portion of the essay was printed in *The Dial* under the title "Poetry and Culture," October 1928; the full essay was published as a chapbook by The Book Club of California, San Francisco, 1929

Index

· ✄✖✄✖✄ ·